Under Prairie Skies

The Plants and
Native Peoples
of the Northern Plains

C. THOMAS SHAY

University of Nebraska Press LINCOLN

The University of Nebraska Press is part of a land-grant institution with campuses and programs on the past, present, and future homelands of the Pawnee, Ponca, Otoe-Missouria, Omaha, Dakota, Lakota, Kaw, Cheyenne, and Arapaho Peoples, as well as those of the relocated Ho-Chunk, Sac and Fox, and Iowa Peoples.

Library of Congress Cataloging-in-Publication Data
Names: Shay, C. Thomas (Creighton Thomas), author.
Title: Under prairie skies : the plants and native peoples of the Northern Plains / C. Thomas Shay.
Description: Lincoln : University of Nebraska Press, 2022. | Includes bibliographical references and index.
Identifiers: LCCN 2021047029
ISBN 9781496223388 (paperback)
ISBN 9781496232144 (epub)
ISBN 9781496232151 (pdf)
Subjects: LCSH: Indians of North America—Great Plains—Ethnobotany. | Ethnobotany—Great Plains. | Human ecology—Great Plains. | BISAC: NATURE / Ecosystems & Habitats / Plains & Prairies | SOCIAL SCIENCE / Anthropology / Cultural & Social
Classification: LCC E78.G73 S438 2022 | DDC 978.004/97—dc23/eng/20211203
LC record available at https://lccn.loc.gov/2021047029

Designed and set in Arno Pro by L. Auten.

Frontispiece a. Drawing by Diane Magill.
Frontispiece b. Tom and Jennifer Shay sieving for plant remains in 1980. Photo courtesy of Joseph Shaw.

To
Jennifer—
my mentor, my partner, my love.
Her fingerprints are all over this book.

CONTENTS

Figures

Maps

Table

Years ago I took a course that changed my life. One fall semester at the University of Minnesota I enrolled in Plants Useful to Man: A Cultural Course in Botany, taught by Professor Donald B. Lawrence. In the dim light of a packed auditorium, Professor Lawrence illustrated his lectures with a seemingly endless series of slides, many of which he had taken himself. I still remember his oft-repeated phrase, "Notice the penny for scale." During the lectures he sailed botanical terms across the room like paper airplanes: leucoplast, alkaloid, ovule, bryophyte, phenology, xanthophyll, double cross. Lawrence's course not only taught me about botany, it opened my mind to new ways of thinking about people and plants. I still refer to the ninety-page course syllabus.

Lawrence's lectures were sprinkled with botanical wonders. In one he listed more than two dozen products derived from the coconut palm (*Cocos nucifera*), the most widely cultivated nut tree in the world. In another he revealed that lignum vitae (*Guaiacum officinale*), a tree native to Central America and the Caribbean, has wood so tough it's used in making bowling balls, mallet heads, and pulley blocks. Moreover, lignum vitae resin is a lubricant so superior to petroleum grease that it is used on the propeller shafts of seagoing vessels and the heavy roller bearings in steel mills.

In his distinctive, high-pitched voice, Lawrence spoke of how, thousands of years ago, people across the globe began to domesticate and cultivate dozens of plants. I sat captivated as he told the story of corn, or maize, that began in Mexico, where a spindly grass known as teosinte gradually evolved to become a giant—Native America's gift to the world and today's second most important cereal. The transformation seemed nothing short of a miracle. I returned to the story of maize years later when my research team found charred kernels in centuries-old deposits near Winnipeg, Manitoba. Impressed by this evidence of early Native agriculture in an area far north of the traditional Corn Belt, I decided to spread the word. With the help of student assistants, I wrote *The Story of Corn* (2003), containing one hundred pages of lesson plans for grade-school students.

But botany was not my only passion.

Early in my college career I discovered anthropology when I took an introductory course. Taught by Professor Elden Johnson, an archaeologist, the course rekindled my love of the ancient past. Professor Johnson's lectures offered a golden opportunity to explore human evolution, early cultures, and exotic societies. The experience got me hooked. With two intriguing areas to study, what could be more sensible than to combine them? My love affair with people and plants had begun.

A pollen course taught by botany professor A. Orville Dahl plus an interest in geology inspired by Professor H. E. Wright resulted in my doing graduate work that combined archaeology, botany, pollen studies, and geology. Early on I was fortunate to spend a year studying pollen on a Fulbright scholarship at the National Museum of Denmark. I later spent a postdoctoral year studying pollen at Cambridge University before moving on to a fulfilling career in education and research. While I worked as an anthropology professor at the University of Manitoba in Winnipeg for the next twenty-five years, much of my research focused on the historical uses of plants by the people of the northern plains. This work gave me a profound love for the land and its history. I traveled its length and breadth, from Saskatchewan's arid grasslands to northern Iowa's rolling prairies, and from the badlands of North Dakota to the oak savannas of southern Minnesota. I spent hot summer days tramping over it, surveying its plant cover, digging into its soil, and later analyzing bits of it under a microscope. These were my ways of seeking answers to the question, "What was everyday life like under those ancient prairie skies?" When I came to write this book, I narrowed my study to focus on the role of plants in the lives of the Native peoples who lived here before the Europeans came. These pages offer shining examples of sustainable living that show a deep love and respect for the land.

A Word of Warning

Even though this book is full of knowledge about how Native peoples used plants in their daily lives, please do not use it as a personal guide to foods and medicines. There is simply too much room for error. Always seek advice from a professional before using a plant medicinally. The author and publisher disclaim liability for any loss or risk, personal or otherwise, resulting directly or indirectly from the use, application, or interpretation of this book's content.

ACKNOWLEDGMENTS

I dedicate this book to Jennifer, my dear late wife, whose botanical expertise, helpful criticism, and love sustained me on this book's lengthy journey. Calling off the names of plants in a sun-drenched prairie or shady forest, verifying a seed under a microscope, editing draft text, and cheering me up when I was down are just a few of the ways she made it happen.

Every book project goes through phases. Mine began decades ago as I, together with a small gaggle of helpers, began a search for plant remains in soil samples from archaeological digs. We wanted to know how much of the local flora was used by early Native peoples living in southern Manitoba and adjacent Saskatchewan—what plant foods they ate, the medicines they used, and the woods they chose for heating and cooking.

In these efforts I owe an enormous debt to my late friend and associate Cole Wilson. Capable and meticulous, with a wicked sense of humor, Cole was an ideal sidekick. He happily helped me sample the plant life around a number of ancient sites, even crawling on his hands and knees in one tangled forest. Over the years he shouldered much of the soil processing, spent hours sorting seeds under a microscope, prepared maps and charts, filled out countless spreadsheets, and applied statistical tests to our data. As the book progressed, Cole also helped with research, writing, and editing.

I have also had excellent help from many students who painstakingly sorted through hundreds of samples or compiled background information for me. Prominent among these were Joan Kleinman, Shirley Lee, Donalee Deck, Anne Moulton, Monica Wiest, Lori Podolsky, Shannon Coyston, Harpa Isfeld, and Mike Waddell. Margaret Kapinga verified seed identifications during the early years, while Janusz Zwiazek and Donalee Deck identified hundreds of charcoal fragments.

While all of this was going on, I succumbed to an urge to share our results with the public, drafting popular text about past plant uses. At that time I was fortunate to have editorial advice from Marion Lepkin, Eva Janssen, and Cheri Fraser.

Later in this book's evolution, after our last soil sample had been washed and we had put away our microscopes, I recruited a number of student researchers, including Jordi Malasiuk, Candace Jorgenson, Jason Jorgenson, Renee Baluta (née Lavallée), Brian Myhre, Andrew McCausland, Karen Kivinen, Amrita Daftary, Calla Grabish, Cassie Davidson, Robert Jackson, Rebecca Simpson, Olga Zikrata, Vera Civiri-Girik, Sara Johnson, Elaine Stocki, Peter Joyce, Dawna Ventura, Eddie Powell, and Chris Powell. Together they amassed a wealth of material that has informed every chapter of the book. During that period, with the help of Sara Halwas and Kimberly Dalton, I wrote *The Story of Corn*—lesson plans for local grade schools—published in 2003.

As the book neared completion, I enjoyed the able assistance of Naomi Bloch, Loris Sofia Gregory, Beth Page, and Allan Jones. Mary Keirstead, Mark d'Almeida, Sarah Powell, and David Kaufman helped edit one or more early draft chapters. Bev Hauptmann then patiently steered me through innumerable writing hurdles. Together with Loris Gregory, Bev also helped me track down and gain permission to use the many illustrations.

Gathering the art for this book put me in touch with many fine photographers, illustrators, and cartographers. Chapter 5 has benefited from the lovely drawings of early domesticates by Diane Magill. Patti Isaacs drew the prairie-forest transition and pollen diagram and also added the common names of plants to the profile of Delta Marsh that had been drawn by my wife, Jennifer. Michael Wiemann was instrumental in finding the wood anatomy images in chapter 8. The attractive maps throughout the book were drawn by Mark Williams of Eureka Cartography. Pat Breen's last-minute photography of aspen leaves was most appreciated, as were Donalee Deck's spruce images. Scott Hamilton and Clarence Surette furnished the photograph of the grinding stone. Katy Chayka of Minnesota Wildflowers (www.minnesotawildflowers .info) provided several plant photos of excellent quality on short notice. I especially want to thank Joseph Shaw for digging in his files to find an image of Jennifer and me that could be used on the dedication page. Others who were especially helpful include Malia Volke, Tom Bean, Glen Lee, Thomas Rosburg, Lynnea Parker, Bryan Kelly-McArthur, and Travis Scheirer.

I am also deeply indebted to my good friend Vanessa Farmery, who helped enormously in refining my draft text.

Lea Galanter capably took over the manuscript's copyediting, while Diana Sawatzky kindly checked all of the scientific names. Elizabeth Punter and Lysandra Pyle also advised on botanical issues.

I am grateful to various people who read and commented on the chapters. Introduction: Fred Schneider, Mary Jane Schneider, and Wendy Geniusz; chapter 1: John Bluemle, Jim Teller, Mark Williams, Harvey Thorleifson, Carrie Jennings, and Jay Bell; chapter 2: Greg Gust, Scott St. George, Barbara Scott, Jay Anderson, Dorian Burnette, and Linea Sundstrom; chapter 3: John Tester, Daryl Smith, and Linea Sundstrom; chapter 4: Mike Newbrey and Kirstie Edwards; chapter 5: John Hart, Gary Crawford, Bill Green, Lance Foster, Mary Adair, Mary Simon, Linea Sundstrom, Michael Blake, Bruce Benz, John Staller, and Leo Pettipas; chapter 6: Nancy Turner, Kelly Kindscher, Peter Jones, James House, Bob Nielsen, and Rachel Laudan; chapter 7: Iain Davidson-Hunt, Linea Sundstrom, Jonathan Ellerby, Colin Briggs, and Joe Kaufert; chapter 8: Anne Lindsay, Rebecca Oaks, Roland Bohr, Mary Jane Schneider, Katherine Jakes, and Wendy Geniusz.

I also wish to thank those who answered my many questions. Among them were Leo Pettipas, Nancy Turner, Fred Schneider, Mary Jane Schneider, E. Leigh Syms, Jack Brink, Alice Kehoe, David Punter, Elizabeth Punter, Karen Noyce, Dean Snow, the Paul Gruchow Foundation, Richard Drass, Colin Wright, and Ruthann Knudson.

Research funding was provided by the Manitoba Heritage Federation, the Saskatchewan Heritage Foundation, St. Paul's College, and Western Heritage Services. I thank Don Lemmen, formerly of the Terrain Sciences Division, Geological Survey of Canada, now with Natural Resources Canada, for arranging radiocarbon dates from the Peg site in Saskatchewan. Laboratory facilities were kindly provided by the Department of Anthropology and St. Paul's College at the University of Manitoba. The anthropology department has also generously allowed me full use of library services, enabling me to access a wealth of scholarly sources.

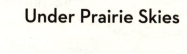

Under Prairie Skies

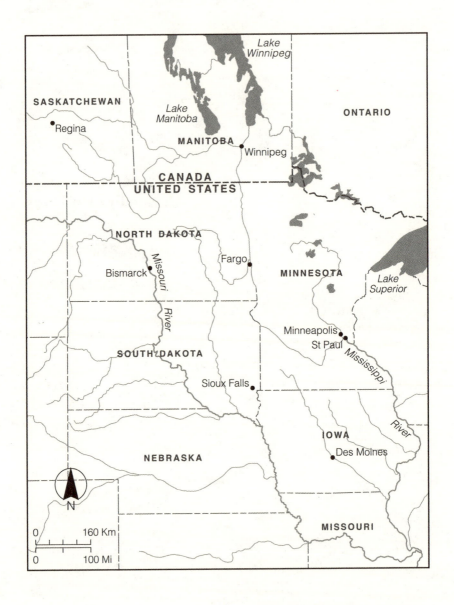

MAP 1. The northern plains region. By Eureka Cartography.

Introduction

No, a prairie is wine-colored grass, dancing in the wind.
A prairie is sun-splashed hillside, bright with wild flowers.
A prairie is a fleeting cloud shadow, the song of a meadowlark.
—DENNIS FARNEY, "The Tallgrass Prairie: Can It Be Saved?"

With vast prairies, wide vistas, azure skies, and refreshing breezes, the northern Great Plains is where Big Sky Country begins. Yet this lovely land is also a land of climatic extremes: devastating floods and searing droughts, raging wildfires and blinding blizzards, violent tornadoes and choking dust storms. Flanked by humid forests on the east and high plains on the west, its rolling hills and broad flatlands stretch over some 220,000 square miles of North America, across parts of two Canadian provinces and four American states, mainly between the Mississippi and Missouri Rivers.[1] In the words of North Dakota geologists John Bluemle and Bob Biek, this land is "no ordinary plain."[2]

The region has been home to humans since the end of the last ice age, when nomadic hunters followed herds of bison and gathered seeds, berries, and roots wherever they went. For hundreds of generations people fished its waters, hunted and trapped its wild animals, and gathered its flora to use as food, shelter, clothing, and medicine and to meet other needs. Eventually some groups began to cultivate seed-bearing annuals, and they later grew fields of maize and other crops.[3]

Writing through the lens of ethnobotany, which is the study of the links between people ("ethno") and plants ("botany"), I explore life in the region's past using a mix of science, cultural narrative, and natural history, focusing upon the partnership of people and their environment. I agree with ethnobotanist Richard Klein, who called this type of study "a fascinating exercise in comparative religion, sociology, philosophy, and history."[4]

I want to portray Native life as it may have been before the Europeans came. Nevertheless, I bid readers to make no mistake. Native people are not museum specimens, frozen in time. After centuries of oppression, they are still here and still active. Many of the cultural ways described in the following pages are still practiced by Native peoples today. Siyotanka (John Two-Hawks), an Oglala Lakota musician and recording artist, expressed it this way: "I cannot tell you the dreamy Indian story of your imagination simply because I am not imaginary—and my story is no dream."[5]

Award-winning ethnobotanist Gary Nabhan summed up the role of plants in relation to humans as "calories, cures, and characters."[6] In discussing Mediterranean Europe, climatologist A. T. Grove and ecologist Oliver Rackham have written that "plants are not just Environment, part of the scenery of the theatre of historical ecology, the passive recipients of whatever destiny mankind's whims inflict upon them. They are actors in the play."[7] In a similar vein, I see the landscape as a stage, and plants and people as a cast of characters interacting upon it.

I use seeds, charcoal, and other plant traces to provide clues about ancient diet, trade patterns, social relations, and medical practices. In a search for this history, I spent years with my small research team analyzing many thousands of plant remains from a couple of dozen archaeological sites spread across the northern plains. When combined with the work of others, the archaeological record of plant use in the region spans more than three thousand years. However, the story is incomplete without striving to understand the beliefs and practices that permeated people's daily routines. We know from modern Native Americans that their traditional beliefs demonstrate a deep connection with the land, the plants they gathered, and the game they hunted. The key idea is that all creatures and all of nature share a kinship, as referenced in a common Lakota prayer: "I acknowledge everything in the universe as my relations."[8]

These pages discuss the practical and spiritual aspects of plants that have served humans in many ways. Cottonwood, for example, was used to build shelters, provided emergency food, served as medicine, and was also a central symbol in sacred ceremonies. In a similar way, wild rice was not simply a food. Writer and cultural specialist Winona LaDuke reminds us that "food itself is medicine, not only for the body, but for the soul. It is the spiritual connection to history, ancestors and the land."[9]

As South Dakota scholar and poet David A. Evans has observed, "To learn about a place or a way of life, especially one that has been nearly obliterated, it is necessary to accommodate all kinds of perceptions, facts and imaginings."[10] To that end, I have cast a wide net in search of information, drawing upon my own research as well as that of others in a variety of fields. Traditional Native stories and the writings of modern Native authors such as Wendy Geniusz and Robin Wall Kimmerer have added vital context to the work of early twentieth-century writers such as Frances Densmore, Melvin Gilmore, and Gilbert Wilson.

In organizing this wealth of information, *Under Prairie Skies* falls naturally into three parts. The beginning sets the stage by looking at the region's glacial history and climate—factors that influence the abundance and distribution of plant resources. It closes with an exploration of today's prairies, woodlands, and marshes. The middle chapters cover the science behind the story, including technical advances such as the analysis of ancient DNA, and go on to show how early peoples managed the land and domesticated crops such as maize. The last part focuses on daily life long ago, exploring in detail how plants have been used for food, medicine, and material goods.

FURTHER READING

Wishart, David J., ed. *Encyclopedia of the Great Plains.* Lincoln: University of Nebraska Press, 2011. Available online at http://plainshumanities.unl.edu/encyclopedia/.

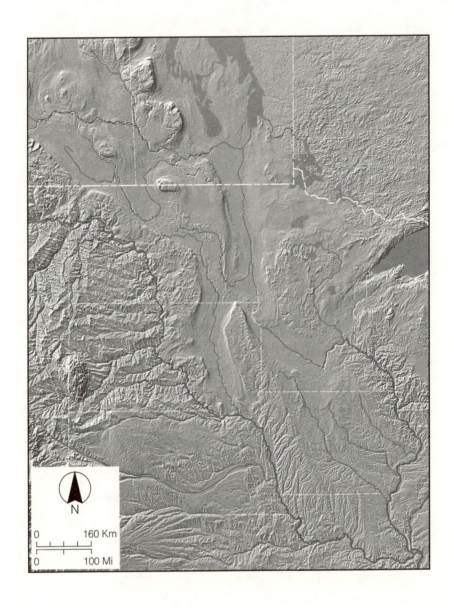

MAP 2. Northern plains region in relief. By Eureka Cartography.

Sculpting the Land

1

The glacier was God's great plough.

—LOUIS AGASSIZ, *Geological Sketches*

Those who know the northern Great Plains are aware of its gorgeous sunsets, rolling hills, and wide vistas, but, depending upon where people live, they may grumble about squishing through gumbo, picking rocks off their fields, or having nowhere to swim or fish. Whatever its charms and quirks, this landscape, smooth in the middle but hilly and rumpled on either side, owes much to the last ice age, which was the earth's most recent major geological epoch.

Over nearly three million years the world repeatedly cooled and then warmed again. As it cooled, massive glaciers advanced southward from the Canadian Arctic, burying much of northern North America under ice a mile or more thick. They made their way south, eventually reaching their southern limits in Kansas or Missouri before melting away as the climate warmed again. The last ice sheet to spread across the northern Great Plains plowed through what is present-day Saskatchewan and Manitoba and into North Dakota along the Red River valley. The ice pushed as far west as the current Missouri River. On its way south, it divided into two broad streams at a bedrock upland called the Coteau des Prairies.[1]

To the west one lobe of the glacier flowed through the low-lying James River valley in North and South Dakota, while in the east the Des Moines lobe spread over southern Minnesota and into Iowa. Both reached their limits about fifteen thousand years ago.

The northern plains looked very different before the glaciers. Although some parts were flat, others featured high plateaus and deep valleys. The glaciers changed all that by filling in the valleys and altering the course of

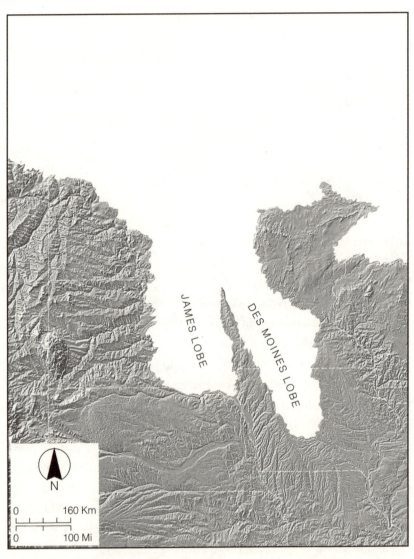

MAP 3. Glacial lobes during the last ice age. By Eureka Cartography.

rivers. Before the last ice age, the Red River valley was more than three hundred feet deep, and the Missouri River did not exist. Back then most streams in what are now the Dakotas and western Canada flowed to the northeast, into Hudson Bay, while those in Minnesota and Iowa ran southward. Today only the Red River flows north.

The study of glacial geology is fairly recent. The idea that masses of ice could shape the land did not take hold until the mid-1800s, largely through the efforts of Swiss-born geologist Louis Agassiz. Fellow geologist Jean de Charpentier persuaded Agassiz that Alpine glaciers once covered the lowlands as well as the mountains. Utterly convinced, Agassiz could think of nothing else to explain the strange gouges on bedrock, boulders found far from their outcrops, and peculiar mounds of rock debris. After he had spent years doing fieldwork, his 1840 book *Études sur les glaciers* argued not only that ice had covered lowland Switzerland but also that "great sheets of ice, resembling those now existing in Greenland, once covered all the countries in which unstratified gravel is found."[2] Skeptics were slowly won over, and now many thousands of researchers study the formation and behavior of glaciers.

A Glacier Is Born

A glacier begins life as untold numbers of tiny snowflakes. When freshly fallen, these delicate ice crystals are about 90 percent air. As more snow falls, flakes pack together in a random fashion. After centuries of buildup, the mass becomes almost solid ice, with less than 10 percent air. Glacial ice is made up of crystals of different sizes and orientations. Specialists call this polycrystalline ice, a type of ice that flows unlike other kinds of ice.[3]

A mass of ice officially becomes a glacier when it grows thick enough to flow outward (think of pouring molasses on a table). Like a river, the surface moves more quickly than its lower depths, and its middle moves faster than its margins. A glacier's pace is generally the very definition of glacial, perhaps only tens to hundreds of feet per year. At times, however, glaciers surge up to a hundred times faster by sliding on a layer of water.[4]

Such an icy world is far from silent. Colossal forces generated by a moving glacier produce a cacophony of cracks and creaks. When a frozen mass hundreds of feet thick advances over rough terrain, crevasses in the ice open and close in what experts call icequakes—seismic vibrations that rend the air with loud reports like gunshots.[5] Icequakes also occur when chunks of ice break off to form icebergs. The noise in this case consists of pops caused by trapped air bubbles that burst as some of the berg melts when it contacts water.[6]

Whatever their speed, these frozen juggernauts erode the surface beneath them. Glaciers abrade the earth when rock fragments frozen into their base act like oversized sandpaper, grinding soft rock into flour and leaving scratches on hard rock to mark their passing. Another means of erosion is plucking. This is when water beneath the glacier seeps into the cracks of surface rock; when it freezes, the ice plucks rock fragments—some as big as boulders—up into the debris layers of the glacier.[7]

After the Ice

As sculptors of the land, glaciers picked up untold tons of debris and then dropped it far from its source. Some debris was laid down as till—a grand mix of boulders, cobbles, pebbles, sand, silt, and clay. This smoothed the land, much as one would frost a cake. In places the ice formed ridges as it picked up and moved huge slabs of material.[8] Groups of oval streamlined mounds are known as drumlins, the name derived from a Gaelic word meaning "rounded hill."

As the climate warmed again, the glaciers stopped advancing and the massive ice sheets began to melt. To mark their maximum extent, they left hilly ridges called terminal or end moraines.[9] Atop the stagnating ice, huge amounts of rock debris accumulated. Melting was faster where the debris layer was thinner, thus leaving a jumbled landscape aptly called a dead-ice moraine. Pioneering plants soon colonized such areas, followed within a few decades by open spruce woodlands, some of which lasted for centuries.[10] Depressions left behind when isolated ice blocks melted became lakes and marshes.[11]

A glimpse into this early world comes from the Seibold Lake site, an ancient lake bed discovered on a farm in southeastern North Dakota.[12] Here, a treasure trove of plant and animal fossils were recovered from organic-rich sediments laid down in a small, deep lake that had formed in the melting ice about 11,500 years ago. This little body of water lasted for about a millennium before gradually becoming a shallow marsh and ultimately disappearing. When excavated in the late 1960s, the lake mud yielded a rich array of remarkably well-preserved fossils: algae, 88 species of insects, 9 aquatic plants, 5 kinds of fish, 11 varieties of freshwater clams and snails, a complete

FIG. 1. Spruce and alder forest growing atop stagnant glacier ice in Alaska. Photo © Tom Bean.

frog skeleton, the skull of a muskrat, signs of beaver (gnawed wood and fecal pellets), and 23 types of upland trees, shrubs, and herbs. Paleoecologists usually find a few scraps of past life at a site, but Seibold ultimately yielded an astonishing 160 examples of flora and fauna.[13] This diverse array shows how quickly plants and animals colonized the melting glacier.

Enormous amounts of debris also washed off the glacier. In summer, muddy streams rushed pell-mell down its front. When the rivulets reached the foot of the glacier, they dumped sand and gravel, forming conical hills called kames (from the Scottish word *kaim*, for "steep-sided hill"). Far more prevalent, however, are broad plains of outwash sands and gravels that can be seen in road cuts or gravel pits in eastern North Dakota, across Minnesota, and in northern Iowa. The outwash sediment, up to several hundred feet thick, is typically layered because, as the velocity of the meltwater stream decreased, it first dumped heavier gravels, then sands and smaller particles.

Snake-like sand and gravel ridges called eskers mark the course of streams that once flowed beneath, or within, a glacier. The word *esker* comes from an Irish word meaning "gravel ridge." Some say they look like abandoned railway embankments. Such former streambeds can be found in southern Manitoba, North Dakota, and northern Minnesota. Other streams flowing under the ice eroded long, U-shaped channels called tunnel valleys.[14]

As the great melt progressed, lowlands beyond the ice became glacial lakes, some covering many thousands of square miles. Among the largest were Lakes Regina in Saskatchewan, Hind in southwestern Manitoba, Souris in northern North Dakota, and Dakota in the James River valley. Large as they were, they all pale in comparison to Lake Agassiz, named after the father of glacial studies, Louis Agassiz. It became the largest of these inland oceans, once covering much of today's Manitoba and parts of eastern Saskatchewan, northwestern Ontario, North Dakota, and Minnesota.[15]

The milky clay and silt-rich meltwater that poured into Agassiz and other lakes built up over time to become the gumbo soil that residents know so well. Tributaries flowing into these lakes also built broad, fan-shaped deltas of sand and gravel.[16] The largest of these, the Assiniboine Delta in south-central Manitoba, covers twenty-five hundred square miles. Sand and gravel from this and other deltas washed into the lake and became worked into beach ridges that stretch for hundreds of miles across the countryside. Where sand was sparse or lacking, the crashing waves cut steep shorelines.

When Lake Agassiz eventually drained, it left three large lakes in southern Manitoba—Lakes Winnipeg, Winnipegosis, and Manitoba, which collectively cover more than thirteen thousand square miles. Most other water bodies are less than forty square miles. Extensive shallow marshlands lie south of Lakes Winnipeg and Manitoba, while millions of small "potholes," often less than two and a half acres in size, dot uplands across the region. Poorly drained expanses in southeastern Manitoba and northwestern Minnesota now support conifer bog forests, mineral-rich fens, and mossy peat lands.

The melting glaciers spewed forth oceans of icy water that carved deep valleys across the northern parts of the region. After the deluge, thousands of years of summer storms and spring snowmelts wore away the land, cutting new channels and washing clay, silt, sand, and gravel into river valleys.

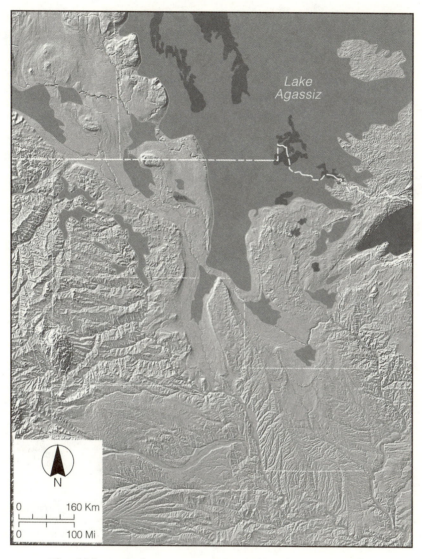

Lake
Agassiz

N

0   160 Km

0   100 Mi

MAP 4. Glacial lakes as the last ice age ended. By Eureka Cartography.

All of this erosion resulted in a complex network of waterways. The major
rivers and their tributaries today form a web so interlinked that you can put
a canoe in the water near Moose Jaw in central Saskatchewan and paddle
more than twelve hundred miles to the Mississippi in southern Minnesota
with only a single portage.[17]

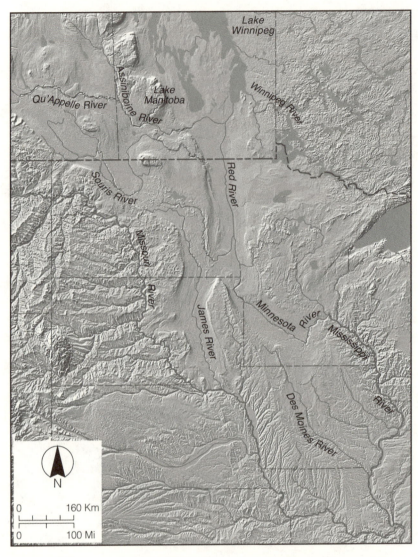

MAP 5. Major lakes and rivers of the northern plains. By Eureka Cartography.

Rivers and streams serve not only as travel routes; they also provide homes to an assortment of plants and animals. In the hills of northeastern Iowa and southwestern Minnesota, where stream gradients are steep, water flows swiftly and supports little aquatic life. At the other extreme are the flat Red and James River valleys, where sluggish rivers and streams are rich in invertebrates, fish, and plant life.

Across parts of southern Minnesota and western Iowa, strong, sometimes gale-force winds built thick deposits of a fine-grained silt called loess (from the German, meaning "loose"). Thicknesses range from about three feet in southern Minnesota to more than three hundred feet in extreme western Iowa.[18]

Soil: The World under Our Feet

The debris the glaciers left became the substrate for plant growth. In the words of soil scientist Wallace Fuller, this was the "thin rind of loose material . . . that stands between life and lifelessness."[19] Over time, this rind was transformed into soil as climate interacted with plants and other organisms present on the inorganic materials. Having had thousands of years to develop, the region's soils are today considered some of the most fertile on earth.[20]

The decay of a single blade of grass offers an example of how soil is created. As the grass stops growing, carbohydrates and amino acids leave the blade and move elsewhere in the plant, while waste products circulate into the dying leaf. As the blade turns brown and falls to the ground, any water-soluble compounds within the leaf dissolve and pass into the soil. Decomposers now begin feeding in earnest. The withered blade is attacked by hundreds of kinds of bacteria and fungi, as well as earthworms and millipedes. After about six months, little is left of the original grass blade.[21]

The best way to become acquainted with a prairie soil is to view it up close and personal. While driving through the countryside, stop where the road cuts through a hill and you will see, just beneath the plants growing on the surface, a thin layer of partially decayed leaves, stems, and other litter. This earthy-smelling mulch teems with life—microscopic bacteria, fungi, worms, millipedes, beetles, mites, rodents, and a host of other organisms— the frontline troops of soil development. (If truth be told, far more species live below the prairie sod than above it.) An army of creatures breaks down dead and dying roots, leaves, and stems into tiny organic particles and ultimately into the chemicals needed by plants.

FIG. 2. A soil profile in North Dakota. The vertical scale is in 10-centimeter intervals (3.9 inches). Photo by USDA.

The next visible layer is called the A horizon. It is a dark gray to black, organic-rich layer six to twelve inches deep and dense with living and decaying roots. Below that is the B horizon, a grayish-brown to brown layer, usually thicker than the A horizon. It has less organic matter and fewer roots. The roots of some prairie plants extend as deep as sixteen feet, ensuring they can survive all but the most severe drought.

To find out more about the plants that helped form these soils, we must turn to the fossil record.

Nature's History in a Pollen Grain

Each year a chronicle of natural events is recorded in lakes and bogs. While many organisms decompose after death, parts of some are preserved. A typical freshwater lake may yield the remains of snails, insects, various invertebrates, algae, and even animal skeletons. Pollen and other airborne particles from the surrounding landscape fall onto the water's surface, finally sinking when waterlogged. Sand, silt, clay, seeds, wood, and various other plant parts are washed in during rains or with melting snow. These aquatic remains, together with the washed-in material built up over thousands of years, store this ecological history. In some places, as much as thirty feet of mud has accumulated since the end of the last ice age.

As an archaeology student at the University of Minnesota, I was interested in Lake Agassiz's huge geological presence, which must have influenced the movements of early inhabitants. We knew from excavations that, after the lake drained, early peoples used the lake's beach ridges as travel corridors, for camping, and for burying their dead.[22] I wanted to learn more about the history of the lake and how changes in plant cover around its shores might have affected the habits of these hunters and gatherers. After discussions with my advisor and others, I chose to focus my thesis study on fossil pollen. This is how I ended up on a frozen pond one Sunday in early January working to retrieve a sediment core.[23]

Bone-chilling winds whipped across frozen Qually Pond as glacial geologist Herbert Wright and I, a raw graduate student, drilled through the thick ice with a hand-held auger. Like Arctic explorers, our breath formed

FIG. 3. Tom Shay and Herbert Wright at Qually Pond, 1961. Photo from author's personal collection.

ice crystals on our eyelashes and the fringes of our parkas. A photo taken that day shows Professor Wright's beard coated with frost.

The pond was located on the eastern edge of the Red River valley, where the highest beach ridge of Lake Agassiz turns 90° to the east. Since Qually seemed to be part of a former lagoon behind the beach, I hoped that radio-carbon dating would confirm that the pond had formed soon after the adjacent ridge. My goal was to collect a core of mud from the bottom for dating and pollen analysis, but why choose a frigid Sunday in January? Why brave such bone-chilling weather when, in a few months, we could return in shirtsleeves? Stability. Cores are best obtained from a stable platform, and there is no more stable platform than ice (in open water you have to use a pontoon boat).

The auger's spoon-shaped blade made a crackling sound as it pushed into the crystal-clear surface. When it had drilled through the thick mass, a puff of steam rose from the water below. To obtain the core, we used a piston sampler developed by freshwater lake specialist Dan Livingstone. The device resembled an oversized hypodermic syringe, consisting of a long, hollow steel tube about the diameter of my wrist with an inner rubber piston. The piston rose up the tube as mud entered the bottom. The entire mechanism was maneuvered with the aid of a metal frame and two chain hoists.[24]

We pushed the sampler into the mud until we had filled the tube, then hoisted it out of the water and used the piston to push a dark, organic-rich "sausage" onto a stout piece of aluminum foil. I wrapped and taped the core segment, using a marker to write its depth range and inscribe an arrow pointing to its top. Sections of lead pipe extended our reach for subsequent samples. When we hit sand, we knew we had reached the pond's bottom.

I began my lab work a few days later. Unwrapping the deepest core segment first, I cut it lengthwise to examine its color and texture, looking for any abrupt changes or conspicuous fossils. A portion was set aside for radiocarbon dating. Next, using a meter stick as a guide, I removed a pea-sized sample of mud at designated intervals and transferred each into a sterilized glass vial to be treated with chemicals that would eliminate extraneous material. Snail shells succumbed to hydrochloric acid, while hydrofluoric acid removed errant sand particles and potassium hydroxide got rid of miscellaneous organic debris. I transferred the resulting residue into tapered glass tubes and placed the tubes into a desktop centrifuge. The high-speed spinning separated solids, such as pollen, from the liquid. The resulting concentrate was then mounted on glass microscope slides for viewing.

On my first look I saw three types of pollen: the filigreed bladders of spruce; the plump, spheroidal birch, with three knob-like protruding pores; and the crumpled shape of a grass. Although thousands of years old, they looked as fresh as yesterday. I had pollen!

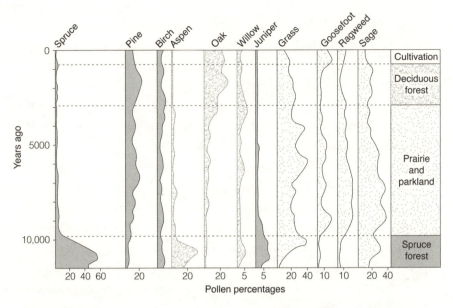

FIG. 4. Simplified pollen diagram of a core taken in the Tiger Hills, southern Manitoba (after Ritchie, "Late-Quaternary Vegetational History," 1801). By Patti Isaacs.

Beginning with that microscopic world from Qually Pond, I set off on a long and fascinating journey in search of traces of ancient plant life. Pollen grains offer an excellent opportunity to chart a site's past vegetation, mainly because they are produced in large numbers and disperse widely. Formed in the male parts of flowers and about the size of dust particles, several dozen can fit on the head of a pin. Most trees and shrubs and some wildflowers, grasses, and other herbs produce large quantities. For instance, the branch of a ten-year-old pine tree may yield 350 million pollen grains! Multiply the number of branches per tree by the number of trees in a forest, and you have a staggering number of particles wafting through the air. Each year between ten thousand and one hundred thousand grains fall on each square inch of ground.[25] Although most eventually decay, those that fall upon lakes and bogs are often preserved.

Fossil pollen grains are identified by their shape, size, and surface features using powerful microscopes. After tallying, the counts are converted into percentages and plotted by depth on a chart called a pollen diagram. Vari-

FIG. 5. The Pembina River valley at Tetrault Woods State Forest, west of Walhalla, North Dakota. Photo © Tom Bean.

ations in the percentages of each type (pine, spruce, grass, etc.) over time indicate an area's changing plant cover. Across the northern plains numerous diagrams show major changes in the percentages of trees, shrubs, and herbs. Most pollen diagrams from northwestern Minnesota show a sequence from spruce forest to prairie and in some places a partial return of forest. A recent abrupt increase in weeds indicates the advent of European-style agriculture.

The northern plains were created over eons, yet today's landscape was largely shaped by ice age glaciers over the past several million years. For example, glacial Lake Hind formed in southwestern Manitoba near the end of the most recent ice age. The lake covered some fifteen hundred square miles, and when it drained a couple of thousand years later, its surging waters created the Pembina River valley.[26] The ice age shaped the land, charted the rivers and streams, gave us our rich soils, and left us countless lakes and ponds. Plants and animals moved in even as the glaciers were melting. This warming period also marked the beginning of the region's human history.

FURTHER READING

Bluemle, John P. *North Dakota's Geologic Legacy: Our Land and How It Formed*. Fargo: North Dakota State University Press, 2016.

Diffendal, R. F., Jr. *Great Plains Geology*. Lincoln: University of Nebraska Press, 2017.

Redekop, Bill. *Lake Agassiz: The Rise and Demise of the World's Greatest Lake*. Winnipeg MB: Heartland Associates, 2017.

Land of the Restless Wind   2

An evil genius could not have devised a more perfect battleground for clashing weather fronts than the prairies of North America.

—DAVID LASKIN, *The Children's Blizzard*

Violent and capricious is the only way to describe the weather across the northern plains. Records prove this statement. Those from recent decades show that the region has the most unpredictable temperatures, precipitation, and severe storms of anywhere on the continent.[1] No wonder a common expression here is, "If you don't like the weather, wait five minutes."

A Restless Atmosphere

From year to year, month to month, day to day, and even hour to hour, changes in the weather can be dramatic. Such sudden shifts stem largely from the region's land-locked position, where moving air masses compete for dominance. As a result, the weather can be cold or warm, wet or dry, depending upon which air mass prevails at the time. Polar air descending from the Canadian Arctic brings dense, dry, icy blasts, provoking such remarks as, "There was only a barbed wire fence between us and the North Pole—and somebody left the gate open."[2] Gentle rain that cools a scorching August afternoon is due to warm, moist winds from the Gulf of Mexico coming up the Mississippi River valley. If this Gulf air collides with cooler air from the Rockies, a storm is likely.

Although distant, both the Pacific and Atlantic Oceans help shape plains weather. Oceans absorb and store an enormous amount of solar heat that is in constant flux, influencing weather patterns elsewhere. For instance, in the equatorial Pacific along the western coast of South America, sea

FIG. 6. Kills Two, a Sicangu Lakota, painting a winter count on buffalo skin. Photo by John Anderson. Courtesy of National Anthropological Archives, Smithsonian Institution NAA Inv. 03494000.

temperatures fluctuate from warm to cool in what climate scientists call the El Niño Southern Oscillation (ENSO). During an El Niño year, warm waters result from weak trade winds that fail to bring cold water up from the ocean depths. In the distant Great Plains, this can mean a warmer winter. The opposite occurs in a so-called La Niña year, when cooler-than-normal seas result in high-pressure conditions on the plains that block moisture-bearing winds and may lead to drought.[3]

Weather Watchers

Native peoples lived on the northern plains for thousands of years and became keen observers of the weather. Some of those observers recorded extreme conditions and important events in pictorial calendars called winter counts.[4] Originally painted on tanned bison hides, some are centuries old.

Count keepers drew images depicting the major event of the year, which might be a flood or drought or even the spectacular Leonid meteor shower of 1833–34.[5] Events could then be remembered and retold as stories. Several counts depict the brutal winter of 1852–53, with its heavy snows and dire conditions, as a "snowshoe winter." One Lakota count noted that "they ate their own horses."[6]

Native people knew that such atmospheric upheavals also affected plant and animal life.[7] The Anishinaabe writer Basil Johnston has observed that "weather, rain, tornado, gale, thunderstorm, cloud, sunshine, winds and their directions, rainlessness, snow, sleet, hail, prolonged cold, sudden warm spells, snowless winters all made some change in the growth of plants and harvest, which in turn altered and had a bearing upon the habits and movement of birds, animals, insects and fish."[8]

Storm

Flowers open to the sun on a prairie summer morning. Insects buzz about and gophers come out of their burrows. A meadowlark sings. Overhead, waves of puffy clouds drift across the sky, yet this day will not remain serene. A storm is brewing. By early afternoon the wind has strengthened as skies darken and animals seek shelter. Flashes of light on the horizon warn of what is to come. Soon, deep rumbles of thunder roll across the prairie.

FIG. 7. A storm approaches at Kalsow Prairie State Preserve, a tallgrass prairie remnant north of Manson, Iowa. Photo © Tom Bean.

Small whirlwinds appear here and there, picking up leaves and debris. These short-lived gusts, sometimes called dust devils, have been known to lift jackrabbits into the air. Clouds turn black as a downpour begins amid jagged lightning flashes and crashing thunder. After an hour or so the tempest subsides, leaving an earthy bouquet of rain-freshened air in its wake.[9]

Given the violence of thunderstorms, it is little wonder that they are featured in mythologies around the world. To the ancient Greeks they signified the wrath of Zeus, while the Norse spoke of hammer-wielding Thor. Similarly, indigenous people across the Great Plains tell of the mythical Thunderbird, a powerful storm spirit who made lightning with its eyes and produced thunder with its flapping wings.[10]

Thunderbird motifs turn up as decorations on pottery vessels, on war shields, and in rock art, which, according to specialist Jack Steinbring, may

FIG. 8. Thunderbird rock art at Jeffers Petroglyphs, Minnesota Historical Society Site, Cottonwood County, 1996. Photo by Eric Mortenson.

be up to several thousand years old.[11] Thunderbirds are among the numerous images pecked into the exposed quartzite outcrops at the Jeffers Petroglyphs site in southwestern Minnesota.

In some Native American stories the Thunderbird is linked with the sacred cedar tree. In the early 1900s pioneering ethnobotanist Melvin Gilmore studied the tree's uses among the Ponca, Pawnee, Omaha, and Teton Dakota peoples. He was told that the fabled creature nested in the cedars of the western mountains. One informant told Gilmore that families placed cedar boughs on their tipi poles to ward off lightning, just "as white men put up lightning rods."[12]

Some storms involve enormous amounts of energy. When colliding air masses generate huge, rotating updrafts around a vertical axis, they are deemed supercell storms. These air currents may persist for long periods, generating lightning, large hailstones, and heavy downpours. When they

FIG. 9. A supercell storm in South Dakota. Photo by Kelly DeLay.

descend to the ground, they can become terrifying tornadoes. Indigenous people had a healthy respect for these devastating whirlwinds, as shown by an Arikara story: "And they came to a place where Mother-Corn stopped and said: 'The big Black-Wind is angry. . . . We must hurry, for the big Black-Wind is coming[,] taking everything it meets. There is a cedar tree. Get under that cedar tree,' said Mother-Corn. 'It cannot be blown away. Get under its branches.' So the people crawled under its branches."[13]

Nani Suzette Pybus has described a Crow legend, part of the "sacred advice" given to young warriors, in which a boy is sucked up into a tornado and embraced by a creature called Bear Up Above.[14] The Bear Up Above shape resembles that of the clouds one might see inside the funnel of such a violent whirlwind. The song the boy hears may have been the tornado's roar, though the song ended when he was set down and the swirling stopped. In Pybus's opinion, "this detailed account agrees with modern descriptions of what happens when someone is caught up in a tornado."[15]

Storms are a mixed blessing. All living things need water, but rain does not always fall in gentle showers. Even spring can be hazardous, especially after heavy snows and a late thaw.

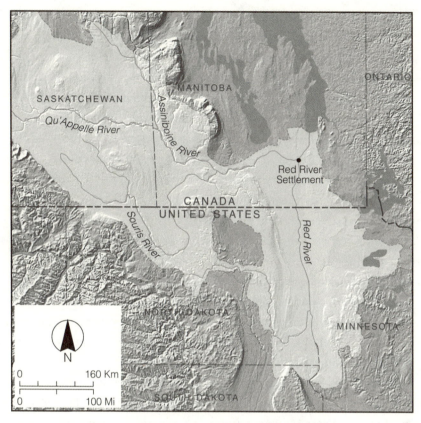

MAP 6. The Red River drainage basin. By Eureka Cartography.

Dark Waters Rising

Without doubt, no place in the northern plains is more susceptible to flooding than the Red River valley. Under adverse weather conditions the valley's flat topography and vast watersheds make a spring deluge inevitable. The most vulnerable part of the valley lies at the confluence of the Red and the Assiniboine Rivers in what is now Winnipeg. It was here in the early 1800s that the Hudson's Bay Company happened to build its regional headquarters.

Settlers arrived in 1812 and began farming at what became known as the Red River Settlement.[16] After a dozen years of struggle, the community of a few hundred was beginning to thrive when the spring of 1826 brought disaster. Nineteenth-century historian Alexander Ross summed up the conditions that led to the deluge: "The previous year had been unusually wet; the country was thoroughly saturated; the lakes, swamps, and rivers, at the fall of the year, were full of water; and a large quantity of snow had fallen in the preceding winter. Then came a late spring, with a sudden burst of warm weather, and a south wind blowing for several days in succession."[17]

The breakup of river ice that year was abrupt, catching even the wariest off guard. Francis Heron, a Hudson's Bay Company clerk, recorded the flood's progress. On May 4, 1826, he recorded that the water under the ice had risen five feet in twenty-four hours but had not broken through. When it finally did, the very next day, there was "an awful rush" that carried away cattle, houses, and everything else in its path. Homes were lost in an instant, and people were left clinging to trees while awaiting rescue. Five days into the flood, ice on the Assiniboine River broke up and added its waters: "The whole population were again in motion, flying to such situations as might afford them a temporary security, leaving in many instances their cattle to perish, and most of their effects to be swept away, happy in escaping with their lives."[18] It was mid-June before people could begin rebuilding their homes and livelihoods.[19]

The flood left more than devastation and bitter memories. More than a century and a half later, physical traces turned up on the river flats near the confluence of the Red and Assiniboine. In the summer of 1991 archaeologists were excavating the remains of Fort Gibraltar, an early fur-trading post built in 1807. Over a number of hot days in July they unearthed a poignant scene frozen in time. From the tracks impressed into the dried mud, it looked as if someone had been leading a team of oxen pulling a heavily laden cart across a muddy field, perhaps the traces of a family fleeing that terrible event.[20]

I can appreciate the settlers' plight—their fears and frustrations, their losses, their fighting spirit. In 1997 my wife (Jennifer) and I fought to save our home on the Red River south of Winnipeg during the worst flooding since 1826. In the end, with a great deal of help, we succeeded, as someone put it, "against all odds." Excerpts from Jennifer's diary tell part of our story, which began in mid-March when we ordered truckloads of sand and hundreds of sandbags to build a dike around our house. While we both worked outside with the dozens of volunteers filling sandbags, Jennifer also fed the hungry mob.

FIG. 10. Unearthed human and animal footprints, possibly made by refugees fleeing the 1826 flood. Photo courtesy of Parks Canada/Quaternary Consultants.

Monday, March 24: Snow, wet snow—the last thing we want. Tom very antsy re flood.

Tuesday, April 1: The boys (4) filled 250 sandbags in two hours. Sorted cookbooks and became quite depressed over the whole packing job.

Saturday, April 5: Rain, sleet, strong winds all day.

Sunday, April 6: Incredible winds and snow, snow, snow. Winnipeg declared an emergency. Highway 75 and most other roads cut off.

Monday, April 7: Snowed in. Packed books and sitting room things all day. Jules ploughed the road at 5 and had a hot brandy and cookies. Tom very worried.

Tuesday, April 8: Still many roads in southern part of province blocked. Apparently the blizzard was the worst ever in Winnipeg.

Thursday, April 10: Flood forecast 1 meter above last year—the flood of the century.

Saturday, April 12: Charles arrived 8:10 shortly after Doug with the front-end loader. From then on the day became more and more chaotic. I did pea soup and spuds for about 16 and juice and cookies all day. Diane packed books most of the day and was a super help.

Sunday, April 13: An overwhelming day. Support from so many— Charles again. . . . I did a lot of bagging and got overtired and a bit weepy. Six stayed for an unexpected supper. Mud everywhere.

Wednesday, April 16: Frantically busy day with sandbagging machine. No students came but six excellent men from Klefeld [*sic*] and Steinbach. Huge influx in pm. . . . I did dinner for 14 and refreshments for three dozen or more. Filled 5,000 bags and did a lot of dike.

Thursday, April 17: What a day. Activity from morn till sunset. The most wonderful Mennonite Disaster Relief workers toiled all day organized by Pat and Rick. An amazing effort . . . what dedicated and wonderful friends.

Friday, April 18: A busy day. Wayne worked on cottage. The movers took away furniture. . . . 29 for lunch 25 for supper.

Saturday, April 19: Charles and Pat came early and coped with the volunteers. 30 or so from all over. Things got chaotic. 19 for lasagna supper brought by Ruth.

Sunday, April 20: An incredibly busy day with loads of people. Built bottom half of huge dike in front of garage. . . . Chaotic afternoon. Little sand or bags. None available. Charles and Pat worked like beavers all day.

Monday, April 21: Feverish work all round . . . 25 plus people worked on bags and stockpiled them. . . . Alex and his crew stayed till 10 pm. We were exhausted. Got some sand.

Tuesday, April 22: Another huge influx of people. Some sand delivered—got people out later in canoes.

Wednesday, April 23: Feverish filling of bags with sand as water rose in afternoon then suddenly in pm, just got cars out in time. . . . Got people out by motor boat by 10 pm.

Thursday, April 24: Began to clean up debris throughout the house. . . . Went to bed very tired. All seemed well until at 3 am we heard water

FIG. 11. Flooding at St. Agathe, Manitoba, near Winnipeg, 1997. Photo © Province of Manitoba.

and found 3–4 feet of water in garage. Bob came and he and Tom found the major piping spot near the garage, plugged it with clay filled bags . . . to slow the flow. Left 3 sump pumps going outside and 2 in the basement. . . . Emptied deep freeze and stowed all remaining things upstairs—left at 8 pm by canoe. St. Mary's Road more or less water covered. Warm welcome and hot baths at Cam's.

We were evacuated for five weeks. When we returned, it took scores of volunteers another two months to remove some thirty thousand sandbags and clean up our property. Our house was saved, although property damage across the Red River valley amounted to billions of dollars. The flood also claimed more than a dozen lives. Of course the experience of area residents in 1997 pales in comparison with the plight of those in 1826. The settlers had neither sand nor sandbags and certainly none of the modern technology we were able to access. Even so, many people suffered in both floods.

The 1997 deluge spawned research projects aimed at deciphering the history of flooding along the Red River. One involved sampling a net-

0   0.5   1   2 mm

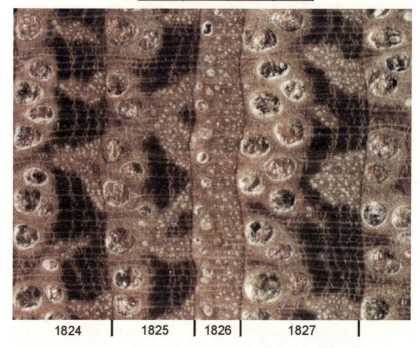

1824 | 1825 | 1826 | 1827 |

FIG. 12. A microscopic view of oak tree rings. In 1824, 1825, and 1827 large circular vessels formed. During the spring of 1826 the vessels failed to develop, indicating the tree must have been standing in water. Photo courtesy of Scott St. George.

work of oak trees of varying ages to identify past floods recorded in their growth rings.

Microscopic examination of the growth rings in a tree's trunk tells us about its past, with wide rings indicating a good year with ample moisture and narrow rings meaning poor growth, most likely due to lack of moisture. The sequence of rings across a series of trees can reveal the local history of wet and dry periods. During a typical spring, oaks form several rows of relatively large, circular vessels that conduct water and other nutrients from the soil to the tree as its branches leaf out. If the lower part of the trunk lies under water during this time, these vessels fail to develop. Seen under a microscope, such shrunken cells are a clear sign of a flood.

Gathering samples for tree-ring analysis is simple but arduous. The first step is to choose a mature tree, preferably one that looks older than eighty years, with a trunk about a foot in diameter. The coring device, called an increment borer, is then assembled. Borers come in various lengths and diameters for different tree sizes, but all consist of three parts: a stout handle; a hollow steel tube called an auger, which is threaded on the outside; and an extractor that fits inside the auger. As the auger is screwed into a tree, the arduous part of the operation, a core of wood is pushed into the extractor. After the auger is unscrewed, the thin cylinder of wood, about 0.2 inch in diameter, is carefully removed from the extractor, wrapped, and labeled with the species, trunk diameter, location, and collection date.[21]

Researchers Scott St. George and Erik Nielsen sampled more than four hundred living oak trees, timbers from historic houses, and trunks buried in river mud. In the end they identified five major floods over the past two hundred years, including the deluge of 1826. They also found eight earlier floods, the earliest dating back to the year 1500.[22]

Clear Skies, Parched Earth

The dreaded word *drought* conjures images of months of rainless skies, blistering heat, searing winds, and choking dust. The semiarid northern plains are no stranger to such calamities. Thankfully, prairie plants can cope with all but the most severe droughts because their extensive root systems enable them to access moisture deep in the soil. In the nineteenth century severe dry spells struck the region every decade or so.[23]

Researchers also turned to tree rings to learn more about early droughts. Just as trees can record past floods, they reflect drought years by laying down narrower rings.[24] An index based on recorded temperature and precipitation data created by W. C. Palmer in the 1960s is now used to estimate the severity of past droughts.[25] Palmer based his index on these data, since both monthly temperatures and rainfall reflect levels of soil moisture, a key limiting factor in plant growth. A map derived from a network of tree-ring histories shows an intense summer drought across the region from 1818 to 1820.[26]

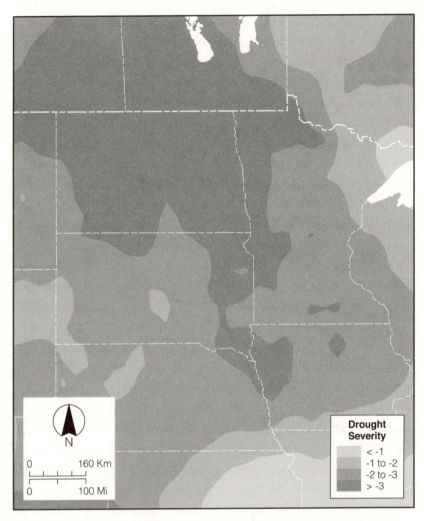

MAP 7. The severe drought of 1818–20 as reconstructed from tree rings. Source: Cook et al., "Megadroughts in North America." By Eureka Cartography.

An Awful Splendor

"Fire!" is surely the most alarming cry in any language. Whether sparked by lightning or set by humans, blazes occur most often in late summer or early autumn, when the grass has become tinder dry. If driven by strong winds, wildfires' terrifying speed demands quick action to escape them. American artist George Catlin traveled across the region during the 1830s and was amazed by what he saw: "The fire in these, before such a wind, travels at an immense and frightful rate, and often destroys, on their fleetest horses, parties of Indians, who are so unlucky as to be overtaken by it."[27]

A fire story captured in a 1762–63 winter count from Coteau des Prairies in eastern South Dakota tells of a Lakota band encamped by the shore of a lake. When the grass caught fire, it killed a woman, her husband, and several children. Others saved themselves by jumping into the lake, but many suffered burns to their lower legs and thighs. Following this incident, the band was given the new name of Sicangu, or Burnt Thighs, known to French traders as the Brulés (the Burned Ones).[28]

William Clark of the Lewis and Clark expedition told how a Hidatsa child was saved from a blaze: "Seeing no hopes of carrying off her son, [the mother] threw him on the ground and, covering him with the fresh hide of a buffalo, escaped herself from the flames. As soon as the fire had passed, she returned and found him untouched, the skin having prevented the flame from reaching the grass on which he lay."[29]

Occasional fires burned for days and scorched huge tracts of land. Canadian explorer Henry Hind described an 1857 fire: "From beyond the South Branch of the Saskatchewan to Red River all the prairies were burned last autumn, a vast conflagration extended for one thousand miles in length and several hundred in breadth."[30]

Modern research helps us appreciate how wildfires affect prairie plants. In one study, Jennifer and her group of ecologists conducted controlled burns over three growing seasons on a mixed-grass prairie in western Manitoba. The team first laid out large rectangular plots, with each plot receiving a different treatment: a control plot with no burn, then other plots burned once, burned twice, and so forth. The results showed that if this mixed-grass prairie burned every three years, its productivity and species composition remained about the same. However, if it burned more frequently, plant biomass declined and its composition changed.[31]

A wildfire can cause devastation, but that might also be a backhanded gift from Mother Nature. As the fire consumes everything in its path, the burning releases nutrients necessary for new growth. Fire also exposes the soil to needed sunlight and rain. Given what we know of ancient climates, fire and grassland have doubtless been partners for millions of years, and, like the fabled phoenix, prairies seem always to rise from the ashes.[32]

Darkened Skies and Rasping Jaws

A swarm of locusts was without doubt the strangest natural calamity the region's early inhabitants faced. Great clouds of them numbering in the trillions swept across the prairie, falling from the sky and devouring every blade of grass. Their rasping jaws sounded like the crackling of a great fire.[33] The size of swarms staggers the imagination. In a July 1806 journal entry, explorer William Clark observed, "Emence Sworms of Grass hoppers have distroyed every Sprig of Grass for maney miles."[34]

While swarms could be devastating, the insects offered an excellent source of protein. Settler Fanny Kelly described the response of a band of Lakotas to a locust invasion in 1864: "To catch them, large holes are dug in the ground, which are heated by fires. Into these apertures the insects are then driven, and, the fires having been removed, the heated earth bakes them. They are considered good food, and were greedily devoured."[35]

Although most nineteenth-century writers called these insects grass-hoppers, entomologists know them as the Rocky Mountain locust (*Melanoplus spretus*)—*Rocky Mountain* for their main breeding grounds and *locust*, derived from the Latin *locus ustus*, meaning "burnt place."[36] During peak years they consumed nearly as much biomass as bison. These ravaging insects became extinct in 1902, most likely because farm fields and pastures had replaced their breeding habitat. With no living specimens to study, entomologist Jeff Lockwood and his associates surveyed glaciers in Montana and Wyoming and found well-preserved remains, a few as old as seven hundred years.[37]

Local Climates

Apart from calamitous floods, fires, and droughts, weather patterns vary widely across the region. To illustrate, if you live around Moose Jaw, Saskatchewan, in the northwestern part of the region, you can expect a short growing season that begins in mid-May and ends in late September with the arrival of snow. July is generally the warmest month with an average high of about 67 degrees Fahrenheit. January is the coldest, at barely above zero. Moose Jaw is dry, with annual precipitation of only around fourteen inches. In short, the area has long, cold winters and short, warm summers.[38]

It is a different story far to the south around Des Moines, Iowa. By mid-April frosts have ended, and temperatures do not usually drop below freezing again until mid-October. In January thermometers maintain near-freezing temperatures, while in July the mercury climbs to the mid-eighties. January is normally snowy, but amounts are modest. Most of the area's three feet of annual precipitation falls as rain. Des Moines thus enjoys a subhumid climate with mild winters and hot summers.

Plants, animals, and people adjust to their local situations. Many plants that grow in the southern part of the region cannot survive in the northern part, whereas those adapted to dry conditions do not do well in humid areas. Nonetheless, a milder climate and longer growing season means that in ancient times Iowa was probably an easier entry point for introducing crops than areas farther north.

Coping with Snow and Cold

By any measure, winters in the northern plains can be harsh, especially in the north. The deadliest of winter storms, the blizzard, supposedly gets its name from early German settlers in Iowa who referred to the sudden snowstorms that rolled across the prairie as *blitzartig*, meaning "the storm comes like lightning." A prairie blizzard can quickly turn a pleasant winter's day into a roaring, swirling, blinding mass of frozen needles. Snow and sky merge in a world of white where no shadow is cast and no horizon can be seen. Anyone caught in such a storm knows how disorienting it can be. After wandering for hours, becoming tired and drowsy, the urge to lie down and rest is irresistible. This could result in being found lifeless and frozen after the tempest abates.[39]

Blizzards can strike even in springtime. Buffalo Bird Woman of the Hidatsa tribe vividly remembered one such violent storm that occurred when she was only six years old. Anthropologist Gilbert Wilson shared the account in *Waheenee: An Indian Girl's Story*. At the end of the winter of 1845–46, the people of her village were lulled into a false sense of security by an apparent early spring. They had moved to the summer village but were surprised by a violent snowstorm that caught several war parties on the open prairie. The account tells of how her father, Small Ankle, survived the storm:

> Two days later Small Ankle and his war party returned. To everyone's relief, all had survived, with only two cases of frostbite. Big Cloud, their leader, had directed them to take shelter in the trees along the Missouri River so they led their ponies single file through the drifts, reaching the river before nightfall. There they found an area of burnt timber among the cottonwoods and camped for the night. With flint and steel, Small Ankle had started a campfire. Soon everyone was warm enough to take off their leggings and wet moccasins and dry them. They toasted dried meat for supper while their ponies fed on green cottonwood branches. After the storm died down, the party headed for home. They were the lucky ones. Sadly, another war party had not fared so well. Unable to reach the trees, they lay down in a coulee and let the snow drift over them. Two men froze to death.[40]

People coped with snow and cold through their choices of what they wore, how they traveled and hunted, the foods they ate, where they lived, and even their sports and games.[41] Adequate body protection was vital for survival. We can glean some hints about early clothing from the tools found to make them—bone awls, stone scrapers, and knives—even though the garments themselves have perished.[42] They most likely used animal skins and furs to tailor their garments, including leggings, mittens, and snug hats, topped by buffalo robes. Clothing not only had to insulate, it also needed to allow free range of motion and regulate body temperature. As archaeologist Ian Dyck has noted, "An important design feature of Aboriginal clothing was the facility with which it permitted the control of body heat generated by exercise. Closures at the wrists, waist, neck and knees could be tightened to contain heat, or loosened to release it into another compartment of the clothing or away from the body altogether."[43]

Bison herds spent winters either on the open prairie or along the forest fringes, moving to where they could obtain enough forage. Native groups followed the herds, camping nearby and hunting as needed.[44] In hilly coun-

FIG. 13. Small bison herd in winter snow. Photo by Lloyd Blunk on Unsplash.

try the people could drive the animals over a cliff or down a steep hill. On flatter ground hunters might force them into a snowbank. Families worked together to erect elaborate corrals, known as "pounds," with the goal of funneling the herd into an enclosed killing field. Hudson's Bay Company trader Matthew Cocking observed one such pound on October 23, 1772, in central Saskatchewan:

> It is a Circle fenced round with trees laid one upon another at the foot of a Hill, about 7 feet high and a hundred yards in circumference: entrance on the Hill side, where the Animal can easily go over; but when in, cannot return: From this entrance small sticks are laid on each side like a fence in form of an angle extending from the pound; beyond these to about 1 1/2 mile distant. Buffalo Dung or old roots are

laid in Heaps in the same direction as the fence; these are to frighten the Beasts from deviating on either side.[45]

Snowshoes helped hunters pursue an animal across soft snow, as George Catlin observed: "In the dead of the winters . . . the Indian runs upon the surface of the snow with the aid of his snowshoes, which buoy him up, while the great weight of the buffaloes, sinks them down to the middle of their sides, and completely stopping their progress, ensures them certain and easy victims to the bow or lance of their pursuers."[46]

Winter activities demanded a great deal of energy. Snowshoeing at even a regular walking pace over soft snow is as energy-intensive as a cross-country run.[47] Native peoples derived calories from eating fresh or dried meat mixed with fat, bone marrow, and dried berries or perhaps seeds or root foods saved from the previous summer. These would go a long way toward satisfying the daily need for three thousand to four thousand calories when one was gathering firewood, checking traps and snares, or hunting game.[48]

If winter dragged on and larders emptied, a meal of sorts could be prepared from the peeled, calorie-rich inner bark of cottonwood or other trees, a food source that could either be cooked or chewed raw.[49] Some say that such bark tastes like the tree it came from: sweet for maple, bland for cottonwood. To add to such meager fare, people searched for overwintering fruits like rose hips or highbush cranberries.[50]

Though bitter, some lichens were also gathered; boiling slightly improved their flavor.[51] Sadly, on rare occasions when food supplies ran out, a diet of lichens, bark, and berries could not save some from starving.[52]

Winter Fun

By no means did cold weather and snow discourage outdoor activities. Edwin Denig tells of Assiniboine women playing a game involving "sliding long sticks on snow."[53] This activity sounds very similar to another game, one that involved throwing a blunt-ended pole (a "snow snake") underhanded along a snowy track, rather like tossing a bowling ball. Poles were about six feet long and tapered; the blunt end became the head of the "snake,"

FIG. 14. Migrating geese in flight. Photo by Raphael Rychetsky on Unsplash.

with incised eyes and a slit for a mouth.[54] A strong slider could toss a snake several hundred yards.

Sledding was popular among Blackfoot children. They made their sled runners out of buffalo ribs tied together at the ends to form a kind of cage. Upon this, they then stretched a hide to make a seat. Some sleds had a rawhide rope tied in front and buffalo tails at the back.[55]

A Lovely Land

To the early inhabitants the prairie was home, a challenging but comfortable place to live. I have spent most of my life on the prairies, first in Minnesota and then in Manitoba. Since leaving, I miss the connections with nature found there: seeing skeins of geese honking across a spring sky, feeling gentle summer breezes waft mosquitoes away, crunching through leaves on golden autumn afternoons, watching softly falling snowflakes and maybe catching some on my tongue. Most of all I miss those starry winter nights that came alive with wondrous shimmering northern lights. In short, the prairie delights in every season.

FURTHER READING

Dewey, Kenneth F. *Great Plains Weather*. Lincoln: University of Nebraska Press, 2019.

Marshall, John, and R. Alan Plumb. *Atmosphere, Ocean, and Climate Dynamics: An Introductory Text*. Cambridge MA: Academic Press, 2016.

Therrell, Matthew D., and Makayla J. Trotter. "Waniyetu Wówapi: Native American Records of Weather and Climate." *Bulletin of the American Meteorological Society* 92, no. 5 (2011): 583–92.

The Land Is Sacred

3

The land is our mother, the rivers our blood.

—MARY BRAVE BIRD, *Ohitika Woman*

For countless generations Native groups called the northern Great Plains home. These lands gave them a livelihood and were a spiritual anchor. Aboriginal peoples everywhere have strong ties to the environment and its relevance for their past, present, and future. The story of the earth beneath their feet became their story or, as Tr'ondëk Hwëch'in (Hän) elder Percy Henry put it, "Our land is our history book."[1] They knew every hill, valley, prairie patch, and tree grove within their territories yet kept in touch with the wider world via well-worn footpaths and the midcontinent's vast network of waterways.

Some notable features—a high butte, an isolated boulder, or an unusual rock formation—became known as places of great spiritual and cultural meaning. According to ethnobotanist Gary Nabhan, "When a place is described as a sacred site, it is not simply located in the landscape, but also located in cultural rules and regulations."[2]

Native peoples have inhabited this region since the melting of the glaciers. In the early years everyone lived in hunting camps on the open plains, but much later some built villages beside rivers and lakes. In the words of Watchemonne ("the Orator"), Ioway: "Search at the mouth of the Upper Ioway River; there see their dirt lodges, or houses, the mounds and remains of which are all plain to be seen, even at this day."[3] Only a few such places survive today.

Their legacy is omnipresent. Many modern highways follow Native trails that European explorers, fur traders, and settlers also trod.[4] Furthermore, the

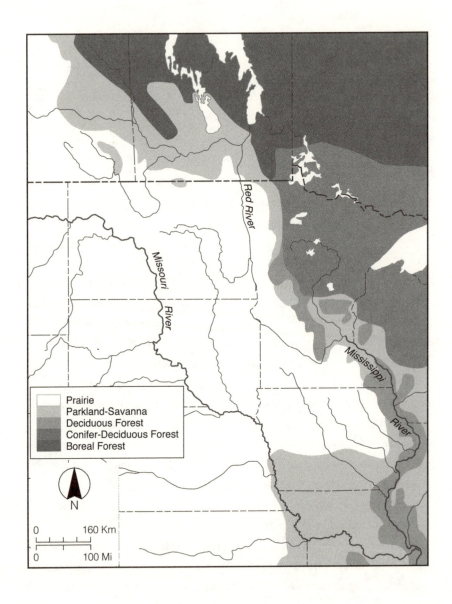

Prairie
Parkland-Savanna
Deciduous Forest
Conifer-Deciduous Forest
Boreal Forest

N

0   160 Km

0   100 Mi

MAP 8. Pre-European vegetation of the northern plains. Based on Rowe, *Forest Regions of Canada*, 1300; and Küchler, *Potential Natural Vegetation of the Conterminous United States*. By Eureka Cartography.

name of every state and province in the northern plains is derived from an indigenous language, as are those of many rivers, towns, and cities. Traces of the natural world can be found in preserved tracts of prairie, woodland, and marsh.

Hundreds of years ago prairies dominated this part of the continent. To the north and east were scattered tree groves of aspen, which botanists label "parkland," or "savanna," where oaks prevailed. Eastward were large tracts dominated by deciduous trees like oaks, maples, and basswood. Farther to the east and north were, and still are, forests made up of both deciduous and coniferous species such as aspen, birch, pine, spruce, and fir.[5] Finally, a traveler moving northward would, then and now, enter what are called "boreal" forests, with mainly coniferous trees but including aspen and birch.[6] This general pattern of vegetation was shaped by temperature and precipitation.[7]

To learn more about this fascinating countryside, this chapter takes us on a virtual tour, exploring both the natural and cultural heritage of a region that has been the backdrop to the shifting kaleidoscope of relations between plants and peoples since the end of the last ice age. We can't visit with the people of the ancient past, but we can walk where they walked and see things they must have seen under those prairie skies of long ago. Driving the scenic route by car from southern Saskatchewan to Des Moines, Iowa, with stops along the way, would take six or seven days. Several centuries ago the same trip took several weeks by horse and wagon or three months on foot. Our tour takes place in midsummer, the height of the flowering season.

We begin near Moose Jaw, about an hour's drive west of Saskatchewan's provincial capital, Regina. The city lies along its eponymous river, whose name is a reference to *moosegaw*, a Cree word meaning "warm breezes." Gentle winds that flow through the sheltered valley, along with abundant water and game, have made this an exceptional place to live for the past thousand years.[8]

The uplands surrounding Moose Jaw form part of a broad swath of rough terrain extending from Alberta to South Dakota. Early French explorers and traders called it Coteau du Missouri, "hills of the Missouri." It was here that

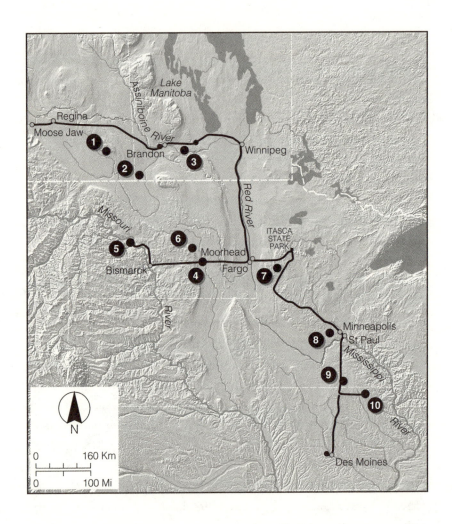

MAP 9. A virtual road trip from Moose Jaw, Saskatchewan, to Des Moines, Iowa. Among the locations visited are (1) Moose Mountain Provincial Park; (2) Southwestern Manitoba Mixed-Grass Prairie; (3) Spruce Woods Provincial Park; (4) National Buffalo Museum; (5) Knife River Indian Villages National Historic Site; (6) Cottonwood Lake Study Area; (7) Bluestem Prairie Scientific and Natural Area; (8) Wolsfeld Woods Scientific and Natural Area; (9) Myre–Big Island State Park; and (10) Hayden Prairie State Preserve. Other stops are shown as black dots. By Eureka Cartography.

ancient sedimentary rocks were laid down in tropical swamps some sixty million years ago. Much later, ice age glaciers moved in and covered the rocks with a thick layer of glacial debris.[9] Looking eastward from the edge of the Coteau du Missouri's eastern face, well above the adjacent plain, we can envisage early hunters scanning for bison, fur traders looking for an easy route east, or perhaps immigrant settlers resting on their westward journey.

We take the Trans-Canada Highway, descending onto the flat bed of former glacial Lake Regina. Some fifteen thousand years ago, its icy waters sprawled across southeastern Saskatchewan from Moose Jaw to Weyburn, south of Regina.[10] The silts and clays left in the lake bed now grow some of the country's highest-quality wheat. Farther along, the highway passes a patchwork of fields and pastures, with shallow ponds sprinkled here and there. Trees are confined to small groves or planted shelterbelts.

Two hours east of Moose Jaw and another hour south is Moose Mountain Provincial Park. From the air, this and a half dozen other isolated uplands scattered across the region resemble an archipelago of giant stepping-stones rising from a prairie sea. Covering an area of five thousand square miles, Moose Mountain is home to several lakes and forests of aspen, balsam poplar, green ash, and box elder (called Manitoba maple in Canada).[11]

Wandering into an aspen grove from the roadside, we stop to listen to the soothing whisper of leaves. Sometimes called quaking or trembling aspen, the tree's flat leafstalks lie at right angles to the leaves, so that the slightest puff of air sets them aquiver. We pick a leaf, and sure enough, it wiggles in our fingers.

To the west of the park, and within Pheasant Rump Nakota First Nation, sits a mound of boulders at the hub of a large circle with five lines of stones radiating outward like spokes in a wheel. Although the origin story of Moose Mountain Medicine Wheel has been forgotten, radiocarbon dating shows that it was laid out twenty-eight hundred years ago.[12] We can easily appreciate the effort it took to carefully place all those stones. Some think these rocks conform to the alignment of celestial bodies at the summer solstice, though others dispute this. Whatever its original purpose, the medicine wheel is still considered sacred and used for Native ceremonies.[13]

FIG. 15. Aspen leaf morphology. Photo by Pat Breen.

East Meets West in Manitoba: Mixed-Grass Prairie

Crossing into Manitoba and turning south at the town of Virden, we come to patches of grassland that make up the Southwestern Manitoba Mixed-Grass Prairie Important Bird Area (IBA) around Melita. This place attracts birders from across the continent because of its rare species, including the reclusive Baird's sparrow, the mockingbird-like loggerhead shrike, and a small but long-legged nocturnal burrowing owl.[14]

Mixed-grass prairies once dominated more than two-thirds of the region but are now quite rare. With an annual precipitation average midway between the humid east and dry west, these grasslands contain species common to both tallgrass prairies to the east and shortgrass prairies to the west. Eastern plants, such as little bluestem and brilliant, reddish-orange wood lilies, prefer low-lying swales, while those common in the west, like the prickly pear cactus, are suited to dry slopes. In between, knee-high grasses prevail. The blue-tinged leaves and compact seed heads of several kinds of wheatgrass make them easy to identify but difficult to tell apart.[15]

FIG. 16. Plains porcupine grass with its sharp awns. Photo by Katy Chayka, Minnesota Wildflowers.

The seed heads of spear or plains porcupine grass feature long bristles called awns. After they drop, the awns twist into the soil like a kind of seed drill, aiding their propagation. Hikers and field botanists beware! These sharp bristles can also bore into flesh. We pick up an awn to see how it has coiled in response to drying out. Amazing. Close relatives, grama grasses, are far more benign. One species, blue grama, has one-sided seed spikes that resemble bushy eyebrows.

Sweetgrass, revered by Native people, also grows here. A short, hardy perennial, it releases a pleasant vanilla scent when burned, which may

FIG. 17. A prairie dog peeking from its burrow. Photo by Moritz Kindler on Unsplash.

explain why this grass features importantly in Native cleansing and healing ceremonies.

Wonderful splashes of color grace this midsummer prairie, including clusters of lemon-yellow hairy golden asters and pale violet moss phlox. The tiny yellow blooms of silverberry shrubs have been out for several weeks, exuding their heavy, insect-attracting scent, while small pink-and-white snowberry flowers are just beginning to show.

These grasslands were once thick with herds of bison, elk, and prong-horn, all preyed upon by grizzly bears and packs of wolves. The only signs of mammals on this day are a few mounds made by pocket gophers and the odd prairie dog peeping out of its burrow. Mind you, if we had come at night, we might have spied a swift fox, restored to the area a few decades ago.

Ancient Hunters and Campers of the Assiniboine

The road from Virden to Brandon partly parallels the southeastward-flowing Assiniboine River, named for a local Native tribe. Like other broad valleys in the northern plains, the Assiniboine is a product of the ice age. When huge glacial lakes overflowed, they released massive torrents of water that carved deep, wide spillways. After the deluge subsided, these channels partly filled with sand and gravel to become today's Assiniboine, Souris, Pembina, and Sheyenne River valleys.[16]

The highway crosses the Assiniboine a short distance before reaching Brandon. Climbing out of the valley, it passes Grand Valley Provincial Park, which features a campground, lookout tower, and interpretive trail. Excavations in the 1980s revealed that more than a thousand years ago hunters drove herds of bison down the valley slope to be killed and butchered. Most of the bones found had been boiled to extract the calorie-rich marrow, though some had been shaped into tools. Families probably roasted meat at their hillside camps, but they may have dried the rest as jerky and pemmican. To make clothing and household items, they used stone knives and scrapers to prepare the hides. Broken pieces of pottery suggest they cooked in clay pots. Apart from bison, their menus also featured freshwater clams, fish, beaver, muskrat, and probably wild plants. Their choices of stone for tools provide clues as to the people's wide-ranging contacts. Some arrow tips and knives were fashioned from Knife River flint, a sought-after stone quarried to the south in western North Dakota, more than a week's journey away by foot.[17]

Spirit Sands of the Assiniboine Delta

East of Brandon we drive across the Assiniboine Delta, an expanse of rolling sand dunes now stabilized by grassy pastures and groves of white spruce

FIG. 18. Skeleton plant, a sand dune survivor. Photo by Bryan Kelly-MacArthur.

trees. Heading south past the town of Carberry, we come to Spruce Woods Provincial Park, covering more than a hundred square miles. Here we climb up to Manitoba's only patch of active dunes, just a few square miles in extent.

Trudging across sand in prairie country feels surreal—in every direction we see gently undulating ripples and waves. This microcosm has its own fauna and flora, an island of desert in a grassland sea. A skittering northern prairie skink or even a slithering hognose snake might cross our path.[18] Pockmarking the sand are tiny blowouts, each surrounding a wiry-stemmed skeleton plant. This member of the daisy family is a stubborn survivor; it keeps growing despite being constantly covered by blowing sand. Buried fragments have been known to emerge from sixteen inches deep.[19]

Anishinaabe people refer to the dunes as Kiche Manitou, from an Algonquin term that means "Great Spirit" or "Great Mystery." Early British explorer David Thompson noted, "On the east side, [the dunes have] very little grass in a few places, no snow lies on them all winter, which is the reason the Natives call them Manito; or preternatural."[20] The area, also known as the Spirit Sands, remains a place of reverence and ceremony.

Sands make strange noises when they move, producing an eerie booming or singing sound, described by scores of desert travelers throughout history.[21] Marco Polo wrote that the Gobi Desert sands "at times fill the air with the sounds of all kinds of musical instruments, and also of drums and the clash of arms."[22] To me, the sound resembles the drone of an Australian Aboriginal bullroarer.

Flatlands of the Red River Valley

We reluctantly leave this otherworldly place and return to the Trans-Canada Highway to continue east. After a quarter of an hour or so, the highway jogs to the north at the small town of Sidney, and over the next few miles it descends more than two hundred feet to the Red River lowlands. We stop by the roadside and marvel at what was once the bottom of enormous glacial Lake Agassiz. Much of the plain spread out before us is planted with wheat, barley, oats, and crops that produces the oil seed canola, though tree groves can be seen scattered among the fields and pastures. These groves were once part of a broad arc of parkland that swept from central Alberta across the Canadian prairies to northwestern Minnesota, marking a transition between the western prairies and the northern forests. French explorers called the parkland *bois brulé*, which roughly translates as "burnt wood," referring to its frequent burning. To locals, the groves are known as bluffs.

Dominated by trembling aspen, a typical bluff might have begun as a border of willow shrubs encircling a shallow pond. Within four to six decades, the pond was replaced by a mature tree grove surrounded by hazel shrubs and berry bushes. Companion trees may include bur oak and green ash, plus balsam poplar in damp areas.

Aspens are aggressive colonizers that produce masses of tiny, cottony seeds wafted by the wind for long distances. If seeds land on moist ground, such as around a pond, they can gain a foothold. As the trees mature, they can easily outstrip competing willows by sending out root suckers. Autumn is the ideal time to pick out those bluffs that are genetically identical, as every tree turns the same lovely hue of yellow, gold, orange, or red.[23]

Delta Marsh: A Birder's Paradise

We continue eastward to Portage la Prairie, where early travelers and fur traders once lifted their canoes from the Assiniboine River and journeyed north to Lake Manitoba. On their way they must have paddled across Delta Marsh, which borders the south end of the lake. Sprawling over forty-nine thousand acres, the marsh is among the largest and most celebrated wetlands on the continent. It attracts more than a hundred bird species, thanks to a variety of habitats: a network of shallow bays and isolated ponds and, especially for songbirds, the wooded dune ridge that separates the marsh from Lake Manitoba. A breeding ground for ducks and geese, Delta Marsh is strategically situated along their migration route between western Canada and the Mississippi Flyway. No wonder spring and autumn skies resound with raucous quacks and honks—the wild music of the prairies.

The ponds and bays of Delta Marsh display several distinct zones of plant life because water levels determine which plants grow where.[24] In shallow water, pondweeds and other aquatics, some with floating leaves, are rooted in the bottom, while mats of bright green duckweed spread across quiet bays. About a half dozen tiny duckweed fronds can fit on a fingernail. We scoop up a handful and savor its fresh taste, a bit like watercress.[25]

Stems of waist-high bulrush grow in ankle-deep water along with the sword-like leaves of cattail. Tall stalks of common reed, the monarch of the marsh, rule the margins.[26] On wet ground that usually dries by summer's end, knee-high sedges and river grass flourish. Where soils are saline, red samphire and grayish-green sea blite prevail. Their salty leaves make a tasty snack.

Thanks to ample supplies of water and nutrients, marshes are among the most productive ecosystems on earth. Reeds, for example, might grow nearly two inches per day in early summer. Yet too much water is not a good thing. For instance, in 1955 water levels rose dramatically and killed

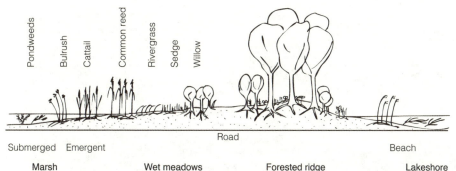

Pondweeds Bulrush Cattail Common reed Rivergrass Sedge Willow

Road

Submerged Emergent   Beach

Marsh   Wet meadows   Forested ridge   Lakeshore

FIG. 19. Schematic of transect from Lake Manitoba to Delta Marsh. Adapted from J. Shay, *Annotated Vascular Plant Species List*, 8, by Patti Isaacs.

wide expanses of reeds and cattails, paving the way for weedy annuals to colonize the bare mud. Still, the former plant life returned within a few years. Occasional flooding and drying are typical in this semiarid region and actually help ensure habitat continuity for waterfowl and other wildlife. T. Albert Sproule studied fossil seeds and pollen from marsh sediments for his master's thesis and found that flooding and drying have been going on at Delta Marsh for several thousand years.[27]

Nearby Lake Manitoba was an isolated basin until the Assiniboine River began to flow into its south end nearly eight thousand years ago. The river shifted to its present course a few thousand years later, after which the lake's waves worked sandy sediments into a barrier beach across its southern shore, separating the lake from what is now Delta Marsh.[28]

Ambling along the lakefront, we can watch sandpipers scurrying among the waves or convoys of pelicans scooping up minnows. If we keep a sharp lookout, the shoreline might also yield ancient treasures, perhaps a scrap of weathered bone or even an arrow point.

From Murky Waters to the Missouri

A little more than an hour's drive east of Delta Marsh is Winnipeg, the capital of Manitoba. Meaning "murky water" in Cree, Winnipeg is a suitable name thanks to the silt-rich rivers that flow through the city. Excavations where the Red and Assiniboine Rivers meet reveal that Cree and earlier Native groups camped there more than two millennia ago.[29]

FIG. 20. Trees line the meandering Red River in southern Manitoba. NRCan photo 2001-032D taken by G. R. Brooks.

South of the city, we continue our journey across the bed of ancient Lake Agassiz. Bright patches of brome grass and wild yellow mustard, both European invaders, mingle along the roadside. Wheat is thriving in nearby fields thanks to ample spring rains. A fox trots across the road, assuring us that some wildlife still thrives in this intensely farmed landscape.

The way south parallels the Red River, marked in the distance by a ribbon of deep green. This verdant corridor contains a rich mix of riverside trees, including American elm, green ash, box elder, cottonwood, peach-leaved willow, and occasionally basswood. This last species is a favorite of wood carvers because it is both soft and straight grained. River valleys like this attracted European settlers looking for abundant fuel and building material. In addition, when steamboats began to ply the Red River after 1859, crews cut thousands of deckloads of wood for fuel-hungry boilers. Such activi-

ties resulted in widespread deforestation. The shift to fossil fuels allowed riverbank trees to return.[30]

Our journey southward into North Dakota follows the Red River along Interstate 29, past towns with names like Warsaw and Oslo, reminders of the Polish and Norwegian immigrants who settled here in the late 1800s. At Fargo we head west along Interstate 94 for an hour and a half until we come to Jamestown.

The National Buffalo Museum's large log structure on the outskirts of town features exhibits celebrating these monarchs of the plains, iconic creatures that once numbered in the millions. Today, after near extinction, bison number in the thousands thanks to a century-long conservation effort. After perusing the exhibits, it is a treat to watch a few cows and calves quietly munching grass in a nearby pasture. They look ragged and patchy at this time of year, having shed only part of their thick winter coat.

On the road again, we drive for another couple of hours through rolling terrain across the rugged Coteau du Missouri to Bismarck.

A Taste of Native Heritage

Two great rivers, the Missouri and the Mississippi, define the middle of the North American continent and, roughly, the boundaries of this book. The Missouri originates in the Rocky Mountains, flowing east and south to drain parts of a half dozen western states. One of its tributaries, the Knife River, meets the Missouri near Stanton, about an hour's drive north of Bismarck. Near the confluence are the remains of agricultural villages built by groups of the Mandan and Hidatsa peoples. These villages were once a thriving trade hub for goods from as far away as the Pacific Ocean, the Gulf of Mexico, and the Great Lakes. Tragically, a smallpox epidemic in the 1830s wiped out thousands of residents.[31] Former resident Buffalo Bird Woman shared her story with ethnographer Gilbert Wilson:

> I was born in 1839 in an earth lodge by the mouth of the Knife River, in what is now North Dakota, three years after the smallpox winter. The Mandans and my tribe, the Hidatsas, had come years before from the Heart river; and they had built the Five Villages, as we called them, on the banks of the Knife, near the place where it enters the Missouri. Here were bottom lands for our cornfields and cottonwood trees for the beams and posts of our lodges. The dead wood that floated down either river would help keep us in firewood, the old women thought.[32]

In order to preserve some of this heritage, the Knife River Indian Villages National Historic Site was established in 1974. At the visitor center we watch the orientation film about the life of this celebrated Hidatsa gardener, tour the exhibits, and then walk the village trail to see a recently built earth lodge. Commodious but dark inside, the dwelling receives its only light from the square smoke hole at the top of the lodge. In former times families would have kept a fire going in a pit below the smoke hole. Maize, squash, pumpkins, beans, sunflowers, and tobacco are growing in the garden outside. Historian Fay Metcalf asks us to picture a once-thriving village: "One can almost hear children splashing in the river's cool waters,

FIG. 22. A reconstructed earth lodge at Knife River Indian Villages National Historic Site. Photo courtesy of National Park Service (NPS).

swimming and playing about in the round bull boats that were used to cross the river."[33]

We return to Bismarck and take the interstate east. After a couple of hours we turn north at the small town of Cleveland and drive twenty miles to the Cottonwood Lake Study Area (CLSA). This two-hundred-acre stretch of prairie is dotted with small marshes known as potholes in the United States and sloughs in Canada. Millions of these water-filled depressions once dotted a broad expanse of countryside from Alberta to Iowa, although most were drained by European immigrant farmers.[34] Local Native groups would have found such areas useful for hunting waterfowl and other game.[35]

While we wait for our tour host, we watch a pair of mallards take off right in front of us, amid a flurry of spray and feverish flapping. As they soar into the sky, our attention turns to a staff member come to explain the CLSA's ongoing ecological research. The team studies, among other

FIG. 23. An aerial glimpse of prairie pothole country. Photo courtesy U.S. Fish and Wildlife Service (USFWS).

subjects, marsh water cycles, water chemistry, plants, and animals, plus the effects of climate change.[36] Being highly sensitive to changes in climate, such marshes will suffer as the earth warms, especially if precipitation stays the same or decreases.[37]

The Headwaters of the Mighty Mississippi

After this sobering scientific assessment, we return to the interstate and continue past Fargo into Minnesota. We make our way east and north and across part of the thirteen-hundred-square-mile White Earth Indian Reservation, home of the White Earth Nation of the Anishinaabe. The road climbs gently, cutting across sandy ridges that were once the beaches of glacial Lake Agassiz, and continues past groves of aspen and oak, then woodlands of sugar maple, basswood, and ironwood.[38] Our ultimate destination is Itasca State Park, home of the headwaters of the mighty Mississippi. The Anishinaabe people call the place Omashkoozo-zaaga'igan, meaning "Elk

Lake," but in the 1830s the American explorer Henry Schoolcraft renamed it Itasca. Schoolcraft derived that name from syllables of the Latin words *veritas* ("truth") and *caput* ("head"), asserting he had found the true place of the Mississippi River's origin.

Established in 1891 to protect the headwaters, Itasca State Park became a sanctuary of plant diversity, as logging and farming had cleared almost all of the surrounding area. The park's rich assortment of trees provides clues as to what northern Minnesota looked like before the onslaught of the ax and plow. It has become a magnet for plant ecologists studying its splendid stands of aspen, balsam poplar, paper birch, basswood, sugar maple, and bur oak, as well as conifer woodlands of white spruce, balsam fir, and jack pine. The park also hosts magnificent groves of stately white and red pines. Black spruce and tamarack flourish in low-lying peat bogs. We visit one such habitat, called Bog D. Donning rubber boots, we gingerly tread on a floating mat of grass-like sedges that surround an open pond a couple of hundred feet in diameter. Gently bouncing on the mat is a treat, but we don't stay long in the black spruce and larch forest that surrounds the bog, as the air is thick with mosquitoes.

An area near the south end of the park merits a mention. In the 1960s I led a small crew of students in excavating a bison kill site adjacent to Nicollet Creek, which feeds into Lake Itasca. We found an array of stone artifacts and masses of bison bone in waterlogged deposits. Our findings suggest that hunters drove the animals down a slope and into a marsh around eight thousand years ago.[39]

Our final stop is a natural jewel and one of the most photographed places in the park. Preachers Grove is a stand of tall red pines overlooking Lake Itasca. It was supposedly named for a group of ministers who camped here in the 1930s. The massive trunks of the pines remind me of the stout pillars of a cathedral, while the sunlight streaming through the canopy brings to mind heavenly light filtering through stained glass. These towering evergreens confer a deep sense of serenity, but these and other red pines in the park have another story to tell—a chronicle of local wildfires.

When a ground fire courses through a forest, the flames tend to scorch the leeward side of trees. Thus, a blackened scar on a trunk is a clear sign

FIG. 24. Red pine trees at Preacher's Grove, Lake Itasca State Park. Photo by dvs.

of a fire. If not killed, the tree will gradually grow new wood over the scar. One can fix the date of a past fire simply by counting the number of annual rings that have grown since the scar was made. Graduate student Sid Frissell did just that when he studied living trees and ancient stumps at Itasca. He was able to compile a local fire history stretching back to the 1600s and to conclude that damaging fires had occurred about every nine years.[40]

A Patch of Tallgrass

We must take leave of Itasca and its wonders and move south to visit the Bluestem Prairie Preserve, located near Glyndon. Tallgrass prairies like this once covered 150 million acres of the midcontinent, from Manitoba to Texas. Striving to grasp the enormity of such a vast ocean of waving green makes one think of the words of celebrated conservationist Aldo Leopold: "What a thousand acres of compass plant looked like when they tickled the bellies of the buffalo is a question never again to be answered, and perhaps not even asked."[41]

It is difficult to fathom such vastness, but we can at least revel in Bluestem Prairie's six thousand acres. Our first discovery is that the ground is squishy, a reminder that so-called "wet prairies" once covered much of the Red River valley before they were drained for farming.[42]

Wet soils support a lush growth of grasses, including the iconic big bluestem, for which the preserve is named. The plant's scientific name, *Andropogon gerardii*, comes from the Greek *andro*, meaning "man" plus *pogon* for "beard," which refers to its hairy seed heads. The species name refers to nineteenth-century French physician and botanist Louis Gérard.

Bluestem has several popular names. The early settlers who plowed the prairie sod called it turkeyfoot because of its drooping, three-part seed heads. The Lakota people call it *pȟeží šašá ókhihe tȟaŋkíŋkiŋyaŋ*, which translates as "very great young red grass."[43] In midsummer bluestem is about waist high, but by season's end it may reach more than three times higher. In autumn stems and leaves turn brilliant copper or orange-brown, appropriate for its Lakota name.

At least two other grasses are obvious on this prairie. Indian grass, which grows almost as tall as bluestem, is easily recognized by its long, feathery

FIG. 25. Big bluestem, once the most common plant across the midcontinent, is abundant at Bluestem Prairie. Photo by Jennifer Briggs provided courtesy of USFWS.

FIG. 26. The western prairie fringed orchid, a rare and threatened prairie gem. Photo by Heather Miltenburg.

seed heads. Bluejoint grass, which is shorter than big bluestem and has a narrow seed head, prefers wet places, something there is no shortage of in some years.

The prairie is alive with a rainbow of hues, from rich reds to deep violets. As we wander among these floral delights, one bloom stands out. Up close, the delicate western prairie fringed orchid's creamy white flowers are clustered near the tops of stems, looking like tiny angels with spreading wings.

Midsummer is also the prime time to savor the prairie's heady scents, though there is much more to it than perfume. Being rooted in one spot, wildflowers communicate by releasing volatile organic compounds into the air as signals to attract insect pollinators, of which there are many. Bees are everywhere, as are bee flies, creatures that look like bees but are actually flies. Butterflies are also common. Even the rare regal fritillary, with its black-spotted, bright orange forewings and white-spotted, dark brown hind wings, calls Bluestem Prairie its home.

Prairies are truly busy places. If we listen intently, we can hear the constant buzzing, munching, and chirping of a host of birds, rodents, beetles, spiders, ants, wasps, dragonflies, and moths. If we add to this multitude the countless billions of invisible bacteria, fungi, and other organisms, we are talking about astronomical numbers of living things in every square yard of prairie. Naming them all would take weeks!

Where Prairie Meets Forest

Exhilarated by our tallgrass experience, we drive south to join Interstate 94 near Barnesville and journey toward Minneapolis and St. Paul. On our way to the Twin Cities, we notice no sharp boundary between the end of the prairie and the beginning of the forest, partly because today's farm fields and planted woodlots blur the transition. Think back to a time before these fields and pastures, when there was open grassland at one end of a line and a closed forest at the other. In between would be a partially treed landscape that nineteenth-century land surveyors described as "oak openings and barrens," meaning grassy areas with scattered oak trees. Today's ecologists call these habitats "oak savanna."[44] These areas were so attractive to early European settlers that most were quickly converted into farm fields, the oaks having been cut for building material and firewood. Once covering 10 percent of the state, these openings are extremely rare today.

The blending of prairie and forest puzzled observers for nearly a century. In 1896 geologist Warren Upham suggested that fire played a role in producing this mixed habitat. In the 1980s Eric Grimm's dissertation research showed that both fire and topography were responsible.[45] In rolling terrain, patches of prairie tended to dominate areas prone to fire, such as

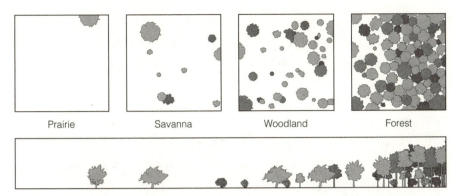

FIG. 27. An idealized transition from open prairie to closed forest. Adapted from Nelson et al., "Presettlement and Contemporary Vegetation Patterns," by Patti Isaacs.

sandy, west-facing slopes, while woodlands were common on heavier soils in lowlands and on the east sides of lakes. An age-old fiery battle had played out on the landscape as prairies held sway over high ground while forests groves controlled the low. The combatants were almost evenly matched. On the one hand, grasses are adapted to burning, as they can regrow from their bases. On the other, oaks have thick, heat-resistant bark, and aspens can send out root suckers far into the grassland.

Before European settlement, when occasional wildfires burned freely, prairies could expand. After settlers suppressed fires, woodlands expanded. Fields become less common and woodland groves larger as we continue eastward. We are entering forested territory that once covered much of south-central Minnesota. Early French fur traders called these old-growth woodlands *bois grand* or *bois fort,* meaning "big woods."[46]

A Family's Legacy

We leave Interstate 94 near Maple Grove and drive south and west to Long Lake and visit nearby Wolsfeld Woods Scientific and Natural Area, two hundred splendid acres of woodland that are one of the largest and best-preserved remnants of the big woods. Named after the German family who homesteaded there, this area is managed by the state's Department of Natural Resources. Here we can amble down a sun-dappled path through tall groves of northern red oak, ironwood, bitternut hickory, sugar maple,

American elm, and basswood and perhaps hear the *rat-tat-tat* of a downy woodpecker drilling for insects. Raccoon tracks in the wet mud beside a creek remind us of the area's nocturnal residents.[47]

A Sacred Site in the Heart of a Metropolis

We drive east from Wolsfeld to the state capital, St. Paul. Here, high above the Mississippi River gorge, is Indian Mounds Regional Park. This sacred site contains a group of burial mounds on a hill and a cave in the rock below. Eroded out of soft, sugary sandstone, most of the cave has been taken over by an underground lake. Dakota people call it Wakaŋ Tipi, a dwelling place for spirits. Its walls were adorned with carved images of humans, rattlesnakes, bears, birds, fish, and turtles. Settlers knew the place as Carver's Cave, after explorer Jonathan Carver, who visited in the 1760s. The cave later became a well-known landmark and tourist attraction but was unfortunately reduced in size by railway construction and damaged by vandals. Now protected, the area is being restored.[48]

Heading south along Interstate 35, we pass rolling hills with fields of chest-high maize to visit Myre–Big Island State Park on the outskirts of Albert Lea, not far from the Iowa state line. The fifteen-hundred-acre park hosts a patch of precious oak savanna. These open woodlands combine waving grasses and sweet-scented prairie flowers with the allure of welcome shade—the best of two natural worlds.[49]

A Tallgrass Bouquet

As the highway crosses into Iowa, the roadside explodes with color. This floral welcome is the result of a diligent campaign to plant wildflowers along the state's highways. Such splendor reminds us that tallgrass prairies once covered most of Iowa, while today it is blanketed by maize and other farm crops. Fortunately, we can visit a noteworthy example, Hayden Prairie State Preserve, about an hour's drive east of the interstate.

Hayden Prairie hosts more than two hundred kinds of grasses and wildflowers.[50] As we enter the preserve, we are confronted with masses of waist-high pinnate prairie coneflowers, also called upright prairie cone-flower.[51] Up close, this flower does not resemble other family members.

FIG. 28. A group of graceful pinnate prairie coneflowers. Photo by Katy Chayka, Minnesota Wildflowers.

The petals of most daisies stick straight out from their centers, but this coneflower's long, narrow petals droop from a dark central dome, reminiscent of a group of hula dancers wearing cheerful yellow skirts. No wonder the scientific name of the species is *Ratibida pinnata*; *pinnata* is Latin for "featherlike."

We soon come across another yellow bloom, the oxeye, or false sunflower. Oxeye flowers look like sunflowers, and, like other daisies, their petals angle slightly upward. The effect is of a shallow, open bowl of yellow. Oxeyes are scattered among the coneflower dancers, an audience of happy faces enjoying the show.

Here and there we see leadplant shrubs, with their small, feathery, grayish-green leaves. Even though its name sounds dull, leadplant has lovely long narrow spikes of bright purple flowers.

The drooping petals of bright orange Michigan lilies resemble delicate Chinese lanterns. Also striking are the clusters of delicate pink-and-white flowers of swamp milkweed, grouped like upside-down chandeliers, holding their treasures aloft. To add to this, the rounded, deep rose-purple flower heads of rough gayfeather are brilliant against the green grass.

The preserve is named in honor of prairie advocate and pioneer plant ecologist Ada Hayden, who devoted her personal and professional life to preserving what remained of Iowa's vanishing grasslands.[52] For more than thirty years Hayden taught botany and curated the herbarium at Iowa State University. In 1919 she wrote, "Iowa is said to be a prairie state, but what is a prairie to the present generation? Within 40 or 50 years, the broad stretches of tall shining grass trembling in the sunlight or tossed by the breezes into billowy waves, gorgeous as the season progresses with its pageant of brilliant hued flowers . . . [are] fast passing."[53]

She was right. In less than a century nearly all of these natural treasures have disappeared.[54] Yet, there is reason for optimism. In 1999 the Tallgrass Prairie Center was founded following state legislation a decade earlier promoting prairie research and restoration, including the planting of native wildflowers along Iowa's roads.[55]

The End of Our Journey

From Hayden Prairie we drive over rolling hills and past sprawling corn-fields to Des Moines, Iowa's capital city. Like many other cities we passed on this trip, it is located at the confluence of two rivers, in this case the Des Moines and the Raccoon. The city is named after the former, a waterway French fur traders called La Rivière des Moines, the "river of the monks."

The area's human history goes back at least six thousand years, when a Native settlement was built on the floodplain. Excavations uncovered depressions that may have been houses, and, if so, they would be among the oldest in the Midwest. Back then, the river and adjacent uplands would have furnished plant foods plus fish, turtles, deer, raccoon, turkey, and bison.[56]

On the outskirts of Des Moines lies Living History Farms, a huge outdoor museum complex that offers visitors a glimpse of what life was like in the 1700s and 1800s. Of special interest is an Ioway farm of 1700. We look into a domed, bark-covered house and then note that the corn, beans, and squash in the garden are much further along than the crops at the Knife River village. The growing season in this area usually begins a month earlier than in western North Dakota.

At journey's end it is time to reflect on our rich experience. This past week has offered us a chance to sample the natural and Native wonders of this vast region, a valuable prelude to later chapters that deal with ancient environments, early plant domestication, foods, medicines, and crafts. We have seen traces of a rich Native heritage—a medicine wheel, hills where early hunters drove bison to their deaths, the remains of once-thriving earth lodge villages, hallowed burial mounds, mystical spirit sands, and a sacred cave. We have listened to the soft whoosh of grasses waving in the wind, watched bees buzzing around a rainbow of prairie flowers, seen marshes teeming with bird life, heard the soothing flutter of aspen leaves, and relaxed in a shady woodland. We have also thought about the effects of a warming climate on some of the region's habitats.

Countless European newcomers have celebrated the beauty of the prairies in poetry, prose, and pictures, but let us not forget that these same lands were treasured by the original inhabitants. White Horse, an Omaha, told Melvin Gilmore, "When I was a youth the country was beautiful. Along the rivers were belts of timberland, where grew cottonwoods, maples, elms, oaks, hickory and walnut trees, and many other kinds. Also there were various vines and shrubs. And under all these grew many good herbs and beautiful flowering plants. On the prairie was the waving green grass and many other beautiful plants."[57]

FURTHER READING

American Automobile Association. AAA Travel Guides. https://www.aaa.com/travelguides/.

Barker, William T., and Warren C. Whitman. "Vegetation of the Northern Great Plains." *Rangelands* 10, no. 6 (1988): 266–72.

Canadian Automobile Association. CAA TourBooks and Travel Guides. https://caaneo.ca/travel/roadtrip-planning/tourbooks-and-guides.

O'Brien, Dan. *Great Plains Bison*. Lincoln: University of Nebraska Press, 2017.

Wishart, David J. *Great Plains Indians*. Lincoln: University of Nebraska Press, 2016.

Among the Ancient Archives 4

Direct observation of the testimony of the earth . . . is a matter of . . .
indefatigable digging among the ancient archives of the earth's history.

—HENRY FAIRFIELD OSBORN, "Evolution and Religion"

In the northern plains the richest archives usually lie in river valleys where
history is written in the layers of sand and silt. The story of one prairie river,
the Souris (French for "mouse") captured my research energies over several
years. The river originates in marshes north of Weyburn, Saskatchewan, and
then meanders into North Dakota and back out again, eventually joining
the Assiniboine near Brandon, Manitoba. As with other prairie rivers, when
winter snows melt, the Souris runs high, but by late summer it can easily be
waded, though it spills its banks about every half dozen years or so.[1] In an
effort to control such flooding and ensure adequate water supplies during
drought, the Saskatchewan Water Security Agency built the Rafferty Dam,
completed in 1991.

A River over Time

I first laid eyes on the Souris River valley at the start of a paleoecological
project a couple of years before the dam was built. Sitting on its grassy
edge, I gazed at the opposite slope dotted with clumps of trees and shrubs
where summer storms had carved numerous ravines. On the valley floor a
dark green ribbon of forest marked the river's course through neat squares
of fields and pastures. This scene would soon disappear under the waters
of a reservoir, but before that happened our research team was determined
to uncover the area's history. First, we wanted to trace its story using river
sediments and soils. Second, we wanted to know what plant foods the

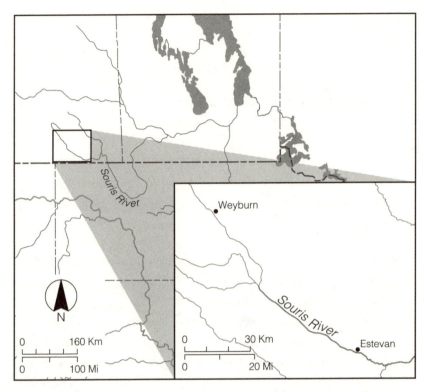

MAP 10. Our study area on the upper Souris River, southeastern Saskatchewan. By Eureka Cartography.

valley's early Native inhabitants ate, what medicines they used, and what woods they chose for heating and cooking.[2]

Our group included Jennifer (my wife), technician Cole Wilson, geomorphologist Larry Stene, and myself working alongside Jim Finnigan's archaeological crews. The study area was a twenty-five-mile stretch of the upper Souris River where the channel was about sixty feet wide and six feet deep. We first hired a tractor-mounted backhoe to dig a dozen or so deep trenches at points along the bank to help us trace the rather confusing parting and merging of sediment layers away from the river's edge.

In years of high water and swifter flow, rivers carry more coarse-textured particles. When a river tops its banks and spreads across the floodplain, the water slows and begins to dump material. Larger particles, like sand, are deposited first, followed by finer silt and clay. This gradation from coarse to fine, called a fining-upward sequence, may be used to chart a river's flood history. Larry Stene detected a dozen of these sequences, suggesting major floods over the past few thousand years. In between floods, dark, organic-rich layers imply that soils began to develop.[3]

Archaeology crews excavated sites throughout the valley, an effort that yielded pottery, stone tools, and quantities of butchered animal bones. Because we wanted to learn about the plant species used by the early inhabitants, we collected two hundred soil samples from eight sites and several backhoe trenches.

Most samples were easy to collect, although one from a soil layer deep in a backhoe trench sticks in my mind. As I hacked away at the rock-hard layer with my stubby Marshalltown trowel, I grew increasingly frustrated. Beads of sweat formed on my forehead and my hand ached with the effort. In the end I collected a measly couple of handfuls that, when processed, contained no seeds. Thankfully, other samples yielded a total of nearly two thousand charred seeds and several hundred pieces of charcoal from more than thirty plant genera.[4]

To make sense of our finds, we needed to learn about the modern vegetation, which meant a botanical survey of local habitats. After consulting aerial photographs and doing some field checking, we chose individual plots randomly to avoid bias. Within each sixteen-by-sixteen-foot plot, we listed the tree species and measured their circumferences, sometimes crawling through tangled undergrowth to get the job done. The abundance of shrubs and herbaceous plants was estimated in smaller plots. We also collected samples of any that could not be identified on the spot. These were laid out on sheets of newspaper, labeled with location and a specimen number, then bundled together with cardboard. Once dry, they could be examined at leisure and identified accurately.

In addition to our own surveys, we also looked at other botanical studies to better grasp the makeup of various plant communities. In all, we listed three hundred species for the valley, distributed among a number of habitats. Forests surrounded the archaeological sites on the floodplain, with marshes and meadows adjacent to the river; grasslands or tree groves covered valley slopes. Some forest plots hosted a few large green ash trees, but young box elders were the most abundant.[5] Other species included aspen and, at one location, American elm. Beneath the trees were chokecherry, juneberry, and western snowberry bushes. A variety of grasses and other herbaceous plants grew in the shade and covered about two-thirds of the ground area.

Even though the seeds and charcoal we found were but a small fraction of the plant species that once grew in the valley, they suggest how it might have looked hundreds of years ago. Our findings fell into four habitats: floodplain forest, marsh, prairie, and disturbed areas. Tree and shrub charcoal consisted of ash, maple, wild cherry, elm, and specimens resembling willow or poplar. Growing among the trees would have been prairie rose, wild cherry, wild strawberry, and brambles. Marsh plants included willows, sedges, flatsedges, and bulrush. Grasses, vetchling, milk vetch, and puccoon grew in prairie patches. The most abundant seeds came from plants typical of areas disturbed by flooding or trampling, like goosefoot and stinging nettle. These are aggressive competitors that produce copious amounts of seed and can thrive in most habitats. Other weedy types found included pigweed, marsh elder, and knotweed. We also identified indicators of soil formation, including small resting bodies formed by fungi, shells and eggs of land snails, and small spheres identified as the cocoons of flatworms.[6]

Some of our finds were most likely foods. The perennial bulrush and the annuals pigweed and goosefoot would have furnished greens. These, along with marsh elder and knotweed, would also offer edible seeds, whereas wild cherry, wild strawberry, and brambles provided summer fruits. Seeds such as wild sage and stinging nettle may have come from plants people used for medicine or crafts.[7] Ash was the most popular firewood. Such inferences came only after countless hours of laboratory work to extract and identify the plant remains.

Uncovering Past Plant Uses

Plant remains are rare in most archaeological sites. The vast majority of the seeds early peoples used have not survived unless they were accidentally charred, such as while cooking. If charred, seeds and pieces of wood will persist in the soil, sometimes for thousands of years. If not, they soon perish.

A further drawback is that, even if charred, such remains are usually scattered throughout the soil, making them almost impossible to recover. This problem dogged archaeology for decades until a breakthrough came in the 1950s, when Hugh Cutler at the Missouri Botanical Garden in St. Louis began to use water to separate light plant remains from heavy soil particles.[8] His "flotation" technique caught on a decade or so later, and since then countless tons of soil have been processed, yielding millions of seeds. It truly became a revolution in recovery.[9]

My personal experience with flotation began in the early 1980s with an old oil drum, a set of sieves, and a garden hose. Within a few years our research group had a custom-made machine we stationed inside a greenhouse on loan from the University of Manitoba's Plant Science Department. One particular night remains in my memory.[10]

The plastic-covered greenhouse creaked and groaned as icy blasts seeped through cracks in its flimsy covering. Inside, a large, blue plastic drum was surrounded by a half dozen steel buckets filled with a soil-and-water slurry. A row of paper trays and plastic bags containing unprocessed soil samples (each about the volume of a large milk carton) covered a nearby bench. Under a string of fluorescent lights, Cole Wilson and I prepared for a session of water flotation.

I began by stirring several tablespoons of Calgon, a branded water softening product, into each bucket to help break up the clay-rich clods. After a few minutes, Cole poured the contents of the first bucket into the blue drum. Made by a local plumbing shop, the contraption was a hybrid of two earlier designs. It had been fitted with a pair of copper rings, and water from a garden hose sprayed through tiny holes in one ring while air from a small compressor bubbled through the other.

As bone fragments, sand, and pebbles sank to a sieve at the bottom of the drum, light material floated up and out through a spout, spilling into a stack of graduated soil sieves. At least that was the theory. In practice, the machine did not cope well with heavy clay, and we spent much of our time up to our elbows in icy water, breaking clods with our hands and coaxing material up and through the spout. As we worked, we presumed the black specks in the flotsam flowing into the sieves were plant remains, but we wouldn't be certain until we had looked at them under a microscope. When a sample was finished, the stuff from each sieve was put to dry on cardboard trays covered with paper towels. The barrel was washed out before processing the next sample.

We didn't realize, as the evening wore on, that a storm was brewing outside. When we finally left the greenhouse, an icy blast of swirling white flakes greeted us. Slip-sliding through mounting drifts, I drove Cole to a bus stop and waited until he got on before I headed home, some twenty miles south. I had only gone a mile or so along the highway before wet snow was sticking to my windshield faster than my wipers could clear it. I slowed to a crawl and leaned out the side window to see, but it was no use; I had to turn back and spend the next two days in a motel until the roads opened.

Over the years our research team floated close to a thousand samples over many sessions. Each marked the beginning of time-consuming lab work. After drying and weighing the findings came hours of patient sorting.[11] Endlessly searching through those tiny mounds of debris brings haystacks and needles to mind. To cope with the workload, I turned to students for help. After training, I told each sorter to pick out anything that looked interesting. Not surprisingly, they found not only seeds but also such oddities as ant body parts.

We sometimes found chipped stone flakes, evidence of stone tool making, in the heavier material that sank to the bottom of the tank. One unusual find came from a site at the junction of the Red and Assiniboine Rivers. The sample contained a variety of charred seeds: goosefoot, prairie rose, raspberry, and marsh elder. It also yielded a rare piece of pottery bearing fingerprints. The student sorter noted, "During laboratory examination . . . researchers recovered a Blackduck potsherd [a type of pottery made eight hundred years or so ago in northern Minnesota, northwestern Ontario, and southern Manitoba] . . . that had thumb and index fingerprints . . . about the right size for a woman." Looking at these impressions hundreds of years later truly puts us in touch with that ancient artisan.[12]

Whenever sorters saw what looked like a seed, they compared it with our lab reference collection. Once tentatively identified, the find went into a small glass vial labeled with its provisional name, sample catalog number, site name, excavation unit, and depth. Later, botanist Margaret Kapinga expertly verified all seed identifications, ensuring accuracy. Details were then entered on computer spreadsheets for further analysis.

Binocular microscopes were essential for our work. When magnified, most finds could be pinned down to a genus based on size, shape, and surface pattern. For instance, to the unaided eye a goosefoot seed is the size of a pinhead. With a magnifying glass, it resembles a tiny comma with a bump that covers the tip of a curled-up embryo. Under 6x magnification the image of the seed swells to the size of a pea, at 25x we see it as comparable in size to a golf ball, and at 50x even more detail of its surface is revealed.

Innovations

Even though binocular microscopes are still the mainstay of seed identification, the technology has come a long way over the last half century. While light microscopes bounce photons (light rays) off objects, a scanning electron microscope (SEM) uses a beam of electrons. The resulting images are superbly detailed, but there are drawbacks. The equipment is expensive, the machine needs shielding since samples are exposed to high levels of radiation, and specimens must first be dried and coated with a thin layer of gold.

Whether it is charcoal found at an archaeological dig or seeds buried in river sediments, a key question is, "How old is it?" Being able to arrange objects and events along a timeline is crucial for telling the story of the past. For decades one dating technique has formed the backbone of archaeological and geological time scales that span the last fifty thousand years.[13]

Developed in 1949 by Willard Libby and his associates at the University of Chicago, radiocarbon dating is based on the fact that, high above the atmosphere, cosmic rays form a radioactive isotope of carbon, C-14. This isotope joins with other carbon atoms in the atmosphere to produce carbon dioxide. Plants take up carbon dioxide from the air as they grow and, through photosynthesis, convert the carbon into chemical compounds for metabolism and growth. Thus, all plants and animals contain a tiny amount of radioactive carbon. When an organism dies, the isotope begins to decay

FIG. 29. A goosefoot seed (*Chenopodium berlandieri* subsp. *jonesianum*) photographed with a scanning electron microscope. Courtesy of Gayle J. Fritz.

at a predictable rate, allowing researchers to determine when it died by measuring the amount of c-14 remaining in a sample.[14]

During our Souris research, we submitted small pieces of ash and maple charcoal from the Peg site for radiocarbon dating. A few months later the lab returned a date of 895 ± 84 years before the present (BP).[15] One drawback of standard radiocarbon dating is that it requires up to several ounces of material, an amount not always available. Accelerator mass spectrometry (AMS), developed in the 1970s, is far more sensitive.[16] Even single goosefoot seeds can now be dated, paving the way to a far more accurate history of plant uses.[17]

In addition to having access to those dating techniques, today's archaeologists can call on a plethora of other specialists and ways to study the earth's treasures. Geoarchaeologists analyze sediments, zooarchaeologists identify bones, paleoethnobotanists (or archaeobotanists) look at plant remains, palynologists study pollen, and so on. Each endeavor may be further subdivided. For instance, some paleoethnobotanists focus on seeds, while others study microfossils such as phytoliths.

Phytoliths are composed of silica that plants take up through their roots. Smaller than the width of a human hair, some are shaped like crosses, others like tiny dumbbells, and still others are rodlike. In a plant stem, phytoliths provide rigidity, as girders do in a skyscraper, strengthening the cell membranes of leaves, stems, roots, and fruit. Like sand grains, they also resist degeneration.[18]

A few specialists operate at the molecular level, examining, for example, starch grains. These are units of glucose that store energy in seeds such as maize kernels, in stems, and in underground parts such as tubers (e.g., potatoes). You can see a mass of starch grains in a potato simply by cutting it in half and adding a drop of iodine; the grains will turn blue-black.[19]

Some scientists specialize in identifying chemical residues from cooking pots and other ancient objects. Mary Malainey and colleagues found traces of large herbivores (probably bison) and plants on pottery fragments from eighteen sites in western Canada. Others identified residues on artifacts at an archaeological site at The Forks in Winnipeg, Manitoba, as traces of more than a dozen wild and domesticated plants.[20]

The Double Helix

Some of the most spectacular advances in biology over the past century have come from our increased understanding of deoxyribonucleic acid (DNA), the molecule that carries the genetic code of all living things. The first piece of the puzzle was discovered in the late 1860s, when Swiss chemist Friedrich Miescher isolated what he called nuclein inside white blood cells. "Nuclein" was later changed to "nucleic acid" and eventually to "deoxyribonucleic acid." The X-ray crystallography work of Rosalind Franklin and Maurice Wilkins contributed substantially to the now-famous 1953 visualization by James Watson and Francis Crick of the three-dimensional, double-stranded helix.[21]

Biologists can extract and analyze the DNA in everything from ancient human bones and frozen mammoth flesh to charred plant fossils. For instance, DNA analysis, combined with AMS dating, has clarified the origins of goosefoot domestication. Anthropologist Logan Kistler and biologist Beth Shapiro, from Pennsylvania State University, have concluded that "the chenopod grown in the Eastern Woodlands was locally-derived."[22]

Applying scientific techniques to the study of archaeological materials has given us much greater insights into the past. Nonetheless, even with this abundance of laboratory tools, most archaeology still involves pulling out our shovels and trowels, getting on our knees, and rummaging through the dark earth.

Putting It All Together

Both field work and lab work have been part of my research life, but my passion has been teaching undergraduates and mentoring graduate students at the University of Manitoba in Winnipeg. Drawing from those years, I offer the following imagined account of a dig in the northern plains.

History of a Dig

The windswept hill littered with rocks has been a cow pasture for generations. The father of the current owner used to stroll here on Sunday afternoons, and by the time he retired he had a cigar box full of arrow points, a few pottery fragments, some stone hammers, and many chunks of weathered bone. Last year a graduate student from the local university came to look over the finds, and now a small dig is planned. Several months ago the professor overseeing the dig reviewed satellite images and aerial photographs of the pasture and realized that many of the small boulders strewn across the hill appeared to be arranged in rough circles, suggesting that they had once marked the outer edges of skin tents.

On the first morning the students are issued their digging tools before huddling around the professor to learn a few basic digging and note-taking skills. With help from a graduate assistant, the trainees set up a grid and mark it with global positioning coordinates. Then, working in pairs, they lay out excavation squares in the middle of four of the stone circles. Each pair uses shovels to carefully remove the sod before getting down on their hands and knees to dig with their trowels. Apart from the wind, the only sounds across the dig this morning consist of a mix of murmurs among the diggers overlain by the insistent metallic rasping of trowels scraping the coarse earth. Every once in a while each pair gets up to pour buckets of

FIG. 30. A typical tipi ring with a hearth in the center, excavated from a site in southwestern Alberta. Photo courtesy of John Brumley.

earth through a screen. Just before lunch the pair in Trench 2 come upon a circle of broken and blackened stones.

"That looks like a hearth," says the professor, taking notes on her laptop. The students pause from their digging to describe, measure, and draw a plan of the hearth and surrounding trench. They note that scattered around the area are a few hefty bones that could easily be bison. After some discussion, the hearth area is photographed and the bones removed and bagged. Using tweezers, the students then pick out a dozen or so pieces of charcoal, which they carefully wrap in foil. The hearth rocks are piled beside the trench before being bagged. Finally, the students collect several liters of earth from around the hearth's location for later processing.

The students return to scraping, but before long a trowel scratches something hard. The professor calls out, "Be careful!" The rim of a clay pot is uncovered. It appears to be decorated, although the adhering dirt has blurred the design. Slowly and carefully, the team uncovers several other pieces of the pot, which are then photographed in situ, taken up, labeled, and packed away. At the end of the dig, each trench was carefully filled and the sod replaced.

A couple of months later, as trees across campus began to show off their rich autumn colors, the archaeology lab on the second floor of one large brick building springs into action. The field crew has arrived. Students cover several long tables with brown paper and begin to wash and lay out their finds.

Soon the tables are filled. Several tables are needed for stone: rocks from the hearth, hundreds of stone flakes, arrow points, knives, scrapers, hammers, and the few pieces of pottery. Bones are arrayed on another table. A faunal analyst confirms that most of the large bones and bone fragments are bison, while the tiny ones belonged to small mammals that probably died naturally at the site. The way in which some bones are broken suggests that not only bison meat but also fat-rich bone marrow had been sought.[23]

Another room receives the soil. A portion of each sample is set aside for soil analysis, while the rest is emptied into a flotation tank near the sink and processed to extract seeds and charcoal. A botanist later examines the finds under a microscope. Ten charred seeds are tallied: five goosefoot, two unidentified grass, and three unknowns. Slim pickings for all the effort, but ten seeds are better than none. The botanist also verifies that most of the pieces of charred wood are from ash, a popular firewood among early prairie people. Ash trees would have grown in a low-lying area a few hundred yards from the site. A few grams of charcoal are sent away for radiocarbon dating. Two months later the team will have the result: 1,350 ± 50 years B P.

A geologist examining the stone tools remarks that several types of stone used do not occur in the area of the dig site, suggesting that the people traded for it or collected it from quarries hundreds of miles away. The rocks from the hearth, however, are of local stone and, after being cataloged, are put away for later analysis.

An expert identifies the pottery as a popular style for the region, probably made from local clay. A few fragments resemble pots made in farming villages, suggesting trade with those settled people. Several pieces of the rim that have been carefully cleaned of earth are encrusted with cooking residue. Another specialist examines the residue and identifies traces of maize and Indian breadroot phytoliths along with a few microscopic starch grains of maize. Chemical residue on a stone knife tests positive for bison.

This preliminary analysis of the excavation's findings suggests that the people who camped on the hill hunted bison with bows and arrows and made cooking pots of fired clay. They supplemented their meat diet with plant foods, including Indian breadroot and perhaps goosefoot seeds. They also ate maize, most likely obtained through trade with nearby farming villages. Research on the stone circle camp will continue, but for now the preliminary results are written up in a report to the agency funding the research and the governmental body that issued the excavation permit. The professor will present a summary at the next regional archaeology conference.

As L'Abbé Jean Cochet, a French archaeologist and cleric, wrote in 1866, "When the soil has been questioned, it will answer."[24]

FURTHER READING

Kelly, Robert L., and David Hurst Thomas. *Archaeology: Down to Earth*. 5th ed. Boston: Cengage Learning, 2013.

From Gathering to Growing   5

The exchange between plants and people has shaped
the evolutionary history of both.

—ROBIN WALL KIMMERER, *Braiding Sweetgrass*

The din at the early bird reception grew louder as more and more people
arrived for an annual conference of the Plains Anthropological Society. The
hotel ballroom fairly crackled with excitement amid the shouts and hugs
of joyful reunions. Professionals, students, and enthusiasts from Alberta to
Texas had gathered in Iowa City for the 1996 event to talk about everything
from the geology of early hunter-gatherer sites to Native American women's
issues. I threaded my way through the crowd and sat down next to a young
man with a sleek ponytail. He was Lance Foster of the Ioway (Páxoje) tribe,
then a graduate student at Iowa State University. We talked about his thesis,
something he later described as an attempt to "discover the sleeping form
of the Iowa past under the monotonous blanket of the present."[1] He has
since written a number of articles and a highly praised book, *The Indians
of Iowa* (2010). Thanks to Foster and others, we have begun to understand
the region's storied landscapes and human lifeways.

Lost Landscapes

The indigenous people of the northern plains probably began their exchange
with plants at the end of the last ice age. This long-ago era reaches back
nearly twelve thousand years, seemingly forever, so perhaps it would help
if we instead thought of it as twelve months. During this eventful "year,"
the glaciers were still around in January, but by February they had begun
melting as temperatures began to rise. People arrived in late January or early

February, pursuing bison and gathering wild plants. Temperatures reached a maximum about May, and by June things had begun to cool again. A pattern of hunting and gathering food lasted over most of the region until mid-September, when a few groups began to grow domesticated crops. By the first week in December, many more people were cultivating the land. European fur traders began to arrive about December 20.[2]

Table 1. History of the northern plains

Calendar years before present*	Highlights
15,000 to 10,000	Glaciers melt as ice age ends.
	Glacial Lake Agassiz and other large lakes form.
	Open spruce woodlands advance across the region but are later replaced by prairie and parkland.
	Small groups of hunters and gatherers enter 11,000 to 12,000 years ago and trade with others to acquire useful materials.
10,000 to 9,000	Glacial lakes drain; their waters erode deep valleys.
	Prairie and parkland continue to expand.
	Humans gather a variety of plants; bison is their primary game animal.
9,000 to 7,000	Prairie reaches its eastward extent about 6,000 to 7,000 years ago.
	People use stones for grinding seeds and roots.
7,000 to 4,000	Prairie declines.
	Native population is sparse.
	Bison hunting and plant gathering continue.
	Across eastern North America, people gather wild squash, goosefoot, marsh elder, knotweed, and sunflower.

4,000 to 2,000	Forests continue to expand.
	Squash, goosefoot, marsh elder, knotweed, and sunflower are domesticated in parts of eastern North America and spread into the northern plains.**
2,000 to 300	Native populations increase across the region.
(late 1600s)	Clay pots are employed for cooking.
	Maize cultivation enters the region, becoming a major crop about 1,000 years ago.
	Farming settlements spread along rivers and around lakes.
	Trade and contact between groups increase.
	Europeans arrive about 350 years ago (late 1600s CE), the first being explorers, traders, and missionaries.

* The dates here are approximate and may change with future research.

** Some say that squash and sunflowers may have come from Mesoamerica.

The Great Melt

As the masses of ice stagnated and wasted away, the terrain began to resemble today's subarctic Canada. Plant fossils of pollen, wood, and seeds suggest a landscape with groves of white spruce, birch, and poplar. Between the trees grew buffaloberry, creeping juniper, and wild sage. A crunchy mat of lichens, with pockets of moss, carpeted much of the ground.[3] Willow bushes bordered stream banks and lakeshores, along with black spruce and alder. Swaths of cattail crowded marsh margins, while wet meadows covered with hardy grasses and grass-like sedges supplied prime forage for roaming bison and mammoth.[4]

When small groups of hunters and gatherers moved into the region, they seemed to feel at home, even while glacial ice still lay over much of the land. Anishinaabe author Edward Benton-Banai writes of men who ran over the ice and snow between villages, searching for herbs, medicines, and plant foods. They were the Ohkwamingininiwug, the "Ice People."[5]

Early habitats must have offered these people many useful plants. They already knew, or soon discovered, which species were tasty, which could bring relief from common ailments, which produced aromatic smoke when burned, which types of wood made good spear shafts and digging sticks, and which plants had fibers tough enough to be woven into baskets and carrying bags. The roots and berries of some species produced colorful dyes, while others made enjoyable children's toys or brightly colored love tokens.[6] Although there was some overlap in gender roles, most early gatherers were likely female.[7] As is true of recent groups, women were probably also the botanical experts.

Spruce is the signature tree of the north. Two species, black and white, dominate the broad expanse of evergreen that stretches across the continent today, covering more than two million square miles. At the end of the ice age, their dark green spires were just as prominent south of the glaciers.

Such a widely available plant was bound to be heavily used. Its straight-grained wood made excellent spear shafts, tool handles, and tent poles. Spruce bark could cover a shelter, and its boughs made a soft, refreshing mattress. The pungent resin that oozed from the bark acted as an ideal sealant and a popular chewing gum. Spruce made for a first-rate firewood, especially when gathered from standing trees that had been killed by fire. Even rotten and powdery wood was useful for tanning hides and keeping swaddled babies dry.

Both species of spruce tend to have shallow roots, especially when growing on wet soils. Spreading out ten feet or more in all directions, these pencil-thin root strands, when split, made strong and durable ropes for lashing and, truth be told, were better than leather thongs for sewing. Gathering these roots, however, was a painstaking endeavor. Ethnobotanist Robin Wall Kimmerer explains: "The spruce roots you can tell by feel; they're taut and springy. You can pluck one like a guitar string and it twangs against the ground, resilient and strong."[8]

A fresh balsamic scent, with undertones of damp moss, makes a stand of spruce identifiable by smell alone. Little wonder that products of this aro-

FIG. 31. Needles of white spruce, a versatile species of the boreal forest. Photo by Donalee Deck.

matic conifer found their way into early medical lore. From the root, families brewed tea to be taken as a stimulant and brewed another, made from the needles, to stem fever. Salves made from spruce resin treated skin wounds.[9]

Yet the boreal environment that these early people had settled into was about to change. About twelve thousand years ago, the climate warmed rapidly and became wetter as the ice continued to melt.[10] Over the next few thousand years temperatures continued to rise. This warm and dry interval lasted for about four thousand years, but over the following millennia temperatures cooled and rainfall rose once more.

This climatic story played out with shifts in plant cover. The spruce woodlands could not tolerate the warming trend and were replaced by prairie and groves of aspen and oak beginning about thirteen thousand years ago. The wave of change started in what is now South Dakota and moved northward to southern Saskatchewan over some two thousand years.[11] Spruce forests in Iowa and southern Minnesota also disappeared. Grasslands continued to expand as the climate warmed and became drier. By seven thousand years ago Iowa had truly become a prairie state. Elsewhere, grassland had expanded as far as central Minnesota and southeastern Manitoba. These shifts meant that forest creatures had to retreat, but there was more habitat for bison and other prairie animals.[12] This change greatly altered what types of animals people hunted and which plants they gathered. For instance, the spruce woodland offered only a few dozen useful plants compared with hundreds of species on the prairie. When the climate cooled again, forests reclaimed some areas, but prairies remained dominant.

Across the Midcontinent: 10,000 to 4,000 Years Ago

Even during these early times the people of the northern plains were well connected to the rest of the continent through trade. A clue to these links is the widespread use of a variety of raw materials for stone tools. For instance, a type of translucent brown chalcedony known as Knife River flint, excellent for making sharp knives and spear points, has been found nearly a thousand miles east of its southwestern North Dakota source.[13] We thus have a number of sites with stone tools and bones dating to this early period but, sadly, very few plant remains.[14]

Although we know little about early Plains people, we do know something about those living elsewhere on the continent.[15] To the south and east of the northern plains, far beyond the reach of the glaciers, the terrain was shaped by millions of years of slope wash and stream erosion. Underlain by limestone, much of this countryside is marked by sinkholes, caverns, and rock shelters. Lush green plateaus and deep valleys harbor an assortment of oak, hickory, and walnut trees.[16] People lived in these verdant valleys, hunting and gathering wild fruits, nuts, and the edible seeds of annual plants.[17]

One dwelling place that has been thoroughly investigated is Dust Cave, located above a marshy tributary of the Tennessee River in northwestern Alabama. Over eleven seasons of field work, archaeologist Boyce Driskell and a team from the University of Alabama dug through fifteen feet of debris and found stone tools and spear points, animal bones, seeds, and nutshells. Radiocarbon dating shows that the cave was occupied for six thousand years, beginning about ten thousand years ago. In the lower levels excavators found the bones of fish, ducks, geese, and other water birds, likely taken from the marsh that still exists below the cave's entrance. Charred plant remains included hickory nuts, walnuts, and acorns, along with a few goosefoot and other seeds, perhaps gathered from nearby slopes and bottomlands.[18] A family meal at Dust Cave may have featured roast duck stuffed with walnuts plus a sweet treat made from the oily "milk" of hickory nuts.[19]

Archaeologists found hearths for cooking, rounded stone hammers for pounding roots, and rough stone slabs for crushing seeds and preparing these foods. Obviously missing are objects made of wood, leather, or fiber, but there are a few suggestive finds. Instead of wooden digging sticks like those found in dry caves in the West, microscopic wear on stone tools from Dust Cave suggests that some were used for working wood, even though the wood itself has not survived. Excavators also discovered impressions of a woven mat or basket on pieces of fired clay.[20]

At about the same time that the people of Dust Cave were catching ducks and eating nuts, other foods were on the menu at the Barton Gulch site in southwestern Montana. Excavated over a number of seasons by Les Davis from the University of Montana, the site was once surrounded by groves of trees among sagebrush and grassland. Davis's team uncovered dark stains in the earth where wooden posts may once have stood, suggesting that either drying racks or house structures had been built there. The animal remains found imply that people ate deer, rabbit, and hare. Clusters of hearths and roasting pits contained remains of some thirty kinds of plant foods, including the seeds of prickly pear cactus and a western species of goosefoot called narrowleaf, clearly named for its long, narrow leaves. Harvesting and preparing the cactus fruits must have been a challenge. Covered with sharp spines that can pierce skin like shards of glass, they are a sweet delicacy once peeled.[21]

Wherever they lived, early peoples changed local habitats. They wore paths and trails simply by traveling from place to place. They cleared areas for camps and gathered wood for fuel.[22] Trampling the ground around camps resulted in bare soil where aggressive plants (what we call weeds) could flourish. Families may have simply eaten the leaves or seeds of some of these invaders growing on nearby river flats. Perhaps they altered their surroundings deliberately by burning the vegetation or pruning trees and shrubs.[23] In many ways, families created a more diverse and productive landscape, working with nature while also respecting it.[24]

Shaping the Land: Burning

Humans have long used the powerful force of fire.[25] It features in stories told by cultures everywhere, including the northern plains. One favorite tale tells of an irrepressible trickster character (variously named Coyote or Spider) who steals fire and presents it to humans so they can keep warm. Among the Anishinaabe people, the thief is Nanabozho (or Nanabush). In their culture, fire is key to survival and one of the four sacred elements.[26]

Many European explorers witnessed Native peoples setting the prairies alight. In the 1680s French royal commissioner Bacqueville de la Potherie observed, "They commence at once by setting fire to the dried herbage which is abundant in those prairies."[27] In practical terms, burning managed the land. Fires may have been started to trap bison, to improve habitat for deer and other game, or to promote the growth of useful plants.[28]

Whether set by lightning or humans, woodland fires over the past four or five centuries can be traced by counting the burn scars left on stumps and trees. For example, scars on ponderosa pine in the Black Hills of South Dakota date back to the 1500s.[29] They reveal that fires occurred about every fifteen years. One pine stump showed six burn scars incurred between 1753 and 1890.

The study of charcoal to trace where fires had long ago burned the landscape expanded when researchers realized that microscopic charcoal fragments survived the harsh chemical treatments used to extract pollen from sediment samples. As a result, beginning in the 1960s paleoecologists began to look for such fragments in the northern plains. Hundreds of studies now incorporate charcoal in presenting fossil evidence that prairie fires occurred over many millennia.[30]

Detecting ancient fires is one thing, but deciding if they were ignited naturally or by humans is not easy. In a search for answers, paleoecologist Matthew Boyd has studied grass phytoliths from soil layers in southwestern Manitoba. He calculated the proportion of burned phytoliths and found that they peaked in layers dating to shortly after twenty-six hundred years ago. After eliminating natural causes, he concluded that humans were most likely responsible for these fires. The implication is that Native people were managing their surroundings, probably to improve game animal forage.[31]

Partnering with Plants: The Rise of Domestication

The cultivation of edible plants in a garden or field rather than gathering from the wild must rank among the most profound transformations in human history. Plant domestication altered not only what people ate but their health and their whole way of living. Humans eventually settled into villages, expanded their numbers, and formed more elaborate social and political arrangements. These developments were not confined to one geographical area. In North America, from steamy Louisiana bayous to the breezy shores of the Great Lakes, from the rugged Missouri Ozarks to deep Kentucky valleys, people followed various pathways as they moved from hunting and gathering to farming, even while they also exchanged seeds and ideas.[32]

Some argue that the transformation was a natural result of people shaping their surroundings and partnering with certain plants, while others have advanced rival explanations. For instance, some experts suggest a gradual process of increasing manipulation of selected plants. Others argue that resource depletion led to reliance on less efficient foods such as goosefoot seeds. From recent history we do know that indigenous peoples promoted plant growth in many ways short of full-scale cultivation.[33] Debate continues.

While prairie peoples were hunting bison—and presumably gathering berries and digging roots—those living across forested eastern North America were hunting deer and collecting nuts and seeds. As some of these eastern groups, especially those living in rich river valleys, returned to the same camps year after year, we suspect they began to shape their surroundings.[34]

It seems likely that women and girls led the ensuing horticultural transformation.[35] They no doubt nurtured certain food plants by using digging sticks to weed out unwanted neighbors. Some began to sow seed saved from the previous year. A focus on favored plants such as squash, goosefoot, sunflowers, marsh elder, and knotweed must have resulted in more bountiful harvests.[36] These five plants changed over time: their seeds became larger, goosefoot seed coats thinned, and squash flesh became palatable. The guiding principle seems to have been, "Do something for the plant and it will do something for you."

This idea of forging partnerships counters the old adage that domestication involved "taming" wild things and bending them to the human will.[37] Today's farmers sow seeds and harvest crops for food, textiles, and building materials. Are we not thus the masters of their fate? Do not crops exist solely for our benefit? Yet some take an opposing view, arguing that the plants are really in control and we are mere assistants.[38]

In his book *The Botany of Desire: A Plant's-Eye View of the World*, author Michael Pollan proposes that, while we think of domestication as something we do to other species, we should consider what those species have done to us. The process may actually be a clever way for crops to advance their own interests! By providing us with food, shelter, clothing, medicine, and other useful things, plants persuade us to help them succeed. From this viewpoint, the plants are nature's success stories.[39]

Master, equal, or slave? Perhaps the middle ground is best. Smithsonian zoologist Melinda Zeder and colleagues have written that "domestication [is] a process of increasing mutual dependence between human societies and the plant and animal populations they target."[40]

The Long Road to Understanding

It has taken many decades for botanists and archaeologists to even begin to figure out when, where, and how people partnered with plants. During the early years of the twentieth century most archaeologists did not care about Native American agriculture, favoring instead the traditional focus on stone tools and pottery. Unlike such durable materials, plants are fragile and decompose easily. They *can* survive under extremely dry or waterlogged conditions or if they have been charred, but lack of interest plus lack of evidence made research progress slowly.[41]

A major step forward came in the early 1930s, when botanist Melvin Gilmore and his assistant Volney Jones founded the University of Michigan's Ethnobotanical Laboratory, the first of its kind.[42] At last there was a central place dedicated to the identification and preservation of botanical remains from archaeological sites. The new lab became swamped after a call went out asking archaeologists to submit specimens. From some of the material supplied, Gilmore and Jones published their analyses of exquisitely preserved remains from two ancient rock shelters: one in the Arkansas Ozarks and the other in eastern Kentucky.[43]

Crews led by Mark Harrington of the Museum of the American Indian/Heye Foundation, excavated a number of shelters along the White River of northeastern Arkansas in the 1920s and early 1930s.[44] At Eden's Bluff the diggers found a small bag that told a big story. Tightly woven from strips of pawpaw bark and the leaves of button eryngo, sometimes called rattlesnake master, the bag measured a mere four by eight inches. Attractive as it was—the light brown warp contrasting with a dark brown weft—the bag's contents told the story. It was full of thousands of tiny goosefoot seeds, probably put aside by an ancient gardener.[45] Other rock shelters also contained sheaves of goosefoot and other small-seeded plants. Such finds implied that these plants were, in Gilmore's words, "probably cultivated."[46] These early finds signified that people were growing small-seeded grains for quite some time before maize arrived.

Such crop remains are only part of this fascinating ancient Ozark ethnobotany. In his 1931 article Gilmore described sixty species of wild nuts, fruits, seeds, and fibers. People ate hickory nuts, walnuts, hazelnuts, and oak acorns and consumed wild grapes and other wild fruits. They also collected the inner bark of basswood, elm, leatherwood, dogbane, and Osage orange and the leaves of bulrush, yucca, and button eryngo. They used bark fibers to make mats, sandals, carrying bags, and breechclouts. They used big bluestem grass for binding. Stout stems of the bamboo-like switch cane made sturdy javelin shafts, and its splints were used to make baskets. For necklaces, they strung together delicate, pearly white beads made from the seeds of western false gromwell.[47]

In 1936 Jones published his analysis of the remains from the Newt Kash Hollow Shelter, a rock overhang located along the Red River in eastern Kentucky. Measuring several hundred feet long and fifty feet wide, the shelter contained layers of rockfall, sand, leaves, and ashes that yielded a

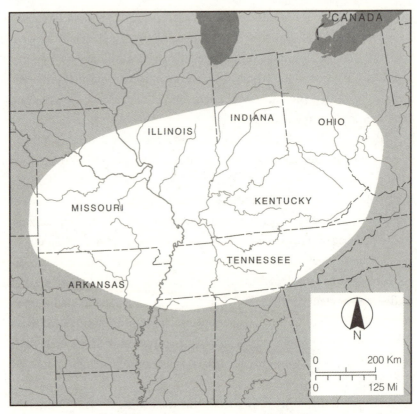

MAP 11. The center of early plant domestication in eastern North America, based on B. Smith et al., *Rivers of Change*; and Patton and Curran, "Archaic Period Domesticated Plants." By Eureka Cartography.

similar floral array, both domesticated and wild. Based on the Ozark and Kentucky finds, Jones went on to propose a premaize agriculture that came to be known as the Eastern Agricultural Complex.[48]

Only a few researchers endorsed the idea of early crop growing over the next few decades, but since the 1960s a growing number of scholars have helped show that people in eastern North America domesticated an assortment of plants thousands of years before maize arrived.[49] This came about thanks in part to better techniques for retrieving plant remains, more detailed methods of studying them, and increasingly accurate means of dating. Advances in genetics and DNA analysis have helped enormously.[50]

Eastern North America can now take its place in world history as a major center of plant domestication.[51]

Plants often play starring roles in Native American oral history. As families came to know these early crops, they may have been given mythological personas, perhaps in the same way that coyotes, eagles, and bears populate Native American stories. Squash and sunflowers are featured in traditional legends, and we can easily imagine goosefoot and marsh elder as quirky supporting characters.

The Squash Saga

Remarkably, a number of squashes, pumpkins, zucchini, and a few gourds all belong to the same genus.[52] Other gourds belong to a different genus and species.[53] Simply put, squashes are just for eating, pumpkins are for both carving and eating, and hard-shell gourds are mainly for rattles, water bottles, and storage containers.

One of the most common types of squash grown today is a subspecies of what botanists call *Cucurbita pepo*. These plants were first domesticated in southwestern Mexico about ten thousand years ago.[54] A few researchers say that squash cultivation later spread northward into the eastern United States.[55] However, most believe that a different *pepo* subspecies was independently domesticated in the eastern United States.[56]

Wild forms of squash still grow along river valleys in several southern states.[57] Their vines can be seen colonizing gravel bars and stream banks or climbing up tree trunks, showing off bright yellow flowers.[58] The hard, ivory-colored fruits, about the size of a tennis ball, contain a mass of flat, oval seeds—but beware! Unlike domesticated types, the rind and flesh of wild squash are bitter and unpalatable to humans. The plant contains cucurbitacin E, which triggers a severe diarrheal illness called toxic squash syndrome.[59] In spite of this, squash fruits must have attracted the attention of human gatherers, possibly for their protein-rich seeds.[60]

People began to gather wild squash in the eastern part of North America about seven thousand years ago, and the plant may have become domesticated about two thousand years later.[61] Archaeologists have recovered charred seeds and rind fragments from open-air sites across much of that

15 - 23mm
9/16 - 14/16 in

FIG. 32. Squash plant. Drawing by Diane Magill.

region, as well as dried specimens from rock shelters. These finds show how, over time, squash fruits grew in size, their shapes became more varied, their rinds thicker, and their seeds larger.[62]

Even with all of that evidence, scientists still did not know when the flesh became palatable to humans (some say it is still not very palatable). DNA provided the answer when anthropologist Logan Kistler and his team analyzed the genetic composition of squash plastids—the parts of plant cells that manufacture and store chemical compounds—from a number of living plants as well as nineteen archaeological specimens. The team correlated a decline in cucurbitacin levels over time, with a corresponding increase in rind (and, we presume, flesh) thickness.[63]

The reasonable explanation is that people selected for these changes.[64] Ancient gatherers must have become skilled at finding plants that contained low or tolerable levels of the dreaded poison we now know as cucurbitacin. This skill would amount to what geneticists call conscious selection. Selection may also have been unintentional. In his award-winning book *Gathering the Desert*, ethnobotanist Gary Paul Nabhan explains, "By repeated sowing of seeds maturing in a cultivated environment, there is automatic, unconscious selection for certain characteristics."[65]

The story of bottle gourds reads more like science fiction. According to DNA studies, these hard-shelled fruits must have floated across several thousand miles of ocean from Africa to reach the Americas.[66] Remains of bottle gourds dating back more than seven thousand years have been found in Florida.[67] A couple of thousand years later they were being used in a number of places across the eastern part of North America.[68] Because they made useful containers long before pottery appeared, gourds might have inspired some early pottery makers.

Today squashes are by far the most diverse of all early domesticates. Thanks to scores of heritage varieties, they display rich shades of orange, yellow, green, and cream, plus green and cream stripes, as well as a slew of shapes: elongated, globular, squat, smooth, and scalloped. They can vary from the size of a baseball to the height and weight of an adult man. Gourds also mature into a bewildering array of sizes and shapes, finding uses as water bottles, bowls, and storage vessels.

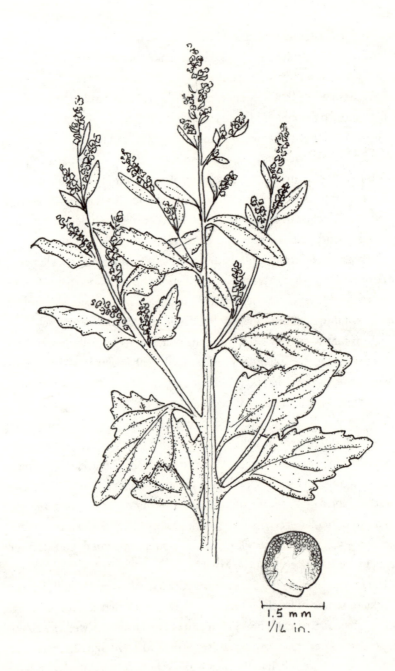

1.5 mm
1/16 in.

FIG. 33. Goosefoot plant. Drawing by Diane Magill.

Goosefoot: Villain and Hero

Goosefoot is both a pernicious weed and a nutritious food. Named for the shape of its leaves, which vaguely resemble a goose's foot, some are reviled as weeds. A gardener friend of mine calls them thugs. One species, lamb's-quarters, is so successful at infesting disturbed soil that it is on a list of the world's worst weeds.[69] In contrast, many consider goosefoot good to eat, referring to it as a "nutritious edible weed."[70]

Goosefoot belongs to the amaranth family, as do a number of other weedy annuals and the familiar garden vegetables spinach and beets. Among hundreds of goosefoot species worldwide, only a dozen grow in the northern plains. These green-gray herbs complete their life cycle from germination to seed set in about three or four months. Attaining heights of three to six feet, their tiny, greenish flowers group in clusters in the leaf axils and at stem tips. When ripe, each plant produces hundreds, if not thousands, of tiny black seeds, each about the size of the head of a pin.

A well-known camp follower, goosefoot would have prospered around early human settlements. Its adaptability, as well as its invasiveness, made it attractive to early plant gatherers who collected what we now know are its vitamin-packed greens and protein-rich seeds. Given all of this, it is no wonder that this small grain has been a prized food among cultures around the world. The Incas, for instance, believed it was sacred, probably because it served as a staple in their diet. Species of goosefoot have been domesticated on four continents, one being today's popular superfood quinoa.[71]

Few seeds have been found at sites in eastern North America dating prior to seven thousand years ago, but then one species, pitseed goosefoot, appeared across the eastern portion of the continent. By forty-four hundred years ago, charred seeds from some sites were showing signs of domestication, such as larger seeds and thinner seed coats. A thinner seed coat means more rapid germination, a desirable trait for any gardener. Researchers refer to these domesticated varieties of *Chenopodium berlandieri* as subspecies *jonesianum*. The subspecies spread and was being grown widely across the midcontinent, from present-day Kentucky to Iowa, by about three thousand years ago.[72]

FIG. 34. Goosefoot seeds. Photo by Sara Halwas.

For reasons unknown, people stopped growing goosefoot before Europeans arrived in North America. Perhaps it fell out of favor as maize rose to dominance.[73]

The Sunflower Story

"How many are there?" wondered Margaret Kapinga, my lab technician, as she prodded the mass of charred sunflower seeds with a dissecting needle.

"There could be hundreds," I replied.

The seeds we were looking at had come from a Mandan village along the Missouri River, where several hundred people lived during the late 1700s.[74] Excavations at the site had also yielded maize, squash, and tobacco seeds.[75] As we sat marveling, we realized that while this was an exciting clue to early Mandan life, it was a sad loss to the family who could have cooked and enjoyed those seeds.

The Pawnees call the sunflower *kirik-tara-kata*, meaning "yellow-eyes," while the scientific name, *Helianthus annuus*, is derived from the Greek *helios* (the sun) and *anthos* (a flower).[76] Botanically speaking, the actual seed is a kernel contained in a hard-shelled achene, or husk. Sunflower

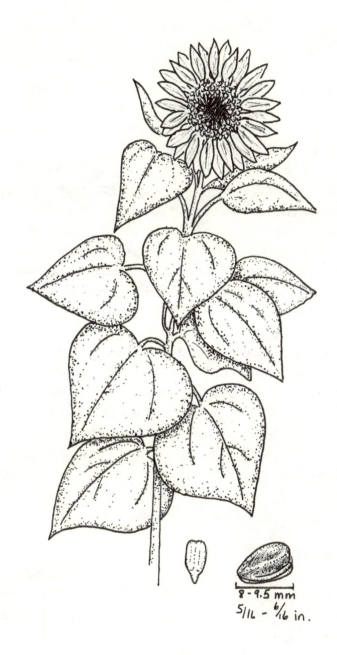

8 - 9.5 mm
5/16 - 6/16 in.

FIG. 35. Sunflower plant. Drawing by Diane Magill.

husks are thin, oval in shape, and gray or black-and-white striped with low ridges. The kernel inside is a rounded oval or teardrop shape with a short, sometimes pointed "stem."

Missouri River tribes and many other Native Americans ate the kernels raw or ground them up before cooking. Some used its oil as a skin lotion and hair conditioner. Pulverized husks made an excellent purple dye for textiles, and the plant's strong stalks found a use in construction. Sunflowers also made their way into rituals. During a Cheyenne animal dance, for example, a tall stem bearing a single flower is brought into the ceremonial lodge.[77]

Sunflowers belong to the aster family, a huge grouping of over twenty thousand species that evolved more than fifty million years ago. Their smiling faces can be seen in open habitats around the globe.[78] The plant has two kinds of flowers. The first is an inconspicuous, tube-shaped kind, numbering in the hundreds; these form a cluster in a head or disk. These flowers mature into seeds. The second type are the brightly colored petals that surround the disk, each a separate flower.

The earliest wild sunflower seeds appear in eight-thousand-year-old deposits in the Illinois River valley. Judging by the gradual increase in seed size across a number of sites, it is surmised that they became fully domesticated as crops about four thousand years ago.[79]

Sunflowers were also first grown as a crop in Mexico about forty-six hundred years ago. Some say they came to North America through trade.[80] The Aztecs called them *chimalsuchitl*, or "shield flower," and they were being widely grown when the Spaniards arrived in the fifteenth century. The plants have been grown on five continents ever since.[81]

Sunflower's Hapless Cousin

A distant relative of the sunflower was also gathered and became domesticated. These rather drab cousins are not showy, nor are they still grown as a crop. Their common name is sumpweed or marsh elder, of the genus *Iva*. As distinguished ethnobotanist and sunflower expert Charles Heiser Jr. has noted, "One would hardly expect any plant with a name like sumpweed to be beautiful."[82]

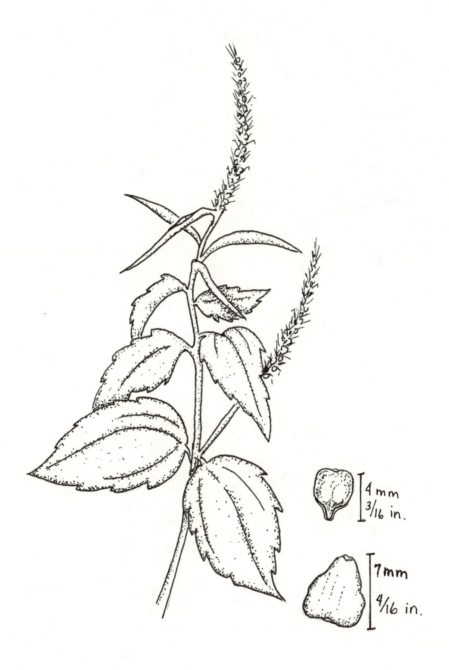

4 mm
3/16 in.

7mm
4/16 in.

FIG. 36. Marsh elder plant. Drawing by Diane Magill.

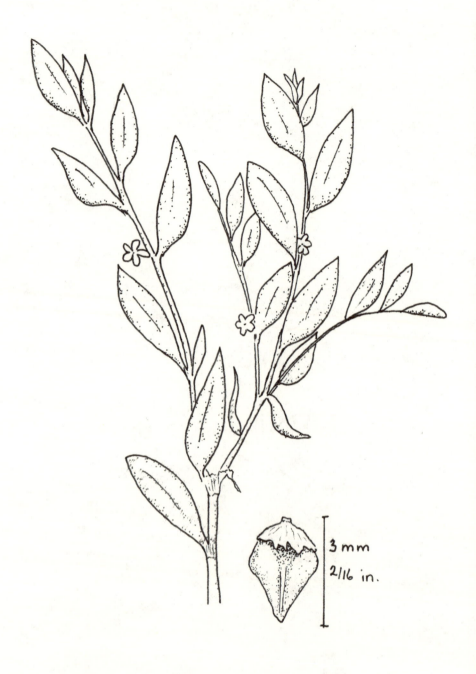

3 mm
2/16 in.

FIG. 37. Erect knotweed plant. Drawing by Diane Magill.

In fact, the whole of genus *Iva* is good, bad, and decidedly ugly. It is good because its seeds are rich in protein and oil, a nutritionist's dream. It is bad because it is closely related to ragweed, and its pollen often causes hay fever. Beyond its drabness, it is ugly due to the painful rash that can result from stripping its seeds by hand. Perhaps this is why the Lakotas call the plant "bad leaves."[83]

One species, the annual marsh elder, reaches up to ninety inches tall and has lance-shaped leaves and tiny flowers in terminal clusters. Like its cousin, the marsh elder has seeds covered by a husk, although the kernel inside is a little more than half the sunflower seed's size. While sunflowers may have many hundreds of seeds per flower head, marsh elder plants produce only a couple of dozen. This means that many more plants must be harvested to gain the same number of seeds.

Marsh elder grows along rivers, in wet meadows, and elsewhere on disturbed ground in moist habitats.[84] Charred seeds of *I. annua* first appear at sites in the Illinois River valley dating to about seven thousand years ago.[85] An increase in seed length suggests that some plants were domesticated about three thousand years later. That cultivar is referred to as *Iva annua* var. *macrocarpa*.[86]

A Kin of Buckwheat

The last of the five plants that indigenous peoples of the region domesticated is erect knotweed, a relative of the familiar cereal buckwheat.[87] Plants grow six to thirty inches high in patches of disturbed ground. With oval-shaped leaves, this plant has clusters of small greenish flowers that emerge from leaf axils.

The tiny, three-cornered seeds, which are less than an eighth of an inch long, are ready to harvest throughout the summer and into the fall. Between about three thousand and two thousand years ago, the seeds increased in size and developed thinner seed coats, implying that these plants were becoming domesticated.[88]

A Pair of Other Crops

The supporting cast in the domestication drama includes two other early cultivars: little barley and maygrass. Little barley grows four to fourteen

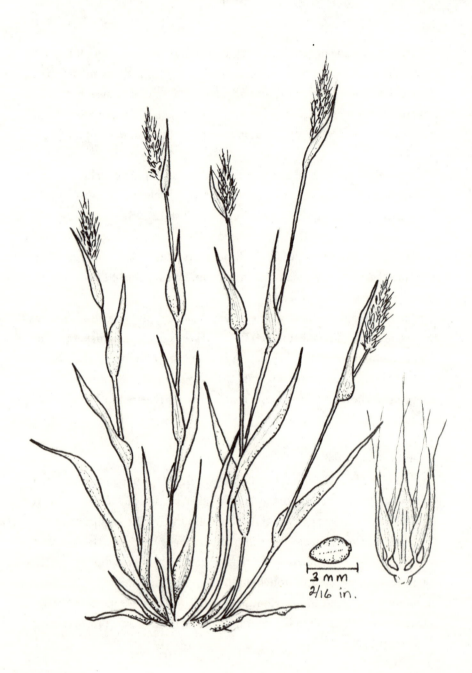

FIG. 38. Little barley plant. Drawing by Diane Magill.

FIG. 39. Maygrass plant. Drawing by Diane Magill.

inches tall, while maygrass stands between twelve and twenty-four inches. Both are annuals, growing throughout the winter, with their seeds ripening in spring. Little barley looks like a pint-size version of cultivated barley, while the heads of maygrass amount to compact cylinders packed with tiny, oval-shaped seeds. Both grow in disturbed places. Maygrass seeds measure about half the size of a grain of wheat.[89] It is not easy to imagine a woman gathering enough of these minuscule seeds to make a meal for her family.

Neither little barley nor maygrass displays the typical traits of domestication. We believe they were crops because their seeds are usually found in quantity, along with goosefoot, sunflower, and marsh elder, and these clutches of seeds date to as early as four thousand years ago.[90]

As crop growing slowly spread westward, most prairie folk remained gatherers, although they traded a variety of goods, including precious raw materials for producing sharp stone tools, such as Knife River flint from North Dakota and super-sharp obsidian glass from Wyoming. Pipestone was quarried in southwestern Minnesota to make pipes and bead necklaces. Shiny copper for tools and ornaments came from rich seams in the igneous rocks around Lake Superior. Farther afield, colorful conch shells from the Gulf of Mexico, long dentalium shells, and small, tapered olivella shells from the Pacific coastline all had decorative uses.[91]

The Sacred Cereal

All of these domesticates would eventually be overshadowed by the queen of crops: maize (*Zea mays*). The word *maize* comes from the Taíno people, who lived on the Caribbean island that the European explorers named Hispaniola. Christopher Columbus met them in 1492 and became fascinated by the cereal crop they called *mahis*, meaning "the source of life." Botanists and archaeologists have traced this annual grass of the Poaceae family back nine thousand years to southern Mexico and a spindly herb called teosinte.[92] Teosinte produces a single, small ear containing a paltry handful of tiny kernels.[93]

We presume that as gatherers in ancient times harvested these tiny kernels, they saved the larger ones to sow for the next year's crop.[94] Over time, and through later selective breeding, maize evolved from a humble dwarf into

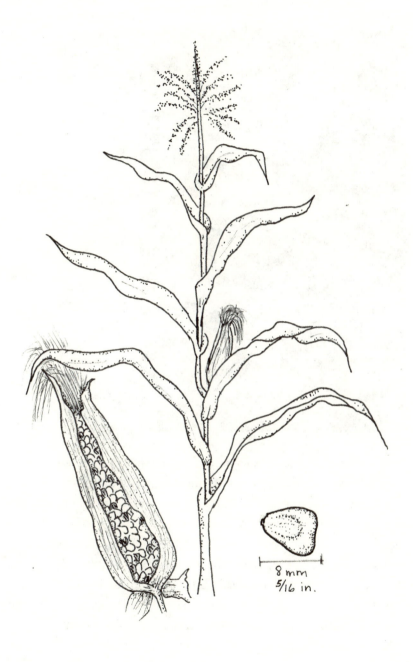

8 mm
5/16 in.

FIG. 40. Maize plant. Drawing by Diane Magill.

FIG. 41. Colorful maize ears. Photo by Markus Winkler on Unsplash.

the giant we know today. Each modern ear contains two hundred to five hundred kernels, making it by far the most productive cereal.[95]

The maize story began in central Mexico and continued in irregular surges southward into South America and northward into what is now the American Southwest, arriving about four thousand years ago. From there it seems to have bypassed the Great Plains to arrive two thousand years later at a few sites to the east. It spread northward into southern Ontario and Quebec, finally reaching the northern plains about a thousand years ago. Five centuries later, maize was a staple across the midcontinent.[96]

Native farmers developed thousands of maize varieties that were genetically diverse and capable of growing in many different habitats.[97] They learned that maize plants grew best when planted in rows of small hills within garden plots. Germination occurs between seven and ten days after planting. During the next three weeks, broad, flag-like leaves form, which efficiently capture sunlight, promoting rapid growth. At maturity, male flowers (tassels) form at the top of the plant. These produce the pollen that fertilizes the female ear (or cob) that emerges from the axil of the leaves. Maize matures in about sixty days, although its kernels can be eaten at every stage of growth. Usually white, they may also be red or purple. Some ears show a mixture of colors.[98]

Maize profoundly altered lifestyles across the Americas. On the Great Plains it was the gift of Corn Mother, a powerful protective spirit often physically represented by an ear of corn.[99]

As maize and bison were important resources for Plains peoples, both figure in many Native stories and ceremonies. We see them represented in a Cheyenne tale about an old woman who shows a pair of young men two fields: one side has corn, the other side has buffalo. Other stories focus on maize. In an Arikara myth, an ear of maize taken from a heavenly garden became a woman sent to help people on Earth. This Corn Woman became a leader and helper, a true cultural hero.[100]

Beans

Around six thousand years ago a protein-rich associate of maize originated as a small-seeded bean in what is now Mexico and Guatemala. It had spread northward into the present-day southwestern United States by two thousand years ago and was present across the Great Plains about nine hundred years ago. Before long, Native American groups across North America were growing several colorful varieties.[101]

Beans are annuals grown for their abundant yield of edible dry seeds (beans) or unripe fruit (green beans). The common bean's ability to climb is legendary. The vine can cling to and rapidly twine around a vertical pole almost before our eyes. Belonging to the Fabaceae (legume) family, most obtain the nitrogen they need from the air through a symbiotic relationship with species of rhizobia bacteria in their root nodules. These microorganisms convert nitrogen into ammonia, which is then made into protein.[102]

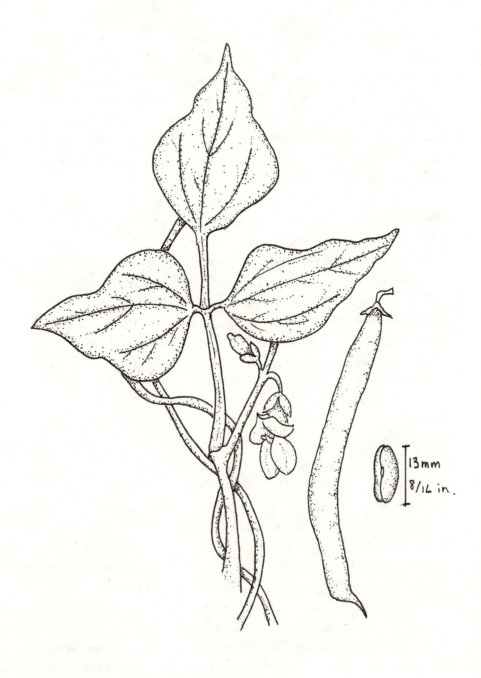

13mm
8/16 in.

FIG. 42. Common bean plant. Drawing by Diane Magill.

The Three Sisters

Corn in the crib, beans by the bushel, and piles of squash and pumpkins are prominent in today's harvest-time celebrations. This trinity of crops is often referred to as the Three Sisters, with the implication being that the trio has always been grown together everywhere.[103] But that is not so. Their relationship across the northern plains and eastern North America began less than a thousand years ago, when maize provided a stalk for beans to climb and squash leaves kept weeds down by shading the soil. For their part, beans' nitrogen-fixing bacteria provided food not only for the plant itself but also for its siblings. As foods, the Three Sisters provide most of the essentials: carbohydrates, protein, and dietary fiber.[104]

People, Plants, and Places

Over countless generations, Native peoples across North America gathered and grew dozens of plants and influenced the abundance of many more through burning, pruning, and weeding. Yet when Europeans first laid eyes on this new land, they pronounced it a pristine wilderness, inhabited by unsophisticated people. Later generations believed the same. Nothing could be further from the truth. We now know that, since last the ice age, indigenous peoples have influenced landscapes from the Amazon rainforests to Alberta's grasslands. Over many millennia Native people transformed plants, just as the plants helped transform their lives.

FURTHER READING

Fritz, Gayle J. *Feeding Cahokia: Early Agriculture in the North American Heartland.* Tuscaloosa: University of Alabama Press, 2019.

Nicholson, Beverley A., ed. *Human Ecology of the Canadian Prairie Ecozone, 11000 to 300 BP*. Regina SK: University of Regina Press, 2011.

Smith, Bruce D., C. Wesley Cowan, and Michael P. Hoffman. *Rivers of Change: Essays on Early Agriculture in Eastern North America.* Tuscaloosa: University of Alabama Press, 2007.

FIG. 43. Tallgrass prairie near Ames, Iowa, with lavender and white asters and yellow goldenrods. Photo by Thomas Rosburg.

Nature's Bounty   6

The acts of hunting, growing, gathering, cooking, and eating
take on a spiritual aspect akin to prayer.

—LOIS ELLEN FRANK, *Foods of the Southwest Indian Nations*

Despite occasional climatic upheavals, Native people thrived across this
lovely land teeming with plant and animal life. Being intimately familiar with
the march of the seasons, their annual rhythm of gathering and growing
aimed to amass enough food to see them through the lean winter. They
pursued bison on the prairie and deer and other game in the woodlands,
hunted ducks and geese in marshes, fished the rivers and lakes, and gathered
roots, seeds, and berries wherever they traveled. Some groups grew crops of
maize, beans, squash, and sunflowers. From this culinary abundance, cooks
prepared hearty roasts and stews, flavorful fruits, and nutritious greens. The
plants they harvested not only provided nourishment, they also became
interwoven into Native spiritual life and were celebrated throughout the
year with feasting and ceremony.

The Bountiful Prairie

Today some fifteen hundred species of wild plants grow across the northern
plains. We know that indigenous peoples employed nearly four hundred of
them, although they were not evenly distributed across the region.[1] Forest
clearings, shrub thickets, and prairies in the humid eastern part of the region
harbor many more species than the dry plains to the southwest. Shady
forests and lowland marshes have few species but often contain quantities
of valuable resources not found elsewhere.[2]

FIG. 44. An expanse of mixed-grass prairie near Lyleton, in southwestern Manitoba. Photo by Lynnea Parker.

On a typical summer day oceans of leaves pulse with activity under the prairie sky. Each leaf contains billions of tiny green chloroplasts that capture the sun's energy and use it to convert carbon dioxide and water into glucose, a simple sugar. This glucose powers the formation of more complex compounds needed for plant growth, a growth that can be impressive. Every square yard of prairie produces almost a pound of fresh plant material each year.[3]

What happens to all this green stuff? From beetles to bison, prairie creatures eat some of it, but humans also benefit. To explore the human portion, my research students put together data on the weight of food produced by a few popular plants. Wild berries yielded up to a half a pound per square yard, underground roots and rhizomes offered two ounces, and wild rice seeds provided less than an ounce. The implication is that plant gatherers could collect more than four edible portions (3.5 ounces or 100 grams) of berries in one square yard, but roots and rhizomes would need almost two square yards and wild rice about five.

A plant's yield of food also depends on how and where it grows. For example, oaks in the open produce more acorns than those growing in a forest, whereas crowded raspberry bushes deliver more fruit than scattered plants. Soil moisture plays a part as well; for example, chokecherry shrubs growing near streams tend to produce more fruit than those on dry slopes.[4]

Sometimes fruit- and nut-bearing plants may not yield as much as expected. In 1979 ecologist Marj Herring helped me sample a young aspen forest in southern Manitoba. We reckoned that hazel shrubs covered more than half the ground in the forest, yet a mere fifth of them bore ripening nuts and only a third of the dogwood shrubs had any fruit at all. Similarly, researchers in the Missouri Ozarks found that only 2 percent of hazel shrubs and 1 percent of wild cherry bushes developed fruits.[5]

Yields can also vary widely over time. Acorn output in an oak grove in central Minnesota deviated sevenfold over seventeen years.[6] In a thirty-year study in northern Minnesota three species varied widely in abundance: raspberry, threefold; hazel, fourfold; and chokecherry, fivefold. Such unevenness proves that key foods are not always available, requiring gatherers to stay flexible and plan ahead.[7]

The Gathering Year
Sugaring

In early spring the woodland trees awaken. Nights are still frosty, but profound chemical changes are under way as starch in the trees' inner bark begins its conversion to a sugary sap. The sap will then surge through the tree, initiating fresh growth. In some trees the watery nourishment is tasty and abundant enough to be collected. Walnut and birch come to mind, but the queen of all is the maple. Its sugar and syrup are so appealing that families still converge on their favorite sugar bush every spring.[8]

One Sunday in April a friend and I rose early and drove south from Winnipeg to the town of St.-Pierre-Jolys, along the Red River, to attend the Sugaring Off Festival held there. We sat at trestle tables in the village hall and breakfasted on eggs and griddle cakes drenched in maple syrup, washed down with steaming cups of coffee. After our meal, we toured a maple grove where every tree sported a tap dripping watery sap into a shiny tin bucket. The Manitoba maple, called box elder in the United States, is common in riverside woods across the western prairies. Its sap is less concentrated and, some say, not as sweet as that of sugar maple or silver maple trees found farther south, in Minnesota and Iowa.[9]

In former times collecting the sap was also an elaborate affair. We do not know when it began, but the practice must be centuries old, originating long before Europeans came to North America.[10] The Menominee people of Wisconsin tell of the time Wenebojo, a trickster spirit known by many names, was standing under a maple tree when it suddenly began to rain maple syrup. In haste, he grabbed a birch bark tray and held it out to catch some. While the sweet liquid was dripping into the tray, Wenebojo thought to himself, "Hmm, this is too easy." There and then he vowed that human folk would have to work if they wanted the sweet stuff.[11]

People did work for it, but they also planned ahead. Nodinens (Little Wind), of the Mille Lacs band of Anishinaabe from central Minnesota, remembers the food her family stored at their favorite sugaring site when she was little: "There were cedar-bark bags of rice and there were cranberries sewed in birch bark makuks [folded and sewn baskets up to about ten inches high and eight inches square, usually heavily decorated] and long strings of dried potatoes and apples. Grandmother had charge of all this."[12]

Families labored together for several weeks, collecting the sap in birch bark containers and spending many hours cooking it down to syrup. To make maple taffy, they heated the syrup above the boiling point for a few minutes and then poured it into containers to harden—sweet treats, especially for the young. Paul Buffalo (Anishinaabe) remembers "how we'd go for that taffy and syrup and sugar cakes. Oh, I ate a lot of that."[13] A longer boil and enough stirring resulted in a granulated sugar. Uncooked, the sweet nectar could be served as a beverage, sometimes mixed with sap from other trees.[14]

Spring Melt

Native peoples delighted in spring, as the words of Sitting Bull (Lakota) reveal: "The earth has received the embraces of the sun and we shall soon see the results of that love! Every seed has awakened and so has all animal life."[15]

Life's annual renewal arrives bursting with sights and sounds, but there is no greater spectacle than the breaking up of river ice. Living south of Winnipeg, Jennifer and I saw the Red River's breakup more than a dozen times. It was never the same; some years brought dramatic floods while others became trivial events, all depending on the thickness of the winter ice, the snow depth, and the pace of warming. In high-water years a rising tide of water, errant tree trunks, and other flotsam turned the Red River into a swollen mass bearing huge rafts of ice that wreaked havoc along the banks, bending trees to near breaking amid groans and cracks. Eventually, the river would calm and shrink into its summer channel.

Native peoples welcomed the opening up of the rivers because it meant, among other things, that fish would soon be spawning. Occasionally some of those awaiting the arrival of the fish were caught off guard by a sudden deluge. A number of Lakotas living along the Missouri were tragically swallowed up in the spring of 1826, the year of a great Red River flood (see chapter 2).[16]

As the land awakens, winter's drab browns and grays give way to the verdant green of spring, with the tiny flowers of elm and box elder trees leading the parade of blooms. They are soon followed by splashes of yellow marsh marigolds in wetlands, blue violets in meadows, and the delicate white blossoms of juneberry in thickets.[17] Native camps and villages across the land also sprang into action. Willow shoots for basketry and other crafts would not be ready for gathering until summer, but this was the time for canoe makers to search in forested areas for the birch bark and cedar wood needed for boatbuilding.

While adults tended to their chores, children and dogs ran everywhere, the laughter and barking mingling with the honks and quacks of returning waterfowl overhead. Some groups followed the birds to the marshes not only to hunt them but also to gather armloads of cattails. Almost every part of this abundant marsh plant was used. Families dug up its starchy underground rhizomes to roast or pound into flour. They chewed the fresh young stalks that, to me, taste like bland celery. Later they picked, boiled, and ate its young flower spikes. Cattail pollen made a protein-rich flour for cooking, while the fluffy down of the ripe seed heads dressed wounds, filled pillows, and padded diapers. Householders also wove the leaves into mats for various purposes. It is thus little wonder that cattail was often featured in ceremonies.[18]

FIG. 45. Marsh marigolds in bloom, an early spring delight. Photo by Travis Scheirer.

FIG. 46. A dense cattail stand showing the hot dog–like seed heads. Photo by Ryan Ready.

FIG. 47. Cattail rhizomes are said to taste slightly sweet. Photo by Ben Lord.

FIG. 48. A grinding stone about the size of a dinner plate from an early site in southwestern Manitoba. Photo courtesy of Clarence Surette, Department of Anthropology, Lakehead University.

Seeds and Fruits

By early summer people could begin harvesting the seeds of annual plants along river flats and marshes. Archaeological evidence suggests that harvesters stripped the seeds from the stems by hand, cut the seed heads off with a knife, or uprooted entire plants.[19] Once gathered, the seeds had to be winnowed to remove excess chaff and other unwanted bits. This could be done by flipping a batch into the air from a shallow basket and letting the wind blow away debris. Gently heating the seeds (parching) helped to loosen tough outer hulls and also served to keep the seeds from sprouting or becoming moldy.

Then came the many hours of work to make the raw foods ready for cooking. As food historian Rachel Laudan points out, "grinding and pounding are some of the heaviest tasks humans have ever undertaken."[20] We know that crushing seeds on a stone into coarse meal takes almost twice the effort of harvesting. Seeds, rough cuts of meat, tough inner bark, woody taproots, nuts, and some berries were all arduously processed.[21] Grinding stones were widely used, though some cooks pounded their foods with a stout wooden pestle in a large mortar made from a hollowed-out tree stump.[22]

People have ground and pounded foodstuffs on the plains for nearly nine thousand years.[23]

Summer ushered in the celebrated berry season. Beverly Hungry Wolf (Blackfoot) notes, "I have seen my Elders receive the first saskatoon [juneberry] of the season. This berry is not just gobbled down; it is taken and held in the air, and a prayer is said. It is then put in the ground as an offering, or as an act of communion with the Earth Mother."[24]

In Gilbert Wilson's *Waheenee: An Indian Girl's Story*, Buffalo Bird Woman (Hidatsa) recalled an afternoon when a young woman named Red Blossom returned to the village with a handful of ripe juneberries. The delicious treat sparked a hastily planned gathering trip for the next day. When morning came, a group of women and teenage girls set off to collect berries, along with a few men to guard the party and help out. Buffalo Bird Woman was delighted when the handsome young warrior Sacred Red Eagle Wing came with her. He kindly broke off some fruit-laden branches and laid them on a hide so she could knock the berries free with a stick.[25]

Such harvesting trips were also teaching moments. An elder recalled, "I would say, 'This tree is full, let's pick them all.' My grandparents would say, 'No[,] we don't do it that way.' . . . We would pick some, we would leave some for others, and we would leave some so the tree would come back next year."[26]

Wild strawberries ripened early. These delicious, juicy berries do not dry easily, so most people enjoyed them fresh.[27] By high summer harvesters could collect bushels of juneberries, raspberries, chokecherries, and blueberries. Paul Buffalo remembered, "When the berries came we were sure of the season. According to our way of reckoning we called that time 'half of the summer.' That was usually the month of July."[28]

Across the prairies July was called the "chokecherry moon."[29]

For early Native peoples, the chokecherry shrub was the very essence of versatility. Before roasting bison steaks, cooks speared them with chokecherry branches, adding a spicy flavor. Mothers made a medicinal tea with the chokecherry shrub's inner bark to ease stomach ailments, coughs, and fevers; crushed hot bark was used as a poultice to draw infection from wounds. A dye made from the bark yielded hues ranging from brilliant red

FIG. 49. A saskatoon shrub with nearly ripe fruit. Photo by Peter M. Dziuk, Minnesota Wildflowers.

to dark purple. Stems made sturdy bows and straight arrows, snowshoe frames, and supports for cooking pots. Both the branches and fruit were used in ceremonies.[30]

Chokecherry thrives in forest margins, clearings, and thickets across much of the continent but is especially well known among prairie residents.

When ripe, the purple-black garlands of bitter and astringent fruit are easy to gather.[31] To retard spoilage once gathered, berries were dried in the warm sun on hides or frames of slender reeds.[32] Some were pounded and mixed with buffalo meat and fat to produce pemmican, the classic trail food.[33]

A Sacred Taproot

An important midsummer event was the digging of Indian breadroot, sometimes called "prairie turnip" or *tipsin* and known to the Lakotas as *timsula* or *thíŋpsiŋla*. It is considered by some to be the most important wild food of the prairies.[34] Harvesting this nutritious staple took time and effort. Alma Snell, Crow historian and herbalist, recalls, "Back when I was growing up, living with my grandmother, we'd spend a few days doing nothing but digging turnips. My sister Pearl, Grandma, and I would bring home three hundred or more roots. We stayed in the turnip area all day. We took our lunch. It was hard work, but we liked it."[35]

The edible taproots were freed from the soil with long, tapered sticks usually crafted from stout ash saplings, the iconic tool of plant gatherers. The stick's business end was trimmed to a three-cornered point, well greased with bone marrow, wrapped in dry grass, and lightly charred to make it nearly as hard as iron.[36]

Back in camp, turnips were peeled, their tops braided together, and the bunch then hung to dry. The spindle-shaped prairie turnip roots, the size of a hen's egg, could be roasted or added to soups and stews. When pounded into flour and fashioned into bread-like cakes, the plant could properly be called the "Bread of the Prairies."[37]

This food was soothing as well. A tasty porridge for convalescents and babies can be made from breadroot meal. Snell offered the following recipe: "Soak two cups of ground turnip meal in two or three cups of water until the particles are soft and swollen. Simmer for about a half an hour. Next add a handful of flour that has been mixed with water to make a smooth paste[;] stir and boil for another five minutes. Take off the heat and add two tablespoons of marrow fat or shortening and sweeten with berries or sugar. Serves about six adults."[38]

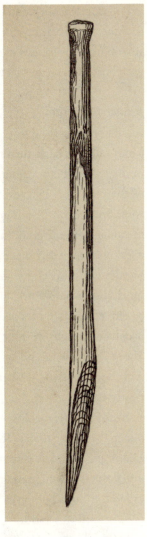

FIG. 50. Prairie turnip. Photo by Philippe Couton.

FIG. 51. Drawing of a Hidatsa digging stick. Gilbert L. and Frederick N. Wilson Papers. Minnesota Historical Society Catalog ID number: 09-00039250. Permission to reproduce courtesy of the Division of Anthropology, American Museum of Natural History and the Minnesota Historical Society.

Manoomin

Wild rice ripens as the days become shorter and the nights cooler. The Anishinaabe call it *manoomin*, meaning "the good berry, a gift from the Creator." This sacred food can be harvested over several weeks in late summer or early fall. Botanically speaking, wild rice (sometimes called "Native rice") is not rice at all but a cereal grain produced by wetland grasses of the genus *Zizania*. The genus emerged about fifteen million years ago and diverged

FIG. 52. A ripening stalk of wild rice (*manoomin*), a sacred food of the Anishinaabe. Photo by Peter M. Dziuk, Minnesota Wildflowers.

into wild rice and northern wild rice during the ice ages.[39] The cereal once grew over much of the northern plains and the forested areas to the east, which explains why so many lakes are called Rice Lake and why many places have names derived from the word *manoomin,* such as Mahnomen County, Minnesota.[40]

Both species of wild rice are wind-pollinated annuals that thrive in clear, shallow lakes or slow-moving waters.[41] Plants grow well in water six to thirty-six inches deep, maturing in around four months. Yields vary from year to year, depending on water levels and other factors. If the water is too high, plants will drown; if too low, they might wither.[42] Paul Buffalo acknowledges the obstacles to a successful harvest: "We know there's much danger ahead: storms, hails, different things might destroy the crops. . . . We're not sure of a crop until we receive it in our hands."[43]

FIG. 53. An American hazelnut ready for picking. Photo by Katy Chayka, Minnesota Wildflowers.

From charred seeds found at archaeological sites in Minnesota, Iowa, and South Dakota and microscopic phytoliths in Saskatchewan and Manitoba, we know that people began gathering manoomin some three thousand years ago.[44] Author Winona LaDuke describes the process: "Two people to a canoe, one poles through the thick rice beds, pushing the canoe forward, while the other, sitting toward the front of the boat, uses two long sticks to gently bend the rice and knock the seeds into the canoe."[45]

After harvesting, manoomin was first dried for a few days on mats or animal skins set out in the sun. The kernels were then parched over a slow-burning fire before being hulled to remove the close-fitting outer husk. Traditionally, men performed the strenuous task of hulling by trampling on the rice in shallow pits. Finally, the grain was winnowed to remove chaff. Collecting and processing wild rice took a lot of time and effort, but the wholesome grain stored well and had an appealing chewy texture and nutty flavor.[46]

The grain still carries deep spiritual meaning for its gatherers.[47] Erma Vizenor, Anishinaabe tribal chairwoman of the White Earth Nation in Minnesota, notes that "wild rice, or *manoomin*, is a sacred food and medicine integral to the religion, culture, livelihood, and identity of the Anishinaabeg."[48]

Nut Harvest

When waterfowl headed south and leaves turned to crimson and gold, the nut harvest began. Bur oak trees and hazel shrubs were the most common nut bearers everywhere, though hickory, black walnut, and several other species of oaks grew in southern Minnesota and Iowa. Hazelnuts are naturally sweet, but acorns need special handling. Cooks first boiled them and then leached out their bitter tannic acid, either by placing the acorns in running water or by burying them in wood ash. After a few days they could be pounded into meal.[49]

Food as Fuel

No doubt gatherers passed over some foods that needed a great deal of energy to harvest in favor of others that were easier to collect. To estimate how much energy it takes to gather some common prairie foods, our research team conducted fifteen field trials over several growing seasons. With the help of twenty volunteers, we focused on Indian breadroot, chokecherry, raspberry, and juneberry. After every trial we weighed what had been collected and converted it into calories, a measure of potential energy.[50] Each food's efficiency was then estimated by comparing "energy gained" with the estimated number of Calories expended.[51]

One hot July day found us on a broad stretch of mixed-grass prairie at the Canadian Forces Base Shilo in western Manitoba.[52] We were there to dig Indian breadroot. Our field methods were simple. First, we laid out several collection areas, the largest about the size of a football field. Next, the diggers fanned out to search for the fuzzy, pale green leaves of the scattered plants.

"Mark!" shouted Heidi. I clicked the stopwatch. She had needed only thirty seconds to locate a plant. Heidi shouted again, and I clicked the stopwatch to time her digging. She took only two minutes to retrieve the precious root. Some taproots took longer because they were buried up to a foot deep. Before we left, we counted all the plants in the different areas to record their abundance.

Back in the lab, we dried and weighed the roots and used U.S. Department of Agriculture tables to calculate our harvest's potential energy. We compared this with our estimate of how much energy the diggers had spent in gathering, concluding that they had gained much more potential food energy than they expended.[53]

Of all our harvesting trials, chokecherry yielded the greatest return on energy expended. Granted, we had collected these fruits from heavily laden bushes, but the way the berries are arranged helped as well. Unlike raspberry and strawberry that nestle their fruits throughout the plant, ten to twenty-five chokecherries are arrayed together along a stalk (called a raceme) near the end of a branch. This layout makes it easy to strip handfuls into a waiting container.

Using our own and others' data, we compared the energy costs of gathering thirteen different foods to the caloric benefits gained. Fruits such as wild plum and chokecherry, the seeds of pigweed, and the roots of cattail ranked highest. Remember, however, that seeds and roots have to be ground into meal or pounded into flour, a lengthy and arduous enterprise, whereas the fruits could be eaten raw. Taste probably drove some gathering choices. Hazelnuts, for example, were the least energy-efficient food that we found, but no doubt their sweet taste warranted the effort.[54]

The Growing Year

Peoples across the prairie gathered the region's seasonal wealth, but some also grew crops for food. If ancient Egypt was a gift from the Nile, then the mighty Missouri bestowed similar offerings on the Hidatsas and their neighbors. In flood years the river deposited nutrient-rich alluvium on its adjacent bottomlands, where Hidatsa families laid out their plots, each one about half the size of a modern-day football field.[55]

We know a great deal about the agricultural year thanks to the memoir of Buffalo Bird Woman. During the summers of 1912 to 1915, with her son Edward Goodbird as interpreter, she described to anthropology graduate student Gilbert Wilson how she grew and prepared maize and other crops

FIG. 54. Chokecherry fruit grows on a raceme, with each fruit hanging on a short stem along a stalk. Photo © Minnesota Department of Natural Resources.

in her village on the Knife River in central North Dakota. First published in 1917, *Buffalo Bird Woman's Garden* remains a classic.

As Buffalo Bird Woman tells it, women and girls did the gardening, with the older men sometimes helping: "It was theirs to plant the corn while the women made the hills; and they also helped pull up weeds."[56] Families worked together when there was much to do. After the frost went out of the ground, women cleared the last year's crop residue, turned over the soil, broke up dirt clods, and piled weeds, roots, and brush to dry. Later,

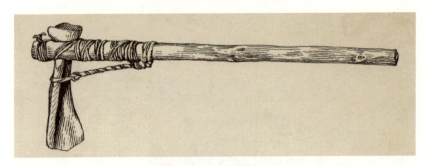

FIG. 55. Drawing of a hoe made from the shoulder blade of a bison. Gilbert L. and
Frederick N. Wilson Papers. Minnesota Historical Society Catalog ID number:
09-00039250. Permission to reproduce courtesy of the Division of Anthropology,
American Museum of Natural History and the Minnesota Historical Society.

burning this debris added nutrients to the soil. Their tools were wooden
digging sticks, rakes made of deer antlers, and hoes crafted from the shoulder
blades of bison. Always methodical, they hoed the soil frequently to keep
it loose, planted in regularly spaced hills, and sowed an equal number of
seeds in the same hills year after year.

Sunflowers were planted first, usually in April. Three seeds were planted
together in widely spaced small hills, eight or nine paces apart, around the
edges of the fields.[57] About a month later families began planting rows of
corn after the wild gooseberry bushes were in full leaf, a good sign that
the young plants would not be killed by frost. A number of varieties might
be grown, but planters would carefully separate them in the field to avoid
cross-pollination. Six to eight kernels were sowed in each hill, with the hills
spaced about four feet apart in all directions.

Squash was planted in late May or early June. Before the seeds were put
into the ground, they were sprouted in a layer of wet sage and silverberry
leaves bundled in a bison hide.[58] Beans were planted next, in hills equidistant
between the corn rows and only half as far apart as the corn. After scraping
away the dry soil, the women formed small hills with the moist soil under-
neath. Into each hill they planted two groups of three seeds.[59]

Buffalo Bird Woman was fussy about her beans: "I was very careful to
select seed for the following points: seed should be fully ripe; seed should
be of full color; seed should be plump, and of good size. If the red was not

a deep red, or the black a deep black, I knew the seed was not fully ripe, and I would reject it."[60]

A typical field in her village looked something like a checkerboard, with about eighty corn hills, forty of beans, twenty of squash, and a border of sunflowers. Harvesting began in late summer as the squash ripened. Families boiled some of it fresh; they sliced the rest and strung it on cords to dry for later use.

A highlight of the growing season came with the harvest of the unripe "green" corn.[61] These tender ears were boiled or roasted and eaten straight from the cob.[62] In a letter from the 1830s, American painter and traveler George Catlin wrote,

> The green corn is considered a great luxury by all those tribes who cultivate it; and is ready for eating as soon as the ear is of full size, and the kernels are expanded to their full growth, but are yet soft and pulpy. In this green state of the corn, it is boiled and dealt out in great profusion to the whole tribe, who feast and surfeit upon it whilst it lasts; rendering thanks to the Great Spirit for the return of this joyful season, which they do by making sacrifices, by dancing, and singing songs of thanksgiving.[63]

The mature corn harvest came a few weeks later and was usually followed by a husking feast. Buffalo Bird Woman explains:

> The next day after the corn was plucked, we gave a husking feast. We took out into the field a great deal of dried meat . . . and boiled it in a kettle near the corn pile. We also boiled corn on a fire near by. . . . Word had been sent beforehand that we were going to give a husking feast, and the invited helpers soon appeared. . . . There might be twenty-five or thirty of the young men. . . . The husking season was looked upon as a time of jollity; and youths and maidens dressed and decked themselves for the occasion.[64]

Beans ripened next, and finally sunflowers ended the harvesting season. The Hidatsas valued the oil-rich seeds, drying them for use in various dishes.[65] For making a nutritious portable snack, anthropologists Fred

Schneider and Mary Jane Schneider offer this Hidatsa recipe: "The seeds were parched in a pot over the fire and then pounded in a mortar to make a meal. This meal could be gathered in the hand and squeezed into a ball [as a] high energy trail food."[66]

Cooking

Cooking improves flavor and makes food more palatable, such as when it converts the inulin-type carbohydrates in onions and Jerusalem artichokes into easily digested simple sugars.[67] Roasting food over an open fire is both satisfying and an ancient practice.[68] Women roasted meat as well as Indian breadroot and hazelnuts. They baked or steamed greens, seeds, and other nuts. The rich aroma of roasting meat or vegetables over a crackling fire is enough to entice even the least hungry to a meal. These heady bouquets are due to the Maillard reaction—the release of hundreds of volatile aromatic compounds.[69]

Hot rock boiling is almost as simple as roasting. After stones are heated in a fire, they are dropped into a container with water and food, thus bringing the liquid to a boil. Cree historian Joseph Dion explains: "A round hole was first dug in the ground and this was lined with green hide; stones were heated red hot and the dish prepared. It consisted of finely chopped meat and fat, the brain and marrow of the buffalo. When no water was available the blood was used."[70] Boiling softens tough fibers and makes food taste better. We also know that the heat kills harmful bacteria and reduces toxins. Steeping aromatic herbs, barks, and roots in hot water to make teas and medicines helps release useful water-soluble chemical compounds.

A new way of boiling appeared almost three thousand years ago, when people in and around the region began to employ vessels of fired clay.[71] While clay pots were bulky and liable to break, they may have allowed for longer heating, letting meals simmer while cooks were busy with other tasks. It is also possible that boiling in a pot used less fuel.[72]

Buffalo Bird Woman shared the following recipe for a winter vegetable dish: To a pot of water placed on the fire add one double handful of beans and one string of dried squash rings, about the length from one's elbow to the tip of the thumb. When the squash is cooked, remove from the pot and cut the grass string. Chop and mash the squash, then return it to the pot after

FIG. 56. Eastern red cedar "berries" are used for flavoring. Photo by Peter M. Dziuk, Minnesota Wildflowers.

beans are soft. Add four to five double handfuls of mixed meal composed of parched sunflower and parched corn. Boil a few minutes and serve.[73]

Cooking means much more than just roasting or boiling, of course. Small additions can lift an ordinary meal into a culinary experience. To flavor their fare, Native cooks added various ingredients. Juneberries and chokecherries gave zest to otherwise bland dishes; rose hips, either fresh or dried, added a light citrus flavor. Wild mint delivered a delicate essence, but wild strawberry leaves carried a sharp, distinctive flavor. Some used crushed red cedar berries, which tasted slightly sweet and resinous, to flavor soups, meats, and stews.[74]

Buffalo Bird Woman tells of an unlikely flavoring. A fungus, corn smut, lives in the soil but migrates upward to infect ripening ears of corn. It replaces kernels with large, tumor-like growths resembling ugly mushrooms. Highly perishable, the smut was quickly gathered, parboiled, and dried for later use.[75] It seems improbable, but today's chefs relish its pungent, earthy, and woody mix of sweet and savory.[76]

At the sweet end of the spectrum, maple sugar was a popular extra among the Plains Cree people. According to anthropologist David Mandelbaum, "The sugar which adhered to the sides of the kettle was then scraped off and placed in a buffalo bladder which, in turn, was placed in a rawhide bag. These scrapings . . . were sprinkled over meat as a condiment. The sugar was eaten as a delicacy, and as might be expected, was consumed largely by the children."[77]

Plant and animal resources varied enough across the region that each area developed its own cuisine, even though some resources, such as roots and berries, were widely traded. Bison, berries, and Indian breadroot were the primary foods on the open prairies. Maize, beans, squashes, and sunflowers were common among agrarian folk living along rivers and around lakes. Moose, deer, berries, and wild rice were staples in the northern forests. Choices were healthy according to modern research, providing ample protein, energy, vitamins, minerals, and protective antioxidants.[78]

Wherever the people of the northern plains lived and whatever they ate, food choices were about more than simply sustenance. Sean Sherman, a chef of Lakota heritage who champions indigenous cuisine, writes, "I found that, more than anything, my ancestors' work was guided by respect for the food that they enjoyed. Nothing was ever wasted; every bit was put to use. This sparked creativity as well as resilience and independence. Above all else, they were healthy and self-reliant."[79]

FURTHER READING

Kindscher, Kelly. *Edible Wild Plants of the Prairie: An Ethnobotanical Guide.* Lawrence: University Press of Kansas, 1987.

Mt. Pleasant, Jane. *The Paradox of Productivity: Lessons from an Indigenous Culture.* Intercontinental American Indigenous Research Association. https://www .americanindigenousresearchassociation.org/wp-content/uploads/2016/11/Mt. -Pleasant-AIRA-2016.pdf.

Sherman, Sean, and Beth Dooley. *The Sioux Chef's Indigenous Kitchen.* Minneapolis: University of Minnesota Press, 2017.

Wilson, Gilbert L. *Buffalo Bird Woman's Garden: Agriculture of the Hidatsa Indians.* St. Paul: Minnesota Historical Society Press, 1987.

Medicinal and Mystical Plants 7

The old life was attuned to nature's rhythm—bound by mystical
ties to the sun, moon, stars; to the waving grasses, flowing streams
and whispering winds.

—LUTHER STANDING BEAR, *Land of the Spotted Eagle*

With a video camera staring me in the face, I reached over and picked up
a gray-green sprig of wild sage, crushing it between my fingers to release
its sharp perfume. I was hunkered down in a patch of tallgrass prairie that
windy August afternoon while a local television reporter asked me about my
talk at the ninth North American Prairie Conference in nearby Moorhead,
Minnesota.[1] Gazing into the lens, I plucked a sprig of green and declared,
"This is sage, one of the most widely used medicines in North America."

The sprig in my hand belonged to prairie sagewort, *Artemisia frigida*. It
is one of the many wild sages of the daisy family. Please don't confuse it
with the sage in your spice racks. That flavorful seasoning belongs to the
mint family.

Among the hundreds of healing herbs of the northern plains, about a
half dozen species belong to the botanical genus *Artemisia*. These peren-
nials possess a history stretching back millions of years. From the parched
plateaus of central Asia, the pale gray plants spread across the temperate
zone, reaching the plains of North America some thirteen million years
ago.[2] Sage became part of the spruce parkland beyond the ice age glaciers
and later found a prominent place in the prairies that replaced the spruce,
especially in more arid parts of the region.[3] Given this deep history and far-
flung abundance, these powerful plants, with their strong aroma and bitter
taste, must be among the oldest and most widely used on earth.[4]

FIG. 57. A twig of prairie sagewort, *Artemisia frigida*. Photo © Mary Ellen (Mel) Harte, Bugwood.org.

The ancient Greeks named the genus after Artemis, goddess of nature. Legend has it that when a plague struck the island of Sicily in the fifth century BCE, Artemis and her twin brother, Apollo, god of healing, used sage to treat the sick. In nineteenth-century France, sage leaves from one species, absinthium, were steeped in alcohol to create the powerful liqueur absinthe, a licorice-flavored potion that intoxicated and inspired scores of writers and artists.[5]

Whereas absinthe altered minds, an Asian species was destined to save lives. Artemisinin, a compound isolated from sweet sagewort, now cures thousands of malaria sufferers. We need only add the ornamental varieties, those with culinary uses (such as French tarragon), and its inclusion as an ingredient in perfumes, soaps, and lotions to round out its versatility. Not bad for a single genus.[6]

Species of *Artemisia* are also a vital part of Native American spirituality and medicine.[7] Used by the Lakotas for burning and smudging, sage is said to clear the air and the spirit. Likewise, those involved in a healing ceremony are encouraged to cleanse with it to remove any negative thoughts.[8] Similarly, Edward Goodbird (Hidatsa) told anthropologist Gilbert Wilson that when a man came out of the river after emptying his fish trap, the trap was felt to be "kind of alive" with power, so he would brush himself with sage to sweep that away.[9] Hunters stuffed sage leaves into the mouth and nose of a killed animal for the same reason.[10]

My own research also shows that this powerful genus has a long history of practical use.[11] A year before his untimely death, my friend Dr. James Wright, of the Canadian Museum of Civilization, asked me to send him seeds of potential medicinal plants from archaeological sites in western Canada that he could photograph for a book he was writing, *A History of the Native People of Canada*. In response, I huddled with my student researchers and we decided that candidates must be popular medicines, their seeds found charred, and in reasonable numbers (more than one or two).

We reasoned that, although healing herbs could be chewed raw, they were most often prepared over a fire, such as when making a tea, thus increasing the chance of any adhering seeds being charred. Of course plants simply growing around a site could have been burned accidentally, so we chose only samples from charcoal-rich deposits that showed signs of cooking or deliberate heating. After weeks of combing through more than eight thousand seeds collected from twenty-one sites, we came up with five candidate species: dogwood, wild prairie rose, western snowberry, nettle, and sage. Among the five, only sage was used mainly for medicine.

More than thirty charred *Artemisia* seeds have turned up at three sites in southeastern Saskatchewan and southern Manitoba in either ash deposits or roasting pits in levels dating from two hundred to twelve hundred years ago. Elsewhere, remains up to three thousand years old have been found in Utah, Wyoming, and western Oklahoma.[12]

These candidate plants are but a small sample of the region's huge pharmacopoeia. Hundreds of trees, shrubs, and herbs, as well as a few feathery ferns and so-called fern allies, like wiry horsetails and ground-pines (tiny

FIG. 58. White sage, *Artemisia ludoviciana*, the most widely used sage species on the Great Plains. Photo © Glen Lee, Regina, Saskatchewan.

plants that resemble miniature conifer trees), had medicinal uses. Many healing plants were also foods or spices, a fact that makes sense since the complex molecules responsible for flavor often possess healing properties.[13]

A Complex Chemistry

Plants manufacture countless complex molecules using only a handful of elements—carbon, oxygen, hydrogen, and sometimes nitrogen, sulfur, or phosphorus. Many are formed on a basic building block: the benzene ring. Seen in two dimensions, the ring, which has six carbon and six hydrogen atoms (C_6H_6), resembles a six-pointed star. Larger molecules are created by linking with other rings, sometimes having five sides, thus creating a chain with oxygen, hydrogen, or other atoms. Among these many compounds, three chemical groups are relevant to Native medicine: phenolics, alkaloids, and terpenes.[14]

Phenolics, or phenols, are important for plant growth and development. This family of chemicals include tannins, flavonoids, and coumarins. We know tannins as the bitter aftertaste in strong tea. Found in the leaves, fruits, bark, and stems of oaks, dogwood, sweet flag, and yarrow, they serve as mild antiseptics that may help treat cuts and bruises.[15]

Flavonoids, the largest group of phenolics, give fruits such as choke-cherries and blueberries their vivid colors. These chemicals also occur in dogwood, sweet flag, and yarrow, where they act as antioxidants to protect cells from damage.[16] Flavonoid glycosides are made from a sugar (often glucose) molecule bonded with a nonsugar molecule. Salicin is such a glycoside, derived from willow (*Salix* spp.) and poplar (*Populus* spp.) bark. It is the chemical precursor of aspirin.[17]

Coumarins smell like new-mown hay and taste bitter. Some reduce the ability of blood to clot, while others counteract muscle seizures. Yarrow, bedstraw, sweetgrass, and some members of the carrot family all contain coumarins.[18]

Alkaloids are a diverse group of chemicals numbering more than twenty thousand. All contain carbon and nitrogen, are alkaline, and taste bitter. Some, such as morphine, quinine, and codeine, are widely used in modern medicine. Across the northern plains, alkaloids occur in species of

FIG. 59. Yarrow, shown here in flower, is a medicinal plant of many uses. Photo by Lynnea Parker.

nightshade and ground plum. Nicotine, a well-known alkaloid, is found in tobacco plants that Native people cultivated and smoked.[19] In small doses, this addictive chemical acts as a stimulant, but in pure form it is extremely toxic.[20]

Terpenes, the third group of alkaloids, number in the tens of thousands.[21] They are found in lemon oil, menthol, and essential oils used in perfumery and aromatherapy. Native healers took advantage of their antibiotic properties when they used the bark of alder or the leaves of sage, yarrow, and sweet flag to clean wounds or reduce pain.[22]

Given this complicated chemistry, it is remarkable that Native peoples apparently matched plants' benefits with specific situations, all without the panoply of today's chemical reagents and elaborate equipment. For instance, the Hidatsas used sage leaves to aid in sprouting squash seeds. We now know a number of species of sage possess antimicrobial properties that would have protected the damp seeds from mold.[23]

Listening to the Plants

Fossil evidence shows that many medicinal species have grown across the region for thousands of years, providing ample opportunity for healers to experiment.[24] If they came across an unfamiliar plant or a new malady appeared, they likely relied first on their existing knowledge but might have resorted to trial and error. They may also have chosen remedies after watching what animals ate or from tasting or smelling a plant.[25] After all, the prairie is a fragrant place. Who can miss the bay-like aroma of sage, the bittersweet of yarrow, the citrusy bouquet of bergamot?

Once a plant was chosen, healers had to decide how to prepare and safely administer it as medicine.[26] In some cases community elders volunteered as test subjects. According to Keewaydinoquay, an Anishinaabe medicine woman of the Crane clan, "It's perfectly true that in times past, when there was some great scourge of disease . . . that a lot of elder people offered themselves to be experimented on." Others thought this a noble gesture for the good of everyone.[27]

Specialists, sometimes referred to as medicine men or medicine women, had a hefty arsenal to draw upon. The Lakotas, for example, made use of nearly a hundred medicines. Most of these could be obtained from the wild locally, but some needed cultivating or were acquired through trade.[28] They harvested roots, leaves, stems, and barks as needed or when they knew a plant's valuable properties were most potent, usually late summer or early fall. The celebrated Anishinaabe writer Basil Johnston wrote that "every plant had a place and a purpose; every plant had a time."[29]

Healing is, according to one Lakota, a "holistic approach to mental, physical, spiritual, and emotional wellness."[30] In a similar vein, author F. David Peat writes that Native medicine embraces "a whole spectrum of concepts that belong to a profoundly different vision of reality and the human body."[31] Jonathan Ellerby, who studied among the Lakotas, echoes this sentiment: "A simple inventory of healing practices, healing ceremonies and medical equipment does not elucidate anything meaningful about the Lakota people and their approach to healing."[32]

The same perspective comes from plant ecologist and ethnobotanist Kelly Kindscher. In his study of the medicinal plants of the Great Plains, Kindscher stresses that, "though the vast majority of medicinal plants Native Americans have used in this region do have pharmacologically active substances, these Native people have not used these plants for the sole purpose of benefiting from their active ingredients. Rather, these plants are primarily used for their spiritual healing properties and they have active ingredients that help heal ailments."[33]

Healers showed respect when they harvested. Ellerby quotes the directive given by his Lakota mentor, Gene Thin Elk: "Take your tobacco and talk to [the plants]. Explain why you need this, thank them. Explain it is to help The People. Let them know that you appreciate what they are making possible."[34]

When choosing a plant and determining how to administer it, a practitioner thought about both the patient and the ailment. Beyond any physical symptoms, what was the sick person's mental state? Were they feeling sad or anxious? How were they getting along with their family and others in their community? Did they trust the healer and the proposed remedies? In this way the curative powers of both plant chemistry and human relationships were harnessed.[35]

In preparing medicines, healers might boil the herbs for a few minutes (a decoction), steep them in hot water (an infusion such as tea), or prepare a poultice or salve to apply directly to the skin. If a patient failed to improve, the dose might be increased, a more powerful medicine tried, or the same medicine continued for a longer period.[36]

Aspiring healers were often apprenticed to well-known medicine men or women, but some obtained their calling through visions. In the book *Black Elk Speaks*, the great Lakota holy man Black Elk told how his first vision put him on the path to becoming a traditional doctor. He fell sick at the age of nine and was unable to walk, with his arms, legs, and face badly swollen. As the boy lay in great pain, a vision lasting several days came to him. Rich in symbolism, the encounter shaped the rest of his life.[37]

Fire and Smoke

Fire has many faces.[38] A cozy campfire may mesmerize, but a blaze out of control can wreak havoc. In *The Mishomis Book*, Anishinaabe elder Edward Benton-Banai tells the people, "Fire is a very special gift from Creator. If you respect it and take care of it, it will take care of you and bring you warmth. But locked up in this goodness is also evil. If you neglect fire or use it in the wrong way, it could destroy the entire Creation."[39]

Native peoples made wide use of smudging to address the spiritual energy of a person or place. To smudge, a healer lit either a tight bundle of herbs or a loose handful in a shallow vessel, then gently blew out the flame and let it smolder. As smoke built up, it was wafted wherever the energy led, over a person or throughout a room. Healers primarily chose three species: sage and cedar, to purge negative forces, and sweetgrass, to attract positive spirits.[40]

The three were also burned during sweat lodge ceremonies.[41] These purification rites could last several days and were performed to give thanks, to heal sickness, or to prepare individuals for a vision quest or other sacred ritual. They were intended to restore a balance among spiritual, mental, and physical well-being. In his detailed study of sweat lodge ceremonies among the Lakotas on the Pine Ridge Reservation in southwestern South Dakota, anthropologist and Jesuit priest Raymond Bucko describes how those entering the sweat lodge cleansed their bodies by rubbing themselves with sage.[42] Other accounts describe fragrant beds of the plant lining the floor of the sweat lodge.[43] Cedar's disinfectant properties aided healing, while the pleasing perfume of sweetgrass evoked positive energy.[44]

FIG. 60. A stalk of
sacred sweetgrass. Photo
by Paul E. Rothrock.

FIG. 61. Eastern
red cedar. Photo by
Krzysztof Ziarnek.

Sacred Tobacco

People inhaled smoke whenever they lit a fire, though we do not know when and why people began to deliberately inhale burning herbs. Tobacco may not have been their first choice. Native Americans smoked about a hundred different plants, probably in various mixtures. The bark of red osier dogwood or the leaves of bearberry, among other plants, may have been used centuries before tobacco appeared in the region about fifteen hundred years ago.[45]

Botanists have counted scores of tobacco species that are mainly found in the Americas and Australia. Indigenous people in North America smoked about a half dozen different kinds. Cultivated by the men of a number of the region's agricultural tribes and even by the nomadic Crow population, the cured leaves were widely traded.[46]

Smoking of the long-stemmed pipe, what non-Natives usually called the peace pipe, was a powerful spiritual act.[47] Black Elk said, "All the things of the universe are joined with you who smoke the pipe—all send their voices to Wakan-Tanka, the Great Spirit. When you pray with this pipe, you pray for and with everything."[48] According to author Patricia L. Kaiser, "The Lakotas did not see the pipe's contents as merely symbolic of universal involvement, although the symbolism is apparent and meaningful; instead, they knew that at the moment of its filling, the pipe really is, the Universe."[49]

Craftspeople fashioned pipe bowls from many different materials, with one of the most prized being a red, clay-rich sedimentary rock called catlinite, or pipestone. This is a type of argillite, midway in hardness between soft shale and hard slate. It was widely traded, partly because it is soft enough to be scratched by a fingernail and easy to carve into pipes, beads, and ornaments. Pipe stems were made from willow, cottonwood, or ash.[50]

The quarry for catlinite is located within Pipestone National Monument in southwestern Minnesota. Excavations reveal that early people quarried there for thousands of years.[51] Native peoples still obtain material there for making pipes and ornaments. Padani-apa-pi, a ninety-year-old Yankton Dakota chief, described his trips to the quarry as a child:

We visited the pipestone quarry annually in the months of July and August, when my fathers were still alive and I was a small boy.... Before we approached the sacred ground, all of us followed a three day long purification of fasting, prayers, sacrifices, imploring the Great Spirit to expose the holy minerals buried beneath the rocks. On the fourth day, we painted ourselves and began working. Each warrior picked up a block of stone and smashed it against the rocks until they crumbled. Hard and thick layers of rock sometimes made this work last days or weeks; rocks were often colored red by the blood of our hands and feet.[52]

Charms

Apart from medicine, many cultures of the region made use of physical tokens or charms for good luck in the hunt, protection in war, or success in love. More than a half dozen plants were put to use in this way. Sweet flag warded off snakes, whereas both dogbane and wild sage guarded against evil or brought about good luck.[53] Young people attracted the opposite sex with wild sage, bloodroot, and red columbine.[54]

Plants as Personalities

One can imagine long winter nights when families settled down around flickering fires and listened to elders' stories. For the most part, such tales had a moral purpose in which good triumphed over evil and bad behavior was punished. When interpreting them, we need to remember that, as writer Basil Johnston points out, Native language "makes liberal and imaginative use of images, metaphors, and figures of speech to express in the concrete abstract ideas and concepts."[55] With this caution in mind, I offer the following Pawnee tale, "A Journey to the Sky."

On a clear summer's night, young Feather Woman left her tipi to sleep under the stars. In the early hours, as she watched the Morning Star on the horizon, she fell in love with it. A few days later, while out collecting firewood, the Morning Star appeared before her as a tall, handsome young man. He declared his love and persuaded the maiden to return with him to his home in the sky.

Morning Star's mother, the Moon, was kind to the new bride and taught her many things—how to tan buckskin and how to make colorful dyes from the juices of herbs and flowers. Moon also gave her a digging stick of ash wood, sharpened and hardened in a fire, and showed her where to find edible plants and roots. There was one prohibition. Moon warned her never to harvest a particular giant Indian breadroot, or *tipsin*, because it was sacred to the Star People. She warned, "Nothing but sorrow and distress will come to anyone who tries to uproot it. You must leave it where it is."

One day, as Feather Woman was out digging roots, she spied the giant tipsin. Overcome by curiosity, she dug it up. When she looked down the hole, Feather Woman was amazed to see her own camp circle on Earth far below. When father-in-law Sun learned what she had done, he became furious and banished her from the sky.[56]

To my mind, several aspects of the story merit attention. In this account Feather Woman falls in love with Morning Star, the heavenly body we know as the planet Venus. What could be more enchanting than seeing a single bright star in all its glory as night gives way to day? The plains countryside, renowned for its clear skies, offers a perfect setting for such heavenly delights. Native groups across the region developed their own astronomies, though the Pawnees have been judged among the most advanced star watchers.[57]

Another striking thing about the story is its cautionary feature, in which the young woman is punished for neglecting her mother-in-law's advice. Mother Moon warned Feather Woman not to touch the sacred tipsin, perhaps out of respect for all such plants. These roots were and are valued as one of the favorite wild foods of the prairie.

Medicinally, various parts of the tipsin were used to treat ailments, from sprains to sore throats. Moreover, the giant root's position in the sky world offers a clue about the plant's spiritual value. Geologist William Keating, who canoed up the Minnesota River in 1823, reported, "The party landed, for a few minutes, to examine a stone which is held in high veneration by the Indians; on account of the red pigment with which it is bedawbed [*sic*], it is generally called the painted stone.... The Indians frequently offer presents to the Great Spirit near this stone; among the offerings . . . the party found the feather of an eagle, two roots of the 'Pomme de Prairie' [tipsin], . . . painted with vermilion; a willow branch whose stem was painted red, had been stuck into the ground on one side."[58] Deemed sacred, the plant also played a role in the Blackfoot Sun Dance ceremony.[59]

Ethnobotanist Melvin Gilmore recorded another plant story. In this Mandan tale, "The Wonderful Basket," a container made of cedar roots helps bring in the harvest:

A weary woman fell asleep under a cedar tree. In her dreams, the tree spoke to the woman and told her how to dig down to find young, pliable cedar roots that she could weave into a basket. When she woke up, she dutifully dug out the roots and wove a basket that turned out to be incredibly light and strong. She couldn't wait to take it with her when she next went out to dig tipsin.

After she had dug up a pile and loaded the basket, she found it so heavy that she could hardly lift it. "Alas," she cried, "I must carry home this heavy load though I am already weary."

The basket whispered to her, "Do not cry. You need not carry your load back to the village. Instead, sing and be glad. I shall carry your load."

From then on, the woman happily sang through her labors with the cedar basket by her side. She also taught other women in her village how to make magic baskets that could ease their burdens when they went out foraging.[60]

The second part of the story is not so happy. It tells how the woman lost the use of the basket after she robbed a mouse's nest of beans without leaving an offering. This angered the basket, and it refused to carry her burden anymore. This seems a simple cautionary tale. In a dream, a woman is taught to make a magic basket that lightens her burden, but the magic is lost when she fails to leave an offering. The story may also underscore the value the Mandans placed on the sacred cedar.

As a part of the landscape, plants have powers far beyond their known physical and chemical properties. They have sustained humans both physically and spiritually across millennia. As plant biologist and author Robin Wall Kimmerer writes, "In some Native languages the term for plants translates as 'those who take care of us.'"[61]

And so they have.

FURTHER READING

Kindscher, Kelly. *Medicinal Wild Plants of the Prairie: An Ethnobotanical Guide.* Lawrence: University Press of Kansas, 1992.

Morgan, George Robert, and Ronald R. Weedon. "Oglala Sioux Use of Medical Herbs." *Great Plains Quarterly* 10 (Winter 1990): 18–35. Available at Digital-Commons@University of Nebraska–Lincoln, https://digitalcommons.unl.edu /greatplainsquarterly/506.

Neihardt, John G. *Black Elk Speaks.* Woodstock IL: Dramatic, 1996.

From Tools to Toys   8

Plants give us everything: food, shelter, well-being, heat.

—MARY B. ANDERSEN, "Plants in a 'Sea of Relationships'"

Take a look around your home and think about what you see: the structure, its furnishings and decorations, cooking and eating utensils, storage containers, bedding, tools, toys, musical instruments. Do you think you could build and furnish your home using only local natural materials? Native people did this for generations.

In addition to self-sufficiency, a spiritual connection was involved every time they collected materials and made and decorated objects. For instance, the Anishinaabe made mats and bags from the bark of the northern white cedar, extracted its volatile oils for medicine, and burned its fragrant branches in ceremonies. However, before they harvested anything from the cedar tree, they had to communicate with it. Professor Wendy Makoons Geniusz (Anishinaabe) cautions, "If we do not know how to properly address the cedar to ask for her physical and spiritual assistance, then we will be missing a key component."[1]

From this perspective, everything in nature has a spiritual essence; all plants and animals are like family and must be respected. Early gatherers showed this respect by leaving a gift every time an animal was killed or a plant harvested, expressing their faith that living things would provide for their needs.[2]

A Vital Resource

No other natural substance can be worked in so many ways, using only hand tools, as wood. Native woodworkers split logs with wedges and a maul,

FIG. 62. A cottonwood forest growing on the floodplain of the White River in South Dakota. Photo courtesy of Malia Volke.

shaped the pieces using stone scrapers and knives, and then smoothed the wood with sandstone. The results were both functional and beautiful. Wood was used to build homes and to make furnishings, weapons, and tools. Musicians played wooden drums and wooden flutes, pipes had wooden stems, and babies lay swaddled on wooden cradleboards.[3]

Although some twenty tree species grew on the northern plains, most were not plentiful.[4] Islands of aspen and groves of oaks were sprinkled across the prairie, mainly along its eastern margin. Woody plants were hard to find in open country, growing mainly in ravines and on north-facing slopes, yet trees like cottonwood, ash, box elder, and elm flourished along rivers. In addition, water-loving shrubs such as willow and red osier dogwood crowded riverbanks and the margins of prairie marshes. Chokecherry bushes formed dense thickets nearly everywhere, while copses of juneberry grew in wooded draws and on the edges of tree groves.[5]

The working properties of these trees and shrubs are not the same. Some are strong and rigid, others weak and bendable. Botanists use microscopic cellular anatomy and laboratory tests to identify these differences, but some features are obvious to the naked eye.[6] Look closely at the end of a piece of scrap lumber. A series of parallel curved lines mark the tree's annual growth rings, and between each line are tiny cells the size of pinpoints. During spring, when water and nutrients surge up and down the trunk, new cells in some trees are large.[7] As the season wears on and growth slows, new cells in these trees tend to be smaller and thicker. Botanists call this kind of wood "ring-porous." Examples include green ash, box elder, and bur oak. In other trees the large conducting cells appear throughout the season. This applies to willow, aspen, and cottonwood, which are labeled "diffuse-porous."[8]

Simply put, ring-porous woods are more rigid and stronger than diffuse-porous woods. This means they are also heavier. People favored the weaker woods such as cottonwood and aspen for tipi poles and lodge timbers, probably because they were light, easily handled, and plentiful. In these applications, quantity and the ability for people to handle lengths with ease were important.

Willow wood is very flexible, making it ideal for baskets, bindings, mats, and fish traps. To catch sturgeon and catfish in the Missouri River, resourceful Mandan and Hidatsa villagers used willow rods to craft funnel-shaped pens. A typical trap was about three feet long, shaped like a cone, and made of rods bound to hoops with strands of bark. When ready to use, the trap was placed with its open end facing upstream, making it hard for fish to escape.[9]

Strong and resilient species were chosen for spears and bows, the best thought to be Osage orange, a ring-porous wood from what is now southeastern Oklahoma and southwestern Arkansas. Both the wood and bows made from it were widely traded in the southern plains, and even the Blackfeet of Montana used this precious commodity.[10]

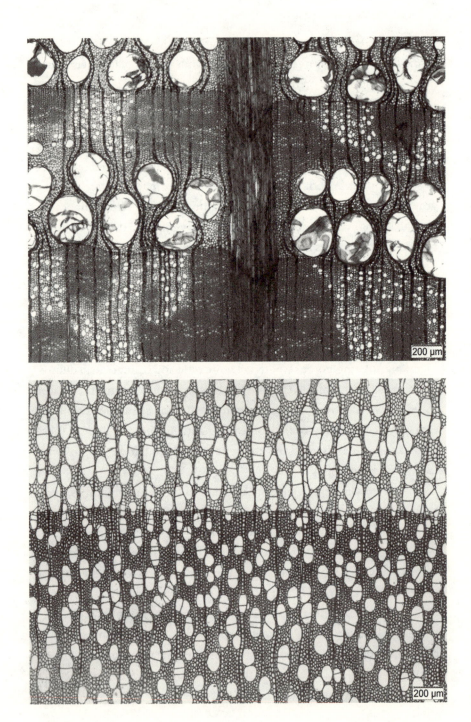

Local woods suitable for creating weapons included box elder, ash, and chokecherry. Late winter, before the sap began to rise, was a good time to look for bow wood, and a sapling about the size of a man's wrist could be split to make two bows. The stave was shaped and then decorated. Animal fat was used to make it waterproof, and to add strength the stave could be bound with sinew.

Arrows came from the straight stems of juneberry and chokecherry.[11] Making them was an art, according to historian and archery expert Roland Bohr: "To assure consistent shooting, the elasticity of every arrow shaft had to precisely match the draw weight and the draw length of the bow and the finished arrows had to be as uniform in size and weight as possible. Therefore, when shaping the arrow shaft, the maker had to keep in mind the weight of the arrowhead, the fletching, the sinew wrapping and glue before the different parts of the arrow were assembled, in order to arrive at the correct weight in the finished arrow."[12]

Home Fires

Wood was everyone's first choice for fuel; it gave light and warmth, cooked food, and fired pottery, though people sometimes resorted to substitutes. For instance, those traveling in treeless country used buffalo chips for fuel.[13] During wet weather the Crees had to burn buffalo skulls packed with fat.[14]

It seems obvious that travelers preferred campsites near sources of timber. Trader Edwin Denig wrote of the Assiniboines, "Owing to the absence of wood on this great plain, they are obliged to place their camp on or near the Missouri in the Winter Season."[15] More settled groups amassed piles of wood when they had the chance. Archaeologists George Will and Herbert

FIG. 63. (*opposite*) Microscopic cross section of ring-porous wood (white oak, *top*) and diffuse-porous wood (cottonwood, *bottom*). White oak cells are 180 to 380 microns in diameter, and cottonwood cells range from 75 to 150 microns in diameter (Brown, Panshin, and Forsaith, *Textbook of Wood Technology*, 517, 546). The scale shows 200 microns. One hundred microns is about the width of a human hair. Photo courtesy of USDA Forest Service, Forest Products Laboratory.

FIG. 64. A bison herd grazing at Triple R Ranch, near Fairburn, South Dakota. Photo © Tom Bean 1998.

Spinden remarked that the Mandans along the Missouri River "collected their whole supply of wood by swimming out [into the icy water] and towing in the driftwood at the time of the spring breakups."[16]

A wood's heating value depends on its density, plus its resin and current moisture content. Dense woods such as ash and oak produce nearly twice the heat of cottonwood, aspen, or willow. Buffalo chips burn slowly and make a hot fire but generate only a fraction of wood's heating value.[17] For tinder, anything dry and fluffy would do: twigs, the inner bark of cedar, broken up buffalo chips, downy feathers, or even fungi. The fleshy insides of large tree bracket fungi made good tinder, as did the low-growing puffball fungus that the Blackfoot called the "fallen stars."[18]

To keep a fire going when traveling, people took along a bit from their previous hearth. The Blackfoot carried live coals in a hollow buffalo horn lined with moist, rotten wood. They placed dry fungus inside this "fire horn" to feed the ember while en route.[19]

On the Move

The earliest people to enter the northern plains were doubtless hunters following bison herds. The bison hunt remained essential, even for those who later settled into an agrarian life. Whether on a hunting or gathering trip or as part of a nomadic life, people hauled everything they needed; they had "an aesthetic of mobility," according to Native American art advocate Ralph Coe.[20]

Waterways offered a great way to carry goods and move around while gathering food, visiting, or trading. The Anishinaabe traveled in birch bark canoes, perhaps the most elegant watercraft on earth. Designs depended upon whether they were built for speed or for carrying heavy loads. Canoe building definitely demanded skill.[21] According to Frances Densmore, "Young men were allowed to assist in the work, but canoe making was regarded as a craft which must be learned by observation and experience."[22]

Raw materials were chosen with care. Large sheets of birch bark were needed for the skin, white cedar strips for the ribs and gunwales, spruce root for sewing, spruce resin for sealing, and cedar or spruce for the paddles. The bark was gathered in early spring, when it was easiest to remove without damaging the tree. Builders first fashioned a frame of cedar strips and then bent large, knot-free pieces of bark around it. They stitched the bark pieces together with the split roots and waterproofed the seams with a mixture of sticky resin and powdered cedar charcoal.[23]

Mandan, Arikara, and Hidatsa villagers crossed the Missouri River in circular, tub-like boats covered with buffalo hide. These "bull boats" were about six feet in diameter and could carry heavy loads yet were said to be light enough to "be carried by a woman on the run."[24] Builders first made a willow frame and then stretched a fresh hide over it, with the hair side facing inward. They sewed the hide to the rim and smeared the exterior with buffalo tallow to waterproof it. Once completed, bull boats were paddled while either kneeling or standing.[25]

Living in open country with few streams, the Blackfoot improvised rafts from the folded skins of tipis braced by wooden crosspieces.[26]

Nomadic groups moved with the seasons, following food supplies and packing their belongings with them as they traveled. Even though agrarian societies lived in long-term settlements, they also left camp for long periods to hunt game or gather wild foods. Native people living in the northern plains acquired horses in the late 1700s by trade from the south. These animals are thought to be descendants of horses the Spaniards had brought to the Americas two centuries earlier. Before horses, dogs were the pack animals—carrying loads on their backs or pulling a travois. According to a Crow story, a small boy captured a pair of wild dogs and showed his mother how, by strapping a pole to each side, they could pull a load. Voilà! The travois was born.[27]

Dragging a travois, a dog could carry about sixty pounds of household goods, sometimes including fuel.[28] Eighteenth-century French explorer Pierre La Vérendrye wrote of the Assiniboines, "They even make the dogs carry wood for fires, frequently being obliged to camp in open prairie, where the islands of timber are distant from one another."[29]

Homes on the Prairies

The tipi is an enduring icon of the Great Plains. Spelled in various ways, *tipi* is derived from the Lakota root words *ti*, meaning "to dwell," and *pi*, meaning "used for." These conical tents were the focus of family life. Nomadic groups lived in them year round, while others took tipis onto the plains when hunting. Traces of camp circles consisting of rings of rocks that likely held down the edges of skin tents imply the pattern may go back thousands of years.[30]

Camp layout was symbolic. Black Elk said, "Everything an Indian does is in a circle, and that is because the Power of the World always works in circles, and everything tries to be round."[31]

These portable homes were strictly a woman's domain. Emma Hansen, member of the Pawnee Nation and curator of the Plains Indian Museum, tells us that "everything related to the tipi belonged to women's areas of authority and responsibility. In addition to setting up their lodges and dismantling and packing them on travois when their bands moved to different locations, women were in charge of acquiring the wood for poles and preparing them for use, creating the tipi covers, maintaining the lodges, and providing the decorative elements and furnishings for the use of the family."[32]

Pretty Shield, a Crow medicine woman, recalled in later life how her tribe had followed the bison across the plains in the late 1800s. When they arrived at a new camp, the women set to work at once. "We didn't only pitch the lodge," she explains. "We gathered wood so that we can make fire right away, so that the water would get hot by the time we get things done, and we're ready to put things into that."[33]

Early tipis were about twelve feet in diameter, a manageable size for transport by dog travois. This offered a little more than a hundred square feet of living space, roughly the size of a family camping tent. Once horses were available as pack animals, the floor diameter increased to about sixteen feet, with double the living space.[34]

Tanned bison hides covered the pole framing and were held in place from top to bottom by wooden pins. Hides were secured at the bottom with larger pins driven into the ground, much like modern tent pegs. These, along with leather ropes guyed to the frame, anchored the structure. Each tipi had a covered doorway and an opening at the top to let light enter and smoke from a hearth escape. Around this opening, adjustable flaps operated by poles kept rain out. In winter extra hides could be added to the inside walls for insulation, and snow might be piled around the outside edges to keep out drafts.[35]

According to Crow historian Alma Snell, the tipi was more than a shelter: "The lodges would be a sanctuary. It actually is a place of refuge."[36] Each lodge expressed the owner's personality. Pretty Shield spoke of a beautiful tipi she knew as a child: "Its poles were taller, its lodge-skin whiter and cleaner, its lining, beautifully painted, reaching all around it. Its back-rests, three of them, were made with head-and-tail robes; and always Kills-good burned in a little sweet-grass, or sweet-sage, so that her lodge smelled nice."[37]

Agricultural peoples such as the Mandans, Arikaras, and Hidatsas lived in villages of dome-shaped earth lodges overlooking the Missouri River or its tributaries. Dozens of dwellings surrounded a central open area used for ceremonies and dances. Some villages had scores of earth lodges that must have housed up to five hundred or more people.[38]

An earth lodge is not an earthen structure but a timber-framed building with an outer layer of earth or sod that gives it the appearance of rising from the earth itself.[39] A brilliant adaptation to the region's variable climate, they were livable in all but the coldest weather. Their history goes back centuries. Supervised by the women of the community, builders first dug a circular pit about a foot deep. Next, four large cottonwood support posts, each a foot or so in diameter and ten feet long, were erected in the center of the shallow pit and joined with crossbeams. A perimeter ring of posts was then installed and topped by more crossbeams. The outer walls of the lodge were made of split logs leaned against the perimeter ring. Dozens of rafters, laid in spoke-like fashion, extended from the perimeter to the center. Builders covered the rafters with a layer of willow stems, then a thick layer of dry grass, followed by a final topping of sod. After the roof was complete, a covered entrance was added, along with a door of buffalo hide. Each lodge had a central hearth vented by a smoke hole. A skin-covered wooden frame enclosed the smoke hole to keep out rain.[40]

These homes were sacred spaces. Before the Mandans completed a lodge, an elder would bless the occupants.[41] Buffalo Bird Woman, who lived in the last of the Hidatsa villages, recalls, "We thought the earth lodge was alive and had a spirit like a human body, and that its front was like a face, with the door for a mouth."[42] Hidatsa tribal member Calvin Grinnell agrees: "Our people thought that they [the lodges] had a spirit . . . that there should be respect given to people's living quarters, because they were made out of natural things."[43]

Other types of homes were built east of the Missouri River, in southern Minnesota, and in parts of Iowa where wood was more plentiful. Depending upon weather and circumstances, these rectangular houses were clad with bark in winter and covered with cattail reed mats in summer. During heat waves, families might erect next to the lodge a wood-framed arbor topped with willow boughs and leaves.[44] In forested country to the north, the Anishinaabe put up bark-covered lodges. Those built for winter were dome-shaped or A-frame dwellings; summer homes resembled bark-covered tipis.[45]

FIG. 65. A cattail leaf in cross section, showing the large, air-filled cells. Photo by Paul Kirtley.

Interiors reflected both utility and comfort. Woven mats of various materials, such as cattail, rush, bulrush, willow, or basswood, covered the ground. Sleeping platforms lined the walls; seats were angled backrests made of willow rods, like beach chairs without legs.[46] A backrest consisted of two parts: a mat and a tripod to support it. The mat, often decorated, was made from slim willow rods sewn together with sinew. When finished, it measured about five feet long and tapered from three feet at the bottom to two feet at the top. Like a straw beach mat, it could be rolled easily into a compact bundle when not in use. The tripod, whose legs were about five feet long and made of stout sticks, would be tied at the top with sinew and set up like an artist's easel, from which the mat was hung. To make backrests and mats, the Hidatsas gathered straight, pencil-thin willow shoots in early summer. According to ethnographer Gilbert Wilson, women used their teeth to strip the bark in a narrow band at each end as well as a band in the middle of the rod. This let the shoots dry without warping. By all accounts these were comfortable seats.[47]

Cattail was ideal for making sleeping mats, floor mats, and thatching. Called "defender of the shoreline" by the Anishinaabe, cattail leaves are long, water repellent, and packed with air-filled cells that resemble foam insulation. The mats could be sewn together or intertwined to cover a summer dwelling or to make a sunshade; shrinking in dry weather, they allow cooling breezes to pass through but will swell during rain showers.[48]

Fiber Arts

Each part of North America had its own textiles, dependent upon regional cultural choices and the raw materials available. Baskets were popular among the agrarian people of the northern plains, while the Anishinaabe wove bags made of nettle and fashioned containers using birch bark.

Few traces of ancient fibers turn up in early sites; most of what we know comes from impressions found on pottery. From these clues and the textiles found in the Ozark bluff shelters of Arkansas, we suppose that early makers twisted plant fibers into ropes and cords, wove them into textiles, or interlaced them to form nets, mats, and baskets.[49]

Creating strong textiles from natural materials is only possible because in some plants the stem and inner bark tissues that transport nutrients have long, strong, thick-walled fibers. This is true of nettle, dogbane, milkweed, cattail, and bulrush stems and the inner bark of willow, cedar, basswood, slippery elm, and cottonwood.

Stinging nettle was well worth harvesting, as its fibers are almost eight times stronger than cotton and twice as strong as hemp. Fortunately, the unpleasant sting that gives the plant its common name vanishes after the fibers dry out or freeze. Nettles have been part of the region's flora since the glaciers disappeared and are still widespread in damp and disturbed places. In former times they were also gathered for food and medicine.[50]

Educator and author Carrie Lyford has described how Anishinaabe women of northern Minnesota prepared nettle fibers for weaving. The

FIG. 66. Ojibwe woven nettle fiber and yarn bag measuring 15⅗ inches tall and 19³⁄₃₂ inches wide. Created not later than 1925. Minnesota Historical Society Collections, The Harry and Jeannette Ayer Collection.

women cut the stalks in October, tied them in bundles, and hung them to dry. When needed, the stalks were "retted." Retting amounts to soaking the plants in water for a couple of days to dissolve the gummy tissue that binds the fibers together. After this, the stalks were beaten with a stick and the separated fibers rolled and twisted together. The resulting cord was then woven into bags of various kinds.[51]

An example of this ancient art form came to light in 2003. Archaeological enthusiasts John and Otto Swennes found a well-preserved nettle bag in a rock shelter on their property in eastern Wisconsin. This find soon came to the attention of the Mississippi Valley Archaeology Center in La Crosse. Surprisingly, the bag turned out to be more than five hundred years old. Anthropology student Amy Karoll studied the bag and found

FIG. 67. The irritating but useful stinging nettle. Photo by Uwe H. Friese.

that its weaving pattern resembled impressions on pieces of early pottery as well as the weave patterns of bags made more recently by the Ioways and Menominees.[52]

Biologist Robin Wall Kimmerer writes about basketry: "The marvel of a basket is in its transformation, its journey from wholeness as a living plant to fragmented strands and back to wholeness again as a basket. A basket knows the dual powers of destruction and creation that shape the world."[53] Those for carrying and storing have been made by agrarian villagers for centuries.[54] When women wanted to carry something, be it the corn harvest or firewood, they fashioned medium-sized baskets that could be slung over their shoulder. Anthropologist Mary Jane Schneider studied such baskets made by Arikara, Hidatsa, and Mandan women. Each typically measured about a foot high and wide. To make a so-called "burden" basket, four flexible saplings were bent into a frame that was then lashed to a rim. Strips of

FIG. 68. Burden basket (Mandan). Photo courtesy of Buffalo Bill Center of the West, Cody, Wyoming; Plains Indian Museum; Chandler-Pohrt Collection, Gift of Mr. William D. Weiss, NA.106.183.

twill-plaited willow, box elder, or cherry bark filled in the frame.[55] When viewed from the side, a finished basket looked like the letter U with flaring sides. When viewed from above, it appeared square.

Twill plaiting differs from that technique familiar to grade-school children who interweave paper strips to form a checkerboard pattern. In twill plaiting, the horizontal materials are woven over two or more verticals, resulting in a stronger weave.[56] The finished products featured a variety of geometric designs, such as chevrons, diamonds, and zigzags. To make different colors, some Arikara women employed black willow bark mixed with the light-colored bark of box elder.

Shallow baskets were ideal for winnowing seeds.[57] Made of coiled willow twigs or roots, these baskets ranged from four to ten inches in diameter. They had flat or rounded bottoms and flared rims. Similar shapes were used for a women's dice game. Instead of the dotted cubes we know, the women used plum stones, walnut shells, or even buffalo bones, each incised with symbols. A player flipped the dice into the air with the basket and scored according to which sides were up when the pieces landed. Totals for each player were tallied with notches on counting sticks made of willow or buffaloberry.[58]

Palettes across the Prairies

The prairie is a rainbow in summer, as deep reds jostle with golden yellows alongside delicate blooms of blue and orange. No wonder people colored their homes, clothing, and ceremonial gear.[59] Each culture had its own palette, and some colors had special meaning. Among the Arikaras, black symbolized north, yellow was associated with the east, red signified south, and white indicated west. The Omahas chose blue for north, red for east, black for south, and yellow for west.[60]

Local raw materials helped guide choices, with the colors coming from minerals as well as many kinds of roots, berries, bark, leaves, wood, flowers, algae, and lichens. For example, the roots of northern bedstraw yield a beautiful deep red. Goosefoot yields yellow or green. Most lichens create shades of brown, though some provide a yellow. The tannic acid from oak bark also creates brown, while red, purple, or blue come from the anthocyanins in fruits such as chokecherry and blueberry.[61]

Dyeing creates chemical bonds between the colorant and the material being colored. If the bond is weak, the color will easily wash out, but if "fixed" it may be long-lasting. Options for fixing include wood ash, salt, and urine.[62]

Artisans mixed materials to achieve certain colors. The Anishinaabe blended dogwood bark together with the ashes of birch, oak, and cedar bark to create a unique red.[63] Ethnobotanist Melvin Gilmore reported that among the Omahas and Winnebagos, young maple twigs were gathered and boiled with a local clay containing iron to create earth tones. Tanned hides were then soaked in the mixture for two or three days. If treated for a short time, the hides became brown; a longer soak turned them black.[64]

FIG. 69. A group of northern bedstraw plants in a mixed prairie. Photo by Lynnea Parker.

In an experiment, graduate student Amanda Thompson and textile specialist Kathryn Jakes tried dyeing milkweed fibers using sumac berries and bedstraw roots, seeking to replicate the dark red color they saw in Native-dyed objects. To help fix their colors, the pair used chemicals found in red ochre (iron oxide), urine (ammonia), and wood ash (potassium carbonate).[65] Some mixtures produced rich red colors but were not colorfast. Other recipes produced colorfast dyes but of a lighter shade than they wanted. When they combined both sumac and bedstraw and used potassium carbonate to fix the color, the outcome was a dark red that was also colorfast. Presto! In the end they succeeded, but only after much effort. Their tests convinced them that "a well-dyed textile requires considerable knowledge of plants, fibers, and dyes."[66]

My research group, which included a number of student assistants, wanted to learn more about dyes, so in 2004 and 2005 we gathered for a couple of workshops led by art major Elaine Stocki. In an effort to replicate early dyeing methods, she had gathered juneberries, oak and dogwood bark, dandelion heads, lilac blooms, and lichens. Each was added to boiling water along with a skein of commercial wool yarn and simmered on a stove for several hours. The resulting colors included

eggplant purple (juneberries)

green-yellow (dandelion heads)

green-brown (lilac blooms)

red-brown (dogwood bark)

light orange-brown (lichens)

light gray-brown (oak bark by itself and oak bark with lichens)

When we added table salt as a fix, the wool dyed with dogwood turned light brown, but that dyed with juneberries stayed eggplant purple.[67] We also tried to dye cotton, leather, birch bark, and porcupine quills. Those results were disappointing. When they all turned a dirty-looking hue, we didn't know what had gone wrong.

I have since learned that cellulose fibers, such as cotton, are especially difficult to dye well compared to the protein fibers of wool, which take dye more readily. In hindsight, the birch bark's waxiness (the same thing that makes it valuable for canoe coverings) would have resisted the liquid dye. It has also been suggested that even though quills are made of protein, they should have been thoroughly washed and cleaned to yield better results.[68]

Bringing Up Baby

Among northern plains cultures, plants were part of childcare from birth. Lakota mothers washed newborn infants with sage tea, a protective gift from Grandmother Earth.[69] Some used the spores of puffball mushrooms much like baby powder, to help prevent skin rashes.[70] Others would rub tallow on their baby's skin and then place the child into a soft leather sack lined with an absorbent material. Inside the sack, Hidatsa women used powdered buffalo chips, dried plant fibers or grasses, and dried moss or milkweed leaves. Astute mothers added the downy fibers of cattail for winter warmth.[71]

When they were a few months old, infants were laced onto cradleboards. First wrapped in a small blanket or skin pouch, the baby was then strapped securely to a flat board. When moving about, a mother secured the cradleboard to her back with a leather band strapped across her chest and upper arms. Cradleboards were often passed down in families. Among the Lakotas "it was an object of art if it was well made, with the leather portion elaborately decorated with the finest quillwork or beadwork. Sometimes the wood frame was decorated as well."[72]

Some mothers tucked their babies into a beaded skin pocket attached to a frame of two sticks. The Blackfoot and Crow people made their carriers using a peeled branch bent into an inverted U-shape tapered toward the bottom. For travel, a baby might be put into a willow basket attached to a travois.[73] Creating a cradleboard was a spiritual endeavor accompanied by prayers, blessings, and thanks for both the newborn and for the materials furnished by nature.[74] Decorative "dream catchers," fashioned with beaded netting across a small ring made of wood or vine, might dangle from the frame.

At Play

Play is part of childhood. A baby's first toy is often a rattle or something hanging over them that jangles. According to nineteenth-century American painter, author, and traveler George Catlin, cradleboards featured "many little tinseled and tinkling things, of the brightest colors, to amuse both the eyes and ears of the child."[75] As babies grow, common household objects that can be banged or crumpled are fascinating, but soon children are engrossed in the world of make believe. In cultures everywhere, a girl's first real plaything is often a doll and a boy's might be some sort of toy weapon. Before long, they create stories that mimic the lives of the adults around them. Melvin Gilmore described how Native youngsters made toy tipis using cottonwood leaves bent into shape and fastened with a splinter or thorn. "These they made in numbers," he wrote, "and placed them in circles like the camp circle of their tribe."[76]

Pretty Shield remembers her childhood tipi: "I carried my doll on my back just as mothers carry their babies; and besides this I had a little tepee that I pitched whenever my aunt pitched hers. It was made exactly like my aunt's, had the same number of poles, only of course my tepee was very small."[77]

Popular children's toys in the late nineteenth and early twentieth centuries were popguns, tops, and whistles.[78] Popguns made from hollowed-out young box elder or ash branches could send a wad of chewed leaf or bark flying with a strong puff of air. Buffalo Bird Woman recalls the Hidatsa version: "Wads were made by chewing the inner bark of the elm. The rod [to tamp down the projectile] was a juneberry shoot."[79]

It is hard to imagine a child without a toy top. Whether made of wood, bone, or clay, tops have captivated children for millennia.[80] The Arapahos, Atsinas (Gros Ventre), Crows, Dakotas, and Omahas made wooden tops of various shapes and sizes. A buckskin or sinew lash made them spin.[81]

Young Hidatsas and Plains Crees fashioned toy whistles. Edward Goodbird recalls, "When I was a boy we used to make whistles of reeds. Boys of eight or twelve years of age liked to do this. We loved to play with them. We cut a reed. . . . It would make a shrill noise."[82]

Play tested dexterity, increased physical prowess, taught lessons in getting along with others, and channeled exuberant energy. Competitions were many. Hidatsa boys played a game called *umakixeke*, loosely translated as "to strike with a glancing blow." Players took turns throwing a dry peeled willow or box elder stick with the forefinger hooked over the smaller end. They threw the stick larger-end down against the ground or a flat stone hard enough to make it spring upward; the winner was the boy whose stick sprang farthest. Edward Goodbird remembers, "I played umakixeke all day, until my forefinger had a sore spot in the middle of the tip. Then I used my second finger. We boys always played against another."[83]

Childhood was a loving time. Anna Lee Walters (Pawnee and Otoe-Missouria) recalls, "I remember hands feeding me from wooden bowls and buffalo-horn spoons. I remember women's voices, lullabies crooned softly into my ears and laughter that fell into each woman's lap."[84]

Families depended upon plants in many ways, and for that help they offered praise and thanksgiving. To outsiders, Native peoples may appear to have worked miracles as they gathered nature's bounty and transformed it into sustenance, medicine, living spaces, and all of their worldly needs.

FURTHER READING

Geniusz, Wendy Makoons. *Our Knowledge Is Not Primitive: Decolonizing Botanical Anishinaabe Teachings.* Syracuse NY: Syracuse University Press, 2009.

Kimmerer, Robin Wall. *Braiding Sweetgrass: Indigenous Wisdom, Scientific Knowledge and the Teachings of Plants.* Minneapolis: Milkweed Editions, 2013.

Roper, Donna C., and Elizabeth P. Pauls, eds. *Plains Earthlodges: Ethnographic and Archaeological Perspectives.* Tuscaloosa: University of Alabama Press, 2005.

Wilson, Gilbert L. *Uses of Plants by the Hidatsas of the Northern Plains.* Edited by Michael Scullin. Lincoln: University of Nebraska Press, 2014.

FIG. 70. Aspen forest in autumn. Photo by Lynnea Parker.

Epilogue Under Autumn Skies

Centuries before Europeans laid eyes on it, the northern plains region was a sprawling grassland sea dotted with islands of trees. On a typical autumn day bison herds appeared as scattered blotches of brown, while here and there circles of hide-covered tipis emitted wisps of smoke from cooking fires. Shiny ribbons of water, flanked by strips of forest, coursed through this vast land, serving as transportation arteries for canoes and bull boats. The banks of one mighty river, the Missouri, were home to farming villages, arranged along the valley as beads on a necklace. Each settlement sat on a bluff high above spring floodwaters, with dome-shaped earth lodges surrounding open plazas and small garden plots nestled in clearings below. Far to the east of the Missouri was a mainly treed landscape, where, along waterways and around lakes, lay other camps and hamlets composed of clusters of bark-covered houses.

As winter approached, the prairie began to shut down. Under the sun's pale disk, a chill breeze blew over the tangled mat of grasses and wildflowers turned to straw. Insects disappeared, many birds flew south, ground squirrels dozed in their burrows, and deer and elk sought wooded shelter where leaves were turning red and gold.

The turn of seasons was also seen in camps and villages. Larders were bulging after a generous summer: racks of buffalo steaks had been cured over smoky fires and leather bags were crammed with dried berries smothered in fat. Sprigs of culinary spices and medicinal herbs festooned the lodges next to where skeins of breadroot hung in heavy garlands. Baskets of parched seeds were safely stowed away from avaricious mice.[1]

In the evenings families gathered around crackling fires yet kept busy as there was still much to do—arrows to fletch, clothing to repair, baskets to weave. When the work was put away, it was storytelling time. It wasn't long before, lulled by a grandmother's soothing voice and the warmth of the fire, young eyelids began to droop as children drifted into dreamland.

As the gathering year ends, so does this book.

Through these pages we have journeyed from glaciers to grasslands, from tornadoes to therapeutic herbs, and from women's work to children's games—all paths leading to a profound verity. Native people have called this land home for thousands of years, ably crafting their societies and material worlds. They learned life skills through experience and developed a know-how that is nothing short of awe-inspiring—choosing, gathering, and preparing nutritious plants and useful medicines, building watercraft from scratch, designing dwellings, making bows and arrows, weaving and dyeing bags and baskets—the ultimate in sustainable living. Their ways are also remarkable for being tied to spiritual life. In their world everything has a purpose, all things deserve respect, and one should never harvest more than what one needs.[2]

Today the region's many Native cultural traditions, as well as its limitless vistas and golden prairies, inspire contemporary artists who work in acrylic, watercolor, bronze, clay, marble, and wood. Others feel at home with digital techniques and use photography, video, and virtual reality to express themselves.[3] Indigenous authors are finding eager audiences for their prose and poetry. Many have won national and international awards.[4]

One must wonder what lies ahead for the prairie and its peoples. Beyond shifts in population, agriculture, or industry, a huge concern is the future climate. As the world warms, the plains may suffer more frequent tornadoes and other wild weather while dreaded droughts may occur more often. Native peoples are not standing by. They are taking action on a number of fronts, such as promoting solar and wind power, protesting against oil pipelines crossing their land, and fighting to protect northern Minnesota's sacred wild rice.

With generous help from Native oral tradition, I have sought to portray life before the Europeans appeared. While much social change has transpired in the years since, I urge the reader to ponder the close connection to the land of those early peoples. Whether ambling across a lush prairie or lounging under a riverside tree, think about this splendid countryside with its rich history and honor those who made it their home for generations.

What is life?
It is the flash of a firefly in the night.
It is the breath of a buffalo in the wintertime.
It is the little shadow which runs across the grass and loses itself in the sunset.[5]

FURTHER READING

Deloria, Vine, Jr. *Custer Died for Your Sins: An Indian Manifesto*. New York: Macmillan, 1969.

Erdrich, Heid E. *New Poets of Native Nations*. Minneapolis: Graywolf Press, 2018.

Erdrich, Louise. *The Round House*. New York: Harper, 2012.

Iverson, Peter. *We Are Still Here: American Indians in the Twentieth Century*. Wheeling IL: Harlan Davidson, 1998.

Lundquist, Suzanne Evertsen. *Native American Literatures: An Introduction*. New York: Bloomsbury, 2004.

Momaday, N. Scott. *House Made of Dawn*. New York: Harper & Row, 1968.

Pratt, Linda Ray. *Great Plains Literature*. Lincoln: University of Nebraska Press, 2018.

Schrag, A. M., and S. Olimb. *Threats Assessment for the Northern Great Plains Ecoregion*. Bozeman MT: World Wildlife Fund, 2012.

Shafer, M., D. Ojima, J. M. Antle, D. Kluck, R. A. McPherson, S. Petersen, B. Scanlon, and K. Sherman. "Great Plains." In *Climate Change Impacts in the United States: The Third National Climate Assessment*, edited by Jerry M. Melillo, T. C. Richmond, and Gary W. Yohe, 441–61. Washington DC: U.S. Global Change Research Program, 2014.

Vermette, Katherena. *North End Love Songs*. Winnipeg MB: Muses' Company, 2012.

Vizenor, Gerald. *Shrouds of White Earth*. Albany: State University of New York Press, 2010.

Based on a spreadsheet created by Cole Wilson in the early 2000s, this table includes data from twenty-two sites analyzed by the author and his group, plus eight sites analyzed by others. The type of archaeological evidence is indicated by number: 1—charcoal; 2—charred seed; 3—charred root; 4—starch grains; 5—chemical residue.

Identification of charred roots (3) of Indian breadroot is from Wood and Woolworth, *Paul Brave Site*, 125; starch grains (4) of Indian bread-root, from Lints, "Early Evidence"; and chemical residue (5) for beeweed and wild onion, from Cummings et al., "Ceramic, Protein, X-Ray Diffraction." Common names come from Flora of North America (FNA), http://floranorthamerica.org. Usage (F = food; M = medicine; C = crafts; CS = ceremony/sacred) is from Moerman, "Native American Ethnobotany" (database).

Plants	Part(s) used	Type of use
ash 1	multiple parts	F, M, C, CS
aspen/cottonwood 1, 2	multiple parts	F, M, C, CS
bee-plant; beeweed 2, 5	multiple parts	F, M, C
bergamot, wild	multiple parts	M, CS
box elder (Manitoba maple) 1	multiple parts	F, M, CS
bulrush 2	underground parts	F, C
cattail 2	multiple parts	F, M, C
chokecherry 2	multiple parts	F, M, C, CS
dogbane 2	multiple parts	M, C, CS

Plants	Part(s) used	Type of use
dogwood, red osier 2	multiple parts	F, M, C, CS
echinacea (purple coneflower)	multiple parts	M
goosefoot 2	multiple parts	F, M, C
groundcherry 2	fruit	F, M
hazel 2	multiple parts	F, M, C
Indian breadroot (prairie turnip or tipsin) 3, 4	underground parts	F, M
juneberry (saskatoon) 2	berries	F, M, C, CS
knotweed 2	greens, seeds	F, M
mint, wild 2	greens	F, M
oak 1, 2	multiple parts	F, M, C
onion, wild 5	underground parts	F, M
pigweed 2	greens	F
plum, wild 2	fruit	F, M, C, CS
raspberry, wild 2	berries	F, M
rice, wild 2	seeds	F, CS
rose, wild 2	multiple parts	F, M, C
sage, wild 2	multiple parts	M, CS
stinging nettle 2	multiple parts	F, M, C, CS
sweet flag	multiple parts	F, M, C, CS
sweetgrass	multiple parts	M, C, CS
willow 1, 2	multiple parts	F, M, C
yarrow	multiple parts	M, CS

GLOSSARY

COMMON AND SCIENTIFIC NAMES OF ANIMALS AND INSECTS

ant Family Formicidae

bear *Ursus* spp.

bear, grizzly *Ursus arctos horribilis*

beaver *Castor canadensis*

bee Superfamily Apoidea

bee fly Family Bombyliidae

beetle Order Coleoptera

bison; buffalo *Bison bison*

butterfly Superfamily Papilionoidea

butterfly, regal fritillary *Speyeria idalia*

clam, freshwater Class Bivalva

deer *Odocoileus*

dog *Canis lupis familiaris*

dragonfly Infraorder Anisoptera

duck Family Anatidae

eagle Family Accipitridae

earthworm Subclass Oligochaeta

elk *Cervus canadensis*

firefly Family Lampyridae

fish Superclass Osteichthyes

fox Family Canidae

fox, swift *Vulpes velox*

frog *Lithobates* spp.

goose/geese Family Anatidae

gopher Family Geomyidae

gopher, pocket *Geomys bursarius*

grasshopper, swarming Family Acrididae

hare *Lepus americanus*

horse *Equus caballus*

jackrabbit *Lepus townsendii*

locust, swarming Family Acrididae

locust, Rocky Mountain *Melanoplus spretus*

mammoth *Mammuthus* spp.

meadowlark *Sturnella* spp.

millipede Class Diplopoda

moose *Alces americanus*

mosquito Family Culicidae

moth Order Lepidoptera

mouse/mice *Peromyscus maniculatus*

muskrat *Ondatra zibethicus*

owl Family Strigidae

owl, burrowing *Athene cunicularia*

prairie dog *Cynomys* spp.

oxen *Bos* spp.

pelican *Pelecanus* spp.

pronghorn *Antilocapra americana*

rabbit *Sylvilagus* spp.

raccoon *Procyon lotor*

rattlesnake *Crotalus* spp.

sandpiper Family Scolopacidae

shrike, loggerhead *Lanius ludovicianus*

skink, northern prairie *Eumeces septentrionalis septentrionalis*

snake Family Colubridae

snake, hognose *Heterodon* spp.

snail, freshwater Class Gastropoda

snail, land Class Gastropoda

sparrow, Baird's *Ammodramus bairdii*

spider Order Araneae

squirrel, ground Subfamily Xerinae

turkey *Meleagris gallopavo*

turtle Order Testudines

wasp Suborder Apocrita

wolf *Canis lupus*

woodpecker, downy *Picoides pubescens*

alder *Alnus* spp.

amaranth Family Amaranthaceae

ash *Fraxinus* spp.

ash, green *Fraxinus pennsylvanica*

aspen *Populus* spp.

aspen, trembling *Populus tremuloides*

aster; daisy Family Asteraceae (formerly Compositae)

aster, hairy golden *Heterotheca villosa* (formerly *Chrysopsis villosa*)

balsam fir *Abies balsamea*

balsam poplar *Populus balsamifera*

barley *Hordeum vulgare* subsp. *vulgare*

barley, little *Hordeum pusillum*

basswood *Tilia americana*

bean *Phaseolus vulgaris*

bearberry *Arctostaphylos uva-ursi*

bedstraw *Galium* spp.

bedstraw, northern *Galium boreale*

beebalm; bergamot *Monarda fistulosa*

beeweed *Peritoma serrulata*

birch *Betula* spp.

birch, paper *Betula papyrifera*

bloodroot *Sanguinaria canadensis*

blueberry *Vaccinium* spp.

bluestem, big; turkeyfoot *Andropogon gerardii*

bluestem, little *Schizachyrium scoparium*

box elder; Manitoba maple *Acer negundo*

brambles; raspberry *Rubus* spp.

buckwheat *Fagopyrum esculentum*

buffaloberry *Shepherdia canadensis*

bulrush *Bolboschoenus* spp., *Schoenoplectus* spp., *Scirpus* spp.

bulrush, softstem *Schoenoplectus tabernaemontani*

button eryngo; rattlesnake master *Eryngium yuccifolium*

cactus, prickly pear *Opuntia polyacantha*

cañihua *Chenopodium pallidicaule*

canola; oil rapeseed *Brassica napus*

carrot Family Apiaceae (formerly Umbelliferae)

cattail *Typha* spp.

cedar *Thuja* spp.

cedar, eastern red *Juniperus virginiana*

cedar, northern white *Thuja occidentalis*

cherry, wild *Prunus* spp.

chokecherry *Prunus virginiana*

club moss *Lycopodium* spp.

coconut palm *Cocos nucifera*

columbine, red *Aquilegia canadensis*

compass plant *Silphium laciniatum*

coneflower, pinnate prairie *Ratibida pinnata*

coneflower, narrow-leaved purple *Echinacea angustifolia*

corn; maize *Zea mays*

corn smut (fungus) *Ustilago maydis*

cottonwood *Populus deltoides*

cranberry, highbush *Viburnum opulus* subsp. *trilobum* var. *americanum*

cup moss *Cladonia/Cladina* spp.

daisy; aster Family Asteraceae (formerly Compositae)

dandelion *Taraxacum officinale*

dogbane *Apocynum* spp.

dogwood *Cornus* spp.

dogwood, red osier *Cornus sericea* (formerly *C. stolonifera*)

duckweed *Lemna* spp.

elm *Ulmus* spp.

elm, American *Ulmus americana*

elm, slippery *Ulmus rubra*

fallen stars; puffball fungus *Calvatia* spp.

flag, sweet *Acorus americanus*

flatsedge *Cyperus* spp.

French tarragon *Artemisia dracunculus*

gayfeather, rough *Liatris aspera*

gooseberry, wild *Ribes* spp.

goosefoot *Chenopodium* spp.

goosefoot, domesticated *Chenopodium berlandieri* ssp. *jonesianum*

goosefoot, Mexican; quinoa *Chenopodium quinoa*

goosefoot, narrowleaf *Chenopodium leptophyllum*

goosefoot, pitseed *Chenopodium berlandieri*

gourd *Cucurbita* spp.

grape, wild *Vitis* spp.

grass Family Poaceae (formerly Gramineae)

grass, blue grama *Bouteloua gracilis*

grass, bluejoint *Calamagrostis canadensis*

grass, grama *Bouteloua* spp.

grass, plains porcupine *Hesperostipa spartea* (formerly *Stipa spartea*)

grass, smooth brome *Bromus inermis*

green ash *Fraxinus pennsylvanica*

groundcherry; tomatillo *Physalis* spp.

ground-pine *Dendrolycopodium dendroideum* (formerly *Lycopodium dendroideum*)

hawthorn *Crataegus* spp.

hazel *Corylus* spp.

hazel, American *Corylus americana*

hazel, beaked *Corylus cornuta* subsp. *cornuta*

hickory *Carya* spp.

hickory, bitternut *Carya cordiformis*

horsetail *Equisetum* spp.

Indian breadroot; prairie turnip; tipsin *Pediomelum esculentum* (formerly *Psoralea esculenta*)

ironwood *Ostrya virginiana*

Jerusalem artichoke *Helianthus tuberosa*

juneberry; saskatoon *Amelanchier alnifolia*

juniper, creeping *Juniperus horizontalis*

knotweed *Polygonum* spp.

knotweed, erect *Polygonum erectum*

larch; tamarack *Larix laricina*

leadplant *Amorpha canescens*

leatherwood *Dirca palustris*

legume Family Fabaceae (formerly Leguminosae)

lichen Kingdom Fungi

lignum vitae *Guaiacum officinale*

lilac *Syringa* spp.

lily, Michigan *Lilium michiganense*

lily, wood *Lilium philadelphicum*

maize; corn *Zea mays*

manoomin *Zizania* spp.

maple *Acer* spp.

maple, Manitoba; box elder *Acer negundo*

maple, silver *Acer saccharinum*

maple, sugar *Acer saccharum*

marsh elder, annual *Iva annua*

marsh elder; sumpweed *Iva* spp.

marsh elder (domesticated) *Iva annua* var. *macrocarpa*

marsh marigold *Caltha palustris*

maygrass *Phalaris caroliniana*

milkweed *Asclepias* spp.

milkweed, swamp *Asclepias incarnata*

mint family Lamiaceae (formerly Labiatae)

mint, wild *Mentha arvensis*

moss Bryophyta

moss, club *Lycopodium* spp.

moss, cup *Cladonia/Cladina* spp.

mustard, wild yellow *Sinapis arvensis*

nettle *Urtica* spp.

nettle, stinging *Urtica dioica* subsp. *gracilis*

nettle, wood *Laportea canadensis*

nightshade *Solanum* spp.

oak *Quercus* spp.

oak, bur *Quercus macrocarpa*

oak, northern red *Quercus rubra*

oats, cultivated *Avena sativa*

oil rapeseed; canola *Brassica napus*

onion, wild *Allium* spp.

orchid, western prairie fringed *Platanthera praeclara*

Osage orange *Maclura pomifera*

oxeye; false sunflower *Heliopsis helianthoides*

pawpaw *Asimina triloba*

pea, garden *Pisum sativum*

phlox, moss *Phlox hoodii*

pigweed *Amaranthus* spp.

pine *Pinus* spp.

pine, jack *Pinus banksiana*

pine, ponderosa *Pinus ponderosa*

pine, red *Pinus resinosa*

plum, wild *Prunus* spp.

pondweed *Potamogeton/Stuckenia* spp.

poplar *Populus* spp.

poplar, balsam *Populus balsamifera*

prairie turnip; Indian breadroot; tipsin *Pediomelum esculentum* (formerly *Psoralea esculenta*)

puccoon *Lithospermum* spp.

puffball fungus; fallen stars *Calvatia* spp.

pumpkin *Cucurbita pepo*

quinoa; Mexican goosefoot *Chenopodium quinoa*

ragweed *Ambrosia* spp.

raspberry, American red *Rubus idaeus* subsp. *strigosus*

raspberry; brambles *Rubus* spp.

rattlesnake master; button eryngo *Eryngium yuccifolium*

reed, common (native) *Phragmites australis* subsp. *americanus*

reed, European (invasive) *Phragmites australis* subsp. *australis*

rice, white *Oryza* spp.

rice, wild *Zizania* spp.

rose *Rosa* spp.

rose, prairie *Rosa arkansana*

rush *Juncus* spp.

sage, fringed; prairie sagewort *Artemisia frigida*

sage, white; silver sage; silver wormwood *Artemisia ludoviciana*

sage, wild *Artemisia* spp.

sagebrush *Artemisia* spp.

sagewort, prairie; fringed sage *Artemisia frigida*

sagewort, sweet; sweet Annie *Artemisia annua*

samphire, red *Salicornia rubra*

saskatoon; juneberry *Amelanchier alnifolia*

sea blite *Suaeda maritima*

sedge *Carex* spp.

silverberry *Elaeagnus commutata*

skeleton plant *Lygodesmia juncea*

spruce *Picea* spp.

spruce, black *Picea mariana*

spruce, white *Picea glauca*

squash *Cucurbita* spp.

strawberry, wild *Fragaria* spp.

sumac *Rhus* spp.

sumpweed; marsh elder *Iva* spp.

sunflower, common *Helianthus annuus*

sunflower, false; oxeye *Heliopsis helianthoides*

sweet Annie; sweet sagewort *Artemisia annua*

sweet flag *Acorus americanus*

sweetgrass, hairy *Anthoxanthum hirtum* (formerly *Hierochloë odorata* subsp. *hirta*)

switchcane *Arundinaria tecta*

tamarack; larch *Larix laricina*

teosinte (ancestor of maize) *Zea mays* spp. *parviglumus*

tipsin; Indian breadroot; prairie turnip *Pediomelum esculentum* (formerly *Psoralea esculenta*)

tobacco *Nicotiana* spp.

tobacco, wild *Nicotiana rustica*

tree bracket fungus *Polystictus* spp., *Fomes* spp.

turkeyfoot; big bluestem *Andropogon gerardii*

vetch, milk *Astragalus* spp.

vetchling *Lathyrus* spp.

violet *Viola* spp.

walnut *Juglans* spp.

western false gromwell *Lithospermum occidentale*

western snowberry *Symphoricarpos occidentalis*

wheat *Triticum* spp.

wheatgrass, crested *Agropyron cristatum*

wheatgrass, western *Pascopyrum smithii* (formerly *Agropyron smithii*)

willow *Salix* spp.

willow, peach-leaved *Salix amygdaloides*

wormwood, common *Artemisia absinthium*

wormwood, silver; silver sage; white sage *Artemisia ludoviciana*

yarrow *Achillea millefolium*

yucca *Yucca* spp.

NOTES

INTRODUCTION

Epigraph: Dennis Farney, "The Tallgrass Prairie: Can It Be Saved?" *National Geographic Magazine* 157, no. 1 (1980): 37.

1. Shay, "Plants and People"; Wishart, "Great Plains Region." Geographers find regions within the Great Plains difficult to define. Areas within the U.S. portion of the northern Great Plains have been variously called the northeastern plains, the Northwest, the Old Northwest, the Middle Border, the Trans-Mississippi West, the Midwest, and the Corn Belt. In Canada, southern Manitoba and Saskatchewan are seen as part of the Canadian Prairies or Canadian Plains.
2. Bluemle and Biek, "No Ordinary Plain."
3. Because of the large number of individual groups that inhabited the region and the span of time involved, naming conventions can be problematic. In addition, a name given to a group by others may or may not be adopted by the group in question. Sometimes the name we find in historical documents is even derogatory. For this book, I have tried to standardize tribal names in consultation with modern-day ethnographers and tribal representatives, although some historical quotations may use alternate names. When I refer to the collective, I use "Native American" or simply "Native." I acknowledge that "Indigenous" is preferred in Canada.
4. Klein, *Green World*, 309.
5. Quoted in Glynne-Jones, *Native American Wisdom*, 74.
6. Nabhan, *Gathering the Desert*, 3.
7. Grove and Rackham, *Nature of Mediterranean Europe*, 45.
8. St. Pierre and Long Soldier, *Walking in the Sacred Manner*, 47.
9. LaDuke, *Recovering the Sacred*, 199.
10. Evans, *What the Tall Grass Says*, 7.

Epigraph: Louis Agassiz, "Ice-Period in America," in *Geological Sketches* (Boston: James R. Osgood, 1875), 99. First published 1864 in *Atlantic Monthly*.

1. Margold, Stokes, and Clark, "Ice Streams in the Laurentide Ice Sheet."

2. Agassiz, *Studies on Glaciers*, 331. Unstratified gravel refers to the jumble of rocks and earth deposited without the layering typical of material deposited by moving water.

3. Duval et al., "Creep and Plasticity of Glacier Ice." Snow more than a year old has only 50 percent air and is called *firn* or *névé*. Polycrystalline ice is made up of crystal aggregates measuring a few millimeters in size with varying orientations. This property allows it to flow relatively easily.

4. Altena, "Observing Change in Glacier Flow." The friction resulting from a glacier's weight induces it to move slowly. Glacial ice streams that slide on a layer of water eventually slow down as the water leaks away, ultimately slowing the ice's progress to a point of stagnation. Debris can then cover and insulate the ice, further slowing melting. Jennings, "Terrestrial Ice Streams."

5. Nansen, *Farthest North*, chap. 7.

6. Podolskiy and Walter, "Cryoseismology."

7. Examples of gouges can be seen on bare rock in the Canadian Shield in eastern Manitoba.

8. Bluemle and Clayton, "Large-Scale Glacial Thrusting."

9. Bluemle, *North Dakota's Geologic Legacy*, 132. End moraines provide clues to the order of ice recession.

10. Florin and Wright, "Diatom Evidence"; Yansa and Basinger, "Postglacial Plant Macrofossil Record"; Bluemle, *North Dakota's Geologic Legacy*, 135–41; Yansa, "Timing and Nature of Late Quaternary Vegetation Changes." As in northern Manitoba today, some trees probably tilted every which way as the ice beneath them slowly melted.

11. T. Winter, "Hydrologic Studies of Wetlands," 16–22; Kantrud and Newton, "Test of Vegetation-Related Indicators," 3.

12. Cvancara et al., "Paleolimnology of Late Quaternary Deposits."

13. Bickley, "Paleoenvironmental Reconstruction"; Cvancara et al., "Paleolimnology of Late Quaternary Deposits," 173; Newbrey and Ashworth, "Fossil Record of Colonization and Response."

14. Bluemle, *North Dakota's Geologic Legacy*, 158–59; Livingstone and Clark, "Morphological Properties of Tunnel Valleys." For a map of tunnel valleys in Minnesota, see Patterson, "Southern Laurentide Ice Lobes," 250.

15. Elson, "Geology of Glacial Lake Agassiz," 37–94; Teller, "Proglacial Lakes"; Teller and Clayton, *Glacial Lake Agassiz*; Teller and Leverington, "Glacial Lake Agassiz"; Redekop, *Lake Agassiz*.

16. The deltas of these extinct glacial lakes contain both active and stabilized sand dunes. For sand dunes in the region, see Hugenholtz and Wolfe, "Recent Stabilization of Active Sand Dunes"; J. Shay, Herring, and Dyck, "Dune Colonization in the Bald Head Hills"; Wolfe, Huntley, and Ollerhead, "Optical Dating of Modern and Late Holocene Dune Sands"; and Wolfe et al., "Holocene Eolian Sand Deposition."

17. The canoe route begins in the Qu'Appelle River. From there, one paddles to the Saskatchewan provincial line and on into the Assiniboine River to Winnipeg, Manitoba. At Winnipeg the route heads southward via the Red River to west-central Minnesota and, after a 6.2-mile portage, it continues down the Minnesota River to join the Mississippi at Minneapolis–St. Paul. It is possible to continue down the Mississippi to its confluence with the Missouri River and then up the Missouri to beyond the North Dakota–Montana state line.

18. For information about bluffs composed of loess, see Mutel, *Fragile Giants*, 3–10, 83–102. For distribution of loess in the Midwest, see Muhs and Bettis, "Geochemical Variations in Peoria Loess"; and Muhs et al., "Impact of Climate and Parent Material."

19. Fuller, *Soils of the Desert Southwest*, xiii.

20. Jay Bell, University of Minnesota Department of Soil, Water, and Climate, email to author, August 16, 2016. It is customary to refer to soils in the plural when including the many different types.

21. C. F. Mason, *Decomposition*, 15–21; Rasse, Rumpel, and Dignac, "Is Soil Carbon Mostly Root Carbon?"; Schaetzl and Anderson, *Soils*, 93–105; Swift, Heal, and Anderson, *Decomposition in Terrestrial Ecosystems*.

22. Elden Johnson, "Prehistory of the Red River Valley."

23. C. Shay, "Postglacial Vegetation Development."

24. Although hand corers are still used for collecting lake mud, today's coring devices are far more sophisticated. Modern corers are capable of obtaining cores 2.75 inches in diameter in plastic liners up to 46 feet long from water depths of nearly 100 feet.

25. Hicks et al., "Some Comments on Spatial Variation in Arboreal Pollen Deposition," 186; Hoyt, "Pollen Signatures," 691.

26. Sun and Teller, "Reconstruction of Glacial Lake Hind."

2. LAND OF THE RESTLESS WIND

Epigraph: David Laskin, *The Children's Blizzard* (Grand Rapids MI: Zondervan, 2009), 118.

1. Silver and Fischer-Baum, "Which City Has the Most Unpredictable Weather?"
2. Luckett, "PS What's News."
3. Marshall and Plumb, *Atmosphere, Ocean, and Climate Dynamics*.
4. Anthropologist James Howard explains: "Generally, a 'winter' was calculated from the first fall of snow and through the ensuing winter, spring, and autumn until the first snowfall the following year, though this does not seem to have been a hard-and-fast rule. Therefore, a variation either way of one year from the western (Gregorian) calendar date is liable to occur, even in the more accurate winter counts." Howard, "Yanktonai Ethnohistory," 2.
5. Therrell and Trotter, "Waniyetu Wówapi."
6. Howard, "Yanktonai Ethnohistory," 2, 52.
7. For the role of variations in precipitation in the condition of grasslands on the plains, see Coupland, "Effects of Fluctuations in Weather." The productivity of marsh plants is related to seasonal water levels. For the effects of seasonal water levels, see Kiel, Hawkins, and Perret, *Waterfowl Habitat Trends*, 36, table 5.
8. B. Johnston, *Honour Earth Mother*, 20.
9. Researchers have tried to isolate what creates this smell. See Bear and Kranz, "Fatty Acids"; Bear and Thomas, "Nature of Argillaceous Odour"; Bear and Thomas, "Petrichor and Plant Growth"; and Gerber, "Three Highly Odorous Metabolites."
10. M. Schneider, "Native American Traditional Art."
11. Steinbring, "Dating Rock Art," 24; Syms, "Devils Lake–Sourisford Burial Complex"; Warren, "Thunderbird Effigies."
12. Gilmore, *Uses of Plants by the Indians of the Missouri River Region*, 18.
13. Pybus, "Whirlwind Woman," 1.
14. Pybus, "Whirlwind Woman," 47–48. This particular version of the legend known as "Bear White Child" was documented in the early twentieth century.
15. Pybus, "Whirlwind Woman," 48.
16. Founded along the Red River north of the junction of the Assiniboine and Red Rivers, in an area known today as The Forks in the heart of Winnipeg, the settlement was the first European farming community in Manitoba. It was set up on land granted to the fifth Earl of Selkirk by the Hudson's Bay Company in 1811. Bumsted, *Collected Writings of Lord Selkirk*, xiii–xxi; Morton, *Manitoba*, 46.

17. A. Ross, "Red River Flood."

18. Heron, "Journal of Occurrences," May 7 entry. Southern Minnesota also suffered that spring. In late April, floodwaters carried away low-lying buildings below the main part of Fort Snelling, located on the bluffs above. The crest continued downstream to wreak havoc on Fort Crawford (now Prairie du Chien, Wisconsin). Farther west, several winter counts record flooding on the Missouri River, with many lives lost. Fisk, "Minnesota Weather History"; Therrell and Trotter, "Waniyetu Wówapi."

19. Bumsted, *Floods of the Centuries*, 7.

20. Kroker, Greco, and Peach, *1991 Investigations at Fort Gibraltar*, 30–34.

21. I prefer the Swedish-made increment borer and consider it the best on the market. The one Jennifer and I used measured about fourteen inches (forty centimeters) in length. Soda straws are ideal for transporting slender cores.

22. St. George and Nielsen, "Palaeoflood Records," 553, 547. The researchers took samples of fourteen bur oaks on my riverside property as well. The trees were relatively young; the oldest began life in 1907.

23. Seager and Hoerling, "Atmosphere and Ocean Origins of North American Droughts." Twentieth-century droughts were somewhat more variable.

24. Pearl et al., "New Frontiers in Tree-Ring Research." Pioneered in the American Southwest by A. E. Douglass, tree-ring analysis has been used across the globe for more than a century to study not only floods, fires, and droughts but also natural events such as insect outbreaks.

25. Heddinghaus and Sabol, "Review of the Palmer Drought Severity Index."

26. Several winter counts report the 1819 drought as the "sand blowing year." See Therrell and Trotter, "Waniyetu Wówapi"; Cook and Krusic, *North American Summer PDSI Reconstructions*; and Dick, *Sod-House Frontier*, 212–13.

27. Catlin, *Letters and Notes*, 427. If a Native encampment was threatened by fire, Catlin claims that the women could take down their tents "in a few minutes" in order to relocate (81). He goes on to say that he witnessed a Sioux encampment of "six hundred of these lodges, struck, and all things packed and on the move in a very few minutes" (83).

28. Hyde, *Spotted Tail's Folk*, 5.

29. M. Lewis and Clark, *History of the Expedition*, 1:185.

30. Hind, *Narrative of the Canadian Red River*, 1:292.

31. Gorrie and Shay, "Effects of Fire and Tank Traffic."

32. Karp, Behrensmeyer, and Freeman, "Grassland Fire Ecology."

33. Locust swarms such as that of 1870 sometimes coincided with years of drought. Hayden, *Report of the United States Geological Survey of the Territories*, 93; Mock, "Rainfall in the Garden," 186. A combination of drought and locusts could create hardship for Native peoples of the upper Missouri. Observers in the mid-nineteenth century noted the decimation of corn crops. For information about locust damage to maize crops, see Will and Hyde, *Corn among the Indians*, 70; and Donovan, "Grasshopper Times," 199.

34. Clark, "July 19, 1806."

35. F. Kelly, *My Captivity among the Sioux Indians*, 123–24.

36. Sutton et al., "Cuticular Hydrocarbons of Glacially-Preserved Melanoplus." DNA analysis showed that Rocky Mountain locusts were not simply the migratory phase of a sedentary species. However, because of similarities in appearance, there is no way of knowing which historical accounts refer to Rocky Mountain locusts and which might refer to other kinds of swarming grasshoppers.

37. Some eighteen extant species, both alpine and lowland, were recovered in the glacier samples, but the researchers also discovered remains from massive die-offs of *M. spretus* dating to the early 1600s. They conjecture that the locusts originated in the Yellowstone River valleys directly to the northwest, where they were likely swept up during inclement weather and blown onto the ice to die. Lockwood, "Fate of the Rocky Mountain Locust," 139; Lockwood, "Voices from the Past," 208; Lockwood et al., "Preserved Insects and Physical Condition of Grasshopper Glacier."

38. Millett, Johnson, and Guntenspergen, "Climate Trends of the North American Prairie Pothole Region."

39. Denig, *Five Indian Tribes of the Upper Missouri*, 9.

40. Paraphrased from G. Wilson, *Waheenee*, 26–34. This book is a simplified narrative of Native life based on Wilson's talks with Waheene-wea, whose name roughly translates to "Buffalo Bird Woman." She has also been called Maxidiwiac, but that name is seldom used in references today. Anthropologist Fred Schneider, email to author, February 16, 2018.

41. Osborn, "Adaptive Responses of Paleoindians."

42. Dyck, "Ancient Cold Weather Adaptations," 197.

43. Dyck, "Ancient Cold Weather Adaptations," 200.

44. Yellowhorn, "Awakening Internalist Archaeology," 124–25.

45. Quoted in Warkentin, *Canadian Exploration Literature*, 12.

46. Catlin, *Letters and Notes*, 384.

47. Connolly, "Energy Expenditure of Snowshoeing"; Passmore and Durnin, "Human Energy Expenditure," 813.

48. Brink, "Fat Content in Leg Bones of *Bison bison*"; Burstein et al., "Energy Expenditure Variations"; Kuhnlein and Humphries, "Traditional Animal Foods of Indigenous Peoples."

49. Östlund et al., "Bark-Peeling, Food Stress"; Kuhnlein and Turner, *Traditional Plant Foods*, 250–52. For a list of which barks are bitter, see Gaertner, *Harvest without Planting*, 3–4.

50. Denig, *Five Indian Tribes of the Upper Missouri*, 12. Some Plains groups considered rose hips miserable food. Hawthorn berries were also collected in difficult times.

51. Kuhnlein and Turner, *Traditional Plant Foods*, 22–23, lists ten edible lichen taxa. In terms of biological classification, lichens are part of the kingdom Fungi. They form a symbiosis of two different kinds of organisms: a fungus and an alga. According to botanist David Punter, personal communication with author, July 12, 2012, three genera occur in the northern plains. Both *Alectoria* and *Cetraria* are members of the family Parmeliaceae. *Alectoria* species hang on trees and appear as grayish tangles of roots, while *Cetraria* are brown or yellow in color and resemble tiny clumps of wild lettuce. *Cetraria* grow on the ground, usually forming mats. *Cladina rangiferina* is also a ground-dwelling lichen. This species looks like miniature clumps of pale gray trees.

52. Therrell and Trotter, "Waniyetu Wówapi."

53. Denig and Hewitt, *Assiniboine*, 566.

54. Hoffman, "Menomini Indians," 244; Nicholson et al., "Function of Ice-Gliders." Snow snakes are still thrown during Native winter games.

55. Dyck, "Ancient Cold Weather Adaptations," 214.

3. THE LAND IS SACRED

Epigraph: Mary Brave Bird and Richard Erdoes, *Ohitika Woman* (New York: Grove Press, 1993), 220.

1. Quoted in Hamilton and Shopes, *Oral History and Public Memories*, 19. The Tr'ondëk Hwëch'in people are a Yukon First Nation based in Dawson City.

2. Nabhan, "Restoring and Re-storying," 3.

3. Quoted in Foster, "Closing Circle," 142.

4. Anfinson, *River We Have Wrought*; Gilman, Gilman, and Stultz, *Red River Trails*; Jackson, *Wagon Roads West*, 1; Meyer and Russell, "'Through the Woods'"; Whelan, "1837 Ioway Indian Map Project"; Wood, "Plains Trade in Prehistoric and Protohistoric Intertribal Relations."

5. Land surveys conducted during the 1800s give some idea of what the plant cover was like in earlier times. See Wendt and Coffin, "Natural Vegetation of

Minnesota." Over the past few centuries, human activities have drastically altered the region's flora and vegetation. Hundreds of crop plants, weeds, and other exotic plants have been introduced, while many herbaceous plant species have been eliminated. The forest composition has also changed. For early settlement as recorded by land surveys and other evidence, see Harms, "Bur Oak"; Boettcher and Johnson, "Restoring the Pre-Settlement Landscape"; and Leichty et al., "Pre-Settlement Vegetation." For the role of large carnivore loss, see Ripple and Beschta, "Hardwood Tree Decline." For fire reduction's influence on forest composition, see Thomas–Van Gundy and Nowacki, "Landscape-Fire Relationships."

6. When Europeans first encountered the region, they needed a vocabulary to describe what they saw. For instance, *prairie* is a French word for a pasture or meadow, *savanna* or *savannah* is derived from the Taíno language, while *boreal* is Latin but derived from Greek, meaning "the god of the north wind."

7. Based on data gathered from 1906 to 2000, the mean annual temperature in central Iowa is 50 degrees Fahrenheit, but it is ten degrees cooler in central Saskatchewan. Mean annual precipitation in central South Dakota is twenty-four inches, but in central Iowa it is thirty-six inches. Millett, Johnson, and Guntenspergen, "Climate Trends of the North American Prairie Pothole Region."

8. Krozser, "Late Prehistoric Period." Oral history and archaeological data show that Cree and earlier groups camped here.

9. Bluemle, *Face of North Dakota*, 4, 45, 47–49; Bluemle, *North Dakota's Geologic Legacy*, 37; Klassen, "Quaternary Geology of the Southern Canadian Interior," 140–41; Trimble, *Geologic Story of the Great Plains*, 34.

10. E. Christiansen, "Wisconsinan Deglaciation."

11. N. Henderson et al., *Climate Change Impacts*.

12. Brumley, *Medicine Wheels*; Vogt, "Medicine Wheels of the Great Plains." For reports on a number of medicine wheels in South Dakota, see Sundstrom, *Boulder Effigy Sites*.

13. Kehoe and Kehoe, "Stones, Solstices, and Sun Dance Structures." According to calculations, the stones would have aligned with six celestial bodies at that time.

14. The Canadian Important Bird and Biodiversity Areas Program was established to identify and conserve sites important to bird species worldwide. See Lindgren and De Smet, "Community Conservation Plan."

15. Lindgren and De Smet, "Community Conservation Plan," 12. A number of wildflower species and more than thirty types of grasses grow in southwestern Manitoba.

16. In an 1868 engineering report, General G. K. Warren attributed the deep and wide Minnesota River valley to the drainage of Lake Agassiz. See Upham, *Glacial Lake Agassiz*, 6–7. R. W. Klassen referred to the Assiniboine valley as a glacial spillway. Klassen, "Wisconsin Events." Glacial geologist Alan Kehew first proposed that a catastrophic flood eroded the Souris River valley. See Kehew, "Catastrophic Flood Hypothesis." For more, see Kehew and Lord, "Origin and Large-Scale Erosional Features"; and Kehew and Teller, "History of Late Glacial Runoff."

17. Badertscher, Roberts, and Zoltai, *Hill of the Buffalo Chase.*

18. McLeod, *Sands of the Assiniboine Delta.*

19. Cuthbertson, "*Chondrilla juncea* in Australia."

20. D. Thompson, *Writings*, 223.

21. Hunt and Vriend, "Booming Sand Dunes."

22. Polo, *Travels*, 101.

23. For aspen reproduction, see Peterson and Peterson, *Ecology, Management and Use of Aspen and Balsam Poplar*, 22–26. In Manitoba the pioneer ecologist of the parkland was Ralph D. Bird. See Bird, "Preliminary Ecological Survey," 207–20; Bird, "Biotic Communities"; and Bird, *Ecology of the Aspen Parkland.*

24. J. Shay and C. Shay, "Prairie Marshes"; van der Valk, *Northern Prairie Wetlands*; Weller, *Freshwater Marshes*, 19–21.

25. Sampling duckweed from a wild pond can be risky, however. For a discussion of duckweed in the human diet, see De Beukelaar et al., "Duckweed as Human Food."

26. Botanists recognize two subspecies of reed: *Phragmites australis* subsp. *australis* and subsp. *americanus*. The *australis* subspecies was introduced from Europe and is considered invasive. Catling and Mitrow, "Recent Spread and Potential Distribution."

27. Sproule, "Paleoecological Investigation in the Post-Glacial History of the Delta Marsh."

28. Teller and Last, "Late Quaternary History of Lake Manitoba."

29. Peach, "Ph.D. Abstract: Faunal Exploitation at the Forks."

30. C. Shay, "Pioneers on the Forest Fringe."

31. Ahler, "Plains Village Cultural Taxonomy," 99–109.

32. Quoted in G. Wilson, *Waheenee*, 7.

33. Metcalf, "Knife River," 34.

34. For the extent of the pothole region, see van der Valk, *Northern Prairie Wetlands.*

35. Chandler et al., *Winged.*

36. U.S. Geological Survey, *Missouri Coteau Wetland Ecosystem*; Mushet and Euliss, "Cottonwood Lake Study Area."

37. W. Johnson and Poiani, "Climate Change Effects on Prairie Pothole Wetlands."

38. For the forest-prairie transition west of Itasca, see Buell and Facey, "Forest-Prairie Forest Transition." For the composition of a deciduous forest near the prairie border, see Buell and Cantlon, "Study of Two Forest Stands."

39. Jenks, "Minnesota Kitchen Midden"; C. Shay, *Itasca Bison Kill Site*; Widga, "Middle Holocene Taphonomy and Paleozoology." The bones may represent a number of individual kills over an extended period of time. It is likely that people have lived in and around the site of Itasca State Park since the last ice age.

40. Spurr, "Forest Fire History of Itasca State Park"; Frissell, "Importance of Fire." See also Gentry et al., "Reanalysis of the Fire History."

41. Leopold, *Sand County Almanac*, 49. The compass plant he speaks of is *Silphium laciniatum*, a species of flowering plant in the aster family. It has many common names.

42. For wet prairies in the Red River valley, see Hanuta, "Mapping Pre-Settlement Landscape." For wet prairies elsewhere in the tallgrass prairie region, see Hewes, "Northern Wet Prairie."

43. L. Black Elk and Flying By, *Culturally Important Plants*. Lakota translation courtesy of Sioux linguist David Kaufman, email to author, August 19, 2019.

44. A few oak savannas can still be seen elsewhere in Minnesota. For a discussion of midwestern oak savannas, see R. Henderson, "Oak Savanna Communities." The surveyors also described aspen groves and mixed aspen and oak woodlands in this area. For the extent of the aspen parkland, see Bird, *Ecology of the Aspen Parkland*, x, map 1. For the prairie-forest transition across North America, see R. Anderson, "Eastern Prairie-Forest Transition," 87.

45. Upham, *Glacial Lake Agassiz*, 604–5; Grimm, "Fire and Other Factors."

46. Gilman, Gilman, and Stultz, *Red River Trails*.

47. For the vegetation history of this part of the "big woods," see Daubenmire, "'Big Woods' of Minnesota"; and Grimm, "Chronology and Dynamics of Vegetation Change."

48. P. Nelson, *St. Paul's Indian Burial Grounds*; Gould and Rock, "Wakan Tipi and Indian Mounds Park." The mounds were excavated more than a century ago.

49. Spencer, "8,000-Year Fire and Vegetation History," 3.

50. P. Christiansen and Leoschke, *List of Flora*. The reserve covers 240 acres. When botanist Daryl Smith led me and Jennifer on a field trip to Hayden Prairie on a hot day in July 2000, Jennifer filled three pages of her field notebook with the names of species.

51. Details of tallgrass wildflowers from Ladd and Oberle, *Tallgrass Prairie Wildflowers*.

52. Iowa has had its share of pioneer plant ecologists, including Ada Hayden, Louis H. Pammel, and Bohumil Shimek. For Hayden, see D. Lewis, "Ada Hayden," 215–19. For all three ecologists, see Egerton, "History of the Ecological Sciences"; and D. Smith, "Iowa Prairie."

53. Quoted in D. Lewis, "Ada Hayden," 215–16.

54. D. Smith, "Iowa Prairie."

55. Laura Jackson, personal communication, April 19, 2020. For more, see D. Smith, *Tallgrass Prairie Center Guide*. The roadside plantings are sponsored by the Iowa Living Roadway Trust.

56. W. Whittaker, "Palace Site."

57. Quoted in Gilmore, *Prairie Smoke*, 11.

4. AMONG THE ANCIENT ARCHIVES

Epigraph: Henry Fairfield Osborn, "Evolution and Religion," *New York Times*, March 5, 1922, 91.

1. Souris Basin Development Authority, *Rafferty/Alameda*, chap. 7. Streamflow in the upper Souris generally peaks in April but quickly drops by almost half in May. It tapers off to less than a tenth of peak levels by midsummer. Between episodes of high water are years with little rainfall—the typical prairie boom-or-bust weather. Water flows out of the channel and across the floodplain about every five years.

2. Finnigan, *Souris Basin Heritage Study*; C. Shay et al., "Final Report of Palaeo-ecological Investigations in the Proposed Rafferty Dam Area," 4; C. Shay et al., "Palaeoecological Studies, Proposed Rafferty Dam Area"; C. Shay et al., "Preliminary Report of Paleoecological Investigations, Proposed Rafferty Dam Area"; C. Shay, Stene, and Wilson, "Palaeoecological Investigations"; C. Shay et al., "Report of Palaeoecological Investigations, Proposed Rafferty Dam Area." Our goals in the upper Souris research were to (1) develop a paleoenvironmental sequence based on channel morphology, sedimentary geology, soils, and plant macrofossils; (2) relate this sequence to the cultural sequence through radiocarbon dates and sediment correlations; and (3) recover small-scale plant and animal remains to help reconstruct past subsistence patterns.

3. Magilligan, Buraas, and Renshaw, "Efficacy of Stream Power"; C. Shay et al., "Final Report of Palaeoecological Investigations in the Proposed Rafferty Dam Area." Estimating the number of floods is difficult because of the complicated links between floods and flood deposits. In years between large floods the litter from surrounding plants decays into humus, ideal for land snails and other tiny

organisms. These raw soils fail to fully mature because they are covered with fresh sediment the next time the river floods.

4. C. Shay et al., "Final Report of Palaeoecological Investigations in the Proposed Rafferty Dam Area." I thank Donalee Deck, now an archaeologist with Parks Canada, for her work in identifying nearly four hundred pieces of charcoal.

5. We surmise that homesteaders had cut the larger trees beginning in the early 1900s.

6. C. Shay and Kapinga, "*Cenococcum geophilum* Sclerotia." Shells of aquatic clams and snails would have been brought in with flood deposits; those of land snails were probably from animals that lived at the site. The flatworm cocoons would have come from leaf litter.

7. Moerman, "Native American Ethnobotany" (database). Some charred seeds may have simply been burned by wildfire or accident.

8. L. Blake and Cutler, *Plants from the Past*; Browman, "Necrology: Hugh Carson Cutler"; Watson, "In Pursuit of Prehistoric Subsistence." Leonard Blake and Hugh Cutler later identified and interpreted the remains of maize and other plants from hundreds of sites across North America.

9. Chapman and Watson, "Archaic Period"; Watson, "Archaeology and Anthropology." Archaeologist Patty Jo Watson coined the term "flotation revolution."

10. Our flotation device was similar in design to those of G. W. Crawford and H. N. Jarman. See Crawford, *Paleobotany of the Kameda Peninsula Jomon*; and Jarman, Legge, and Charles, "Retrieval of Plant Remains." Further details of methods and findings are in C. Shay et al., "Palaeoecological Studies, Proposed Rafferty Dam Area."

11. Back in the lab, each sample was cataloged and its contents dried and weighed. To save time, we then subsampled those fraction sizes of one millimeter or less containing large amounts of residue. Densities ranged from no seeds at all to more than one hundred per liter. See C. Shay, "Medicinal Plant Remains," 448.

12. Mather, "Situating the Pot and Potter"; Gibson and Stratton, "In Search of the Individual."

13. R. Kelly and Thomas, *Archaeology*, 81.

14. This rate of decay is called a half-life, which is defined as 5,730 years for C-14. Our charcoal had about 85 percent of its radioactive atoms remaining, making it much younger than the half-life.

15. The estimate is from Lab No. GSC-5842 (Geological Survey of Canada 5842). The charcoal came from a depth of twenty to twenty-two inches (fifty to fifty-five centimeters) below the surface, just below a layer of coarser sediments. The

date received was converted to calendar years before the present (BP) using the Cologne Radiocarbon Calibration and Paleoclimate Research Package, available at http://www.calpal-online.de. Technically, BP means before 1950, when radiocarbon dating was introduced; see Townsley, "BP: Time for a Change."

16. The technique uses a particle accelerator to count single atoms of radioactive carbon.

17. Hellborg and Skog, "Accelerator Mass Spectrometry"; Muller, "Radioisotope Dating." The technique involves accelerating the sample to a high level of kinetic energy and then actually counting the number of C-14 atoms.

18. Hastorf and Archer, "Paleoethnobotany"; Messner, *Acorns and Bitter Roots*; Piperno, *Phytoliths*; Thorn, "Phytoliths in Paleoecology."

19. Cortella and Pochettino, "Starch Grain Analysis."

20. Malainey, Przybylski, and Sherriff, "Identifying the Former Contents"; Cummings et al., "Ceramic, Protein, X-Ray Diffraction."

21. Klug, "Discovery of the DNA Double Helix."

22. Kistler and Shapiro, "Ancient DNA Confirms a Local Origin," 3549.

23. Brink, "Fat Content in Leg Bones of *Bison bison*."

24. Cochet, *La Seine-Inférieure historique et archéologique*, 388, quoted in translation in Schmid, "Archaeological Applications," 89.

5. FROM GATHERING TO GROWING

Epigraph: Robin Wall Kimmerer, *Braiding Sweetgrass: Indigenous Wisdom, Scientific Knowledge and the Teachings of Plants* (Minneapolis: Milkweed Editions, 2013), 124.

1. Foster, "Tanji na Che," 178.

2. "Radiocarbon Calibration," Oxford Radiocarbon Accelerator Unit, University of Oxford, https://c14.arch.ox.ac.uk/calibration.html. Throughout this book, ages are given in calendar years before the present.

3. Ritchie, "Vegetation of Northern Manitoba," 216–18.

4. M. Hill, "Variation in Paleoindian Fauna Use."

5. Benton-Banai, *Mishomis Book*, 26.

6. For useful plants, see Clavelle, "Ethnobotany of Two Cree Communities"; Moerman, "Native American Ethnobotany" (database); and Uprety et al., "Traditional Use of Medicinal Plants." For fiber uses, see Adovasio et al., "Perishable Fiber Artifacts and Paleoindians"; and Horton, "Ties That Bind."

7. Although the traditional thinking has been that men hunted and women gathered, studies of recent hunter-gatherers show that there is much overlap between

the roles of men, women, and children in acquiring food. Also, archaeological evidence across the Americas suggests that some women were hunters. Hawkes, O'Connell, and Jones, "Hunter-Gatherer Studies"; Haas et al., "Female Hunters."

8. Kimmerer, *Braiding Sweetgrass*, 234–35.

9. Moerman, "Native American Ethnobotany" (database).

10. Roberts, *Holocene*. The climate scenario is based on fossil pollen, seeds, and sediment chemistry from thirty-eight lakes between the Rocky Mountains and the Atlantic coast. Shuman and Marsicek, "Structure of Holocene Climate Change." The time of high temperatures and low moisture between nine thousand and five thousand years ago has been called the Holocene Climatic Optimum. For a summary of the optimum, see Summerhayes and Charman, "Introduction to Holocene Climate Change." For a more recent paleoenvironmental and archaeological summary of the Canadian Plains plus North Dakota, see Rychlo, "Camp Rayner Site."

11. Strong and Hills, "Late-Glacial and Holocene Palaeovegetation."

12. C. Shay, *Itasca Bison Kill Site*; McAndrews, "Holocene Environment of a Fossil Bison"; Widga, "Middle Holocene Taphonomy and Paleozoology."

13. Tankersley, "Variation in the Early Paleoindian Economies," 15. One writer has remarked that Knife River flint has "properties in spades," implying both its beauty and its superb working qualities. G. Gade, "Knife River Flint," 1.

14. Kornfeld and Larson, "Bonebeds and Other Myths." For periods before about three thousand years ago, judging what plants grew in the area is mainly guesswork.

15. R. Walker and Driskell, *Foragers of the Terminal Pleistocene*.

16. Liu et al., "Vegetation History in Central Kentucky"; Veni, "Revising the Karst Map"; McNab and Avers, "Eastern Broadleaf Forest"; Braun, *Deciduous Forests*; Homsey, Walker, and Hollenbach, "What's for Dinner?"

17. Hollenbach, *Foraging in the Tennessee River Valley*, 207–17.

18. R. Walker, "Late Paleoindian through Middle Archaic Faunal Evidence from Dust Cave."

19. Sherwood et al., "Chronology and Stratigraphy at Dust Cave"; R. Walker et al., "Berries, Bones, and Blades"; Hollenbach and Walker, "Documenting Subsistence Change." Some say the hickory nut milk has a buttery quality, as sweet and rich as fresh cream.

20. Sherwood and Chapman, "Identification and Potential Significance of Early Holocene Prepared Clay Surfaces."

21. Prickly pear spines can also be singed over a fire to remove them. For more about Barton Gulch findings, see Armstrong, "Alder Complex Kitchens."

22. Marzano and Dandy, "Recreationist Behaviour."

23. It seems most likely that women led the way in these pursuits. See Watson and Kennedy, "Development of Horticulture."

24. In some cases analysis of soil chemistry, particularly phosphates, can identify habitation areas long after they have been abandoned. Roos and Nolan, "Phosphates, Plowzones, and Plazas."

25. Bowman et al., "Fire in the Earth System."

26. Cabrera and Jacobs, "Conversations about Fire." The four sacred elements are fire, water, earth, and wind.

27. Quoted in Perrot, Marston, and Forsyth, *Indian Tribes of the Upper Mississippi Valley*, 121.

28. Williams, "References on the American Indian Use of Fire." The evidence is slim, but it is likely that early hunters used fire across the continent; see Pinter, Fiedel, and Keeley, "Fire and Vegetation Shifts." The Assiniboines explicitly prohibited deliberate burning; see Denig and Hewitt, *Assiniboine*, 408–9.

29. P. Brown, "Climate Effects on Fire Regimes."

30. For early counts of charcoal particles, see C. Shay, "Postglacial Vegetation Development." Excavators at a site near the junction of the Red and Assiniboine Rivers in Winnipeg found fifteen charcoal-rich layers in sediments spanning the last fifteen hundred years. In our lab Janusz Zwiazek identified that charcoal as coming from ash, poplar, willow, elm, and maple trees. C. Shay, Coyston, and Waddell, "Paleobotanical Studies at The Forks." For a review of the techniques, see Whitlock and Larsen, "Charcoal as a Fire Proxy."

31. Boyd, "Identification of Anthropogenic Burning."

32. Fritz, "Multiple Pathways to Farming."

33. Hollenbach and Carmody, "Agricultural Innovation and Dispersal"; Gremillion, *Food Production in Native North America*; Miller, *From Colonization to Domestication*; Weitzel, "Declining Foraging Efficiency."

34. Abrams and Nowacki, "Native Americans as Active and Passive Promoters of Mast"; Zeder, "Domestication as a Model System for Niche Construction Theory."

35. Roth, "Role of Gender in the Adoption of Agriculture," argues that females were the likely cultivators of domesticated crops in what is now the southwestern United States.

36. For a discussion of how people shaped their habitats, see B. Smith, "Neo-Darwinism"; Yarnell and Black, "Temporal Trends"; and Simon et al., "Regional and Chronological Synthesis." New research extends the geographic range of early sites with domesticates to southeastern Ohio. See Patton and Curran, "Archaic Period Domesticated Plants"; and Buchanan, "Archaic Period Domestic Econ-

omy." Such ongoing research makes it difficult to be definitive about early gathering and cultivation. Patton, "People, Places, and Plants"; and Mueller, "Seeds as Artifacts," 5, fig. 1.1, provide dates for domesticates.

37. For a critique of Western versus Native American ideas about domestication, see Deur and Turner, *Keeping It Living*; and Sayre, "Chronicling Indigenous Accounts."

38. For different definitions of domestication, see Zeder et al., "Documenting Domestication."

39. Pollan, *Botany of Desire*, xvi.

40. Zeder et al., "Documenting Domestication," 139 (quote); Zeder, "Extended Evolutionary Synthesis," 1.

41. This was the case even though a few plant remains had been found at a handful of sites. Ford, "Paleoethnobotany in American Archaeology," 292.

42. Ford, "New Ideas about the Origin of Agriculture," 346–47.

43. Gilmore, "Vegetal Remains of the Ozark Bluff-Dweller Culture"; V. Jones, "Vegetal Remains of Newt Kash Hollow."

44. Harrington, *Ozark Bluff-Dwellers*.

45. It could be argued that the seeds had been gathered, but later analysis confirmed that these seeds belonged to a cultivated subspecies. Fritz and Smith, "Old Collections and New Technology," 7.

46. Gilmore, "Vegetal Remains of the Ozark Bluff-Dweller Culture," 98. The remains of maize, beans, squash, and sunflowers, some stored in bags, were found in the upper levels of some shelters.

47. Densmore, *Uses of Plants by the Chippewa Indians*, 376. The Anishinaabe also reportedly used these seeds in recent times as love charms.

48. Jones's pioneering report lent credence to Gilmore's idea that a large-seeded goosefoot, perhaps the Mexican species *Chenopodium nuttalliae*, was cultivated along with the genera *Ambrosia*, *Iva*, *Phalaris*, and *Helianthus*. He also concluded that this agricultural complex was more important than the tropical American agricultural complex. See Ford, "Ethnobotany in North America"; and V. Jones, "Vegetal Remains of Newt Kash Hollow."

49. E. Anderson, *Plants, Man and Life*; Fowler, "Origin of Plant Cultivation"; V. Jones, "Vegetal Remains of Newt Kash Hollow"; Quimby, "Possibility of an Independent Agricultural Complex." See also Fritz, "Eastern North America"; Fritz, "Multiple Pathways to Farming"; Gremillion, "Paleoethnobotany"; B. Smith, "Eastern North America as an Independent Center"; and Struever, *Prehistoric Agriculture*.

50. During these decades there were debates about whether early agriculture was truly indigenous or if the crops were imported from Mesoamerica. See Riley et al., "Cultigens in Prehistoric Eastern North America"; and B. Smith, Cowan, and Hoffman, *Rivers of Change.*

51. Larson et al., "Current Perspectives and the Future of Domestication Studies." Archaeologist Peter Bellwood called this "one of the major recent achievements of U.S. archaeological research." Bellwood, *First Farmers,* 158.

52. "Cucurbita," Flora of North America, http://floranorthamerica.org/Cucurbita. The gourds *Cucurbita maxima* and *C. moschata* were probably introduced to North America from the New World tropics by humans. Domesticated bottle gourd has been identified at a site in southern Illinois. B. Smith, Cowan, and Hoffman, *Rivers of Change,* refer to these wild plants as squashes; Asch and Hart, "Crop Domestication," use the term "gourds." See also Monaghan, Lovis, and Egan-Bruhy, "Earliest Cucurbita."

53. The other gourd genus is *Lagenaria.* The classification of the squash family is complicated.

54. B. Smith, "Initial Domestication."

55. Bischoff, Schröder, and Misof, "Differentiation and Range Expansion."

56. Asch and Hart, "Crop Domestication"; B. Smith, Cowan, and Hoffman, *Rivers of Change.*

57. The classification of these iconic plants is ongoing. Kates, Soltis, and Soltis, "Evolutionary and Domestication History of Cucurbita."

58. B. Smith, Cowan, and Hoffman, *Rivers of Change,* 89–90.

59. For squash toxicity, see Kirschman and Suber, "Recent Food Poisonings from Cucurbitacin."

60. It is feasible to treat the seeds to remove the cucurbitacin. See Kistler et al., "Gourds and Squashes"; and J. P. Hart, "Can *Cucurbita pepo* Gourd Seeds Be Made Edible?"

61. Dates for the cultivation and domestication of squash are from Mueller et al., "Growing the Lost Crops."

62. Cowan, "Evolutionary Changes."

63. Kistler et al., "Gourds and Squashes"; B. Smith, Cowan, and Hoffman, *Rivers of Change,* 42. Squash with lower cucurbitacin achieved a rind thickness of one-sixteenth of an inch around three thousand years ago. Seed size also increased. See B. Smith, "Eastern North America as an Independent Center."

64. See Zeder et al., "Documenting Domestication"; and Zohary, "Unconscious Selection."

65. Nabhan, *Gathering the Desert*, 143; Rhindos, *Origins of Agriculture*.

66. Kistler et al., "Transoceanic Drift."

67. Doran, Dickel, and Newsom, "7,290-Year-Old Bottle Gourd."

68. Asch and Hart, "Crop Domestication."

69. Holm et al., *World's Worst Weeds*.

70. Hall, "Gardening Nettle-Leaf Goosefoot."

71. Lev, Kislev, and Bar-Yosef, "Mousterian Vegetal Food"; Heiser, *Of Plants and People*; Partap and Kapoor, "Himalayan Grain Chenopods"; B. Smith, Cowan, and Hoffman, *Rivers of Change*. For current distribution of goosefoot, see Jellen et al., "Chenopodium." Quinoa, pronounced "KEEN-wah," was a valuable staple of the ancient Incas. It was featured in their religious ceremonies and revered as the "mother of grains." D. Brown et al., "Characterization of the Granule-Bound."

72. B. Smith, Cowan, and Hoffman, *Rivers of Change*, 42. Research in southern Manitoba suggests that *C. berlandieri* may have been cultivated there in pre-European times. See Halwas, "Domesticating *Chenopodium*."

73. Fritz et al., "Cultigen Chenopods in the Americas," 65.

74. F. Schneider, "Corn in the Crib"; Wedel, "George Francis Will"; Will, *Archaeology of the Missouri Valley*, 315.

75. Adair, "Tobacco on the Plains," 181; F. Schneider, "Prehistoric Horticulture in the Northeastern Plains," 37.

76. The Integrated Taxonomic Information System (ITIS) lumps a number of sunflower subspecies and varieties together under the heading *H. annuus*. Botanists previously recognized three varieties: *H. annuus* var. *lenticularis*, the "wild" sunflower; *H. annuus* var. *annuus*, the "weed" or "ruderal" sunflower; and *H. annuus* var. *macrocarpus*, the "giant" sunflower. Native Americans cultivated the last, and it is now grown worldwide. See Heiser, "Sunflower," 432.

77. J. A. Hart, "Ethnobotany of the Northern Cheyenne Indians," 21.

78. Katinas et al., "Trans-Oceanic Dispersal."

79. B. Smith, Cowan, and Hoffman, *Rivers of Change*; Wales et al., "Ancient DNA Reveals the Timing."

80. Lentz et al., "Sunflower (*Helianthus annuus* L.) as a Pre-Columbian Domesticate."

81. Mueller, *Mound Centers and Seed Security*; B. Smith, Cowan, and Hoffman, *Rivers of Change*, 42. Arbitrary as it seems, the line between wild and domesticated has to be drawn at some point. In the case of sunflowers, measurement of ten samples from archaeological sites shows an increase in seed size between three thousand and four thousand years ago, with seeds becoming larger than a quarter of an inch in length, establishing a differentiation between wild and domesticated types.

82. Heiser, *Of Plants and People*, 163. Another species in the same genus has the English common name of deathweed or devil's weed. See Best, "Biology of Canadian Weeds," 293.

83. For the good, see Carrington, "History, Taxonomic Status, and Nutritional Components"; and B. Smith, Cowan, and Hoffman, *Rivers of Change*, 290. For the bad, see Heiser, *Of Plants and People*, 163. For the ugly, see McKay et al., "Intradermal Positivity"; and Munson, "Osage and Lakota Ethnobotany."

84. Distribution information from the herbarium of the Illinois Natural History Survey (INHS) database, courtesy of Paul B. Marcum, assistant project leader for the Botany in the Wetlands science program.

85. Mueller, *Mound Centers and Seed Security*, 11. The sumpweed seeds are not oval, like those of sunflowers, but have a small knob at the end.

86. B. Smith, Cowan, and Hoffman, *Rivers of Change*, 42. Sizes of charred *Iva annua* seeds from a dozen early archaeological sites show a wide variation in length. See Weiland, "Marshelder (*Iva annua* L.)." In some areas sunflowers later replaced marsh elder. See Wymer, "Trends and Disparities," 73, fig. 9.8.

87. It is possible that erect knotweed tastes like buckwheat, which has been described as nutty and like darkly toasted bread.

88. Mueller, "Extinct Domesticated Subspecies."

89. For little barley, see Hitchcock, *Manual of the Grasses*, 269, 271, and for maygrass, 552–54.

90. Mueller, *Mound Centers and Seed Security*, 11. For a review of little barley, see Adams, "Little Barley Grass."

91. Pettipas, "Introducing Manitoba Prehistory"; C. Shay, "Perspectives on the Late Prehistory."

92. Several studies indicate that some varieties of teosinte are capable of forming fully fertile hybrids with maize, but molecular analyses have identified *Zea mays* spp. *parviglumis* as the original progenitor. Doebley, "Genetics of Maize Evolution," 37.

93. Teosinte is the common name for a group of grasses of the genus *Zea* that are native to Mexico and Central America. Teosinte is from the Aztec language Nahuatl and roughly translates as "grain of the gods." Doebley, "Genetics of Maize Evolution."

94. Benz, "Evidence of Teosinte Domestication"; Flint-Garcia, "Kernel Evolution"; Lorant et al., "Potential Role of Genetic Assimilation"; Piperno and Flannery, "Earliest Archaeological Maize"; Swarts et al., "Genomic Estimation of Complex Traits." Teosinte evolved into maize no later than six thousand years ago and

perhaps earlier. Although bitter in taste and difficult to hull, teosinte seeds can be eaten. Doebley, "Teosinte as a Grain Crop."

95. The astonishing increase in the size of teosinte ears in the transition to early maize is almost two hundred times. Teosinte ears are about one-fourth of an inch in diameter and about three inches long, and they taper to a point, while early ears of maize are a slightly tapered cylinder that is one inch in diameter and four inches long. See Dorweiler and Doebley, "Developmental Analysis of Teosinte," 1314.

96. This geographical history is based upon nearly six hundred radiocarbon dates on corn remains from archaeological sites in Mexico, the United States, and Canada spanning fifty years. See M. Blake, "Dating the Initial Spread of *Zea mays*"; M. Blake et al., "Ancient Maize Map"; and Gajewski et al., "Canadian Archaeological Radiocarbon Database." It is unclear why maize was so late reaching the plains, since sites to the east show signs of it eight hundred years earlier. Ongoing research might provide earlier dates for the plains. According to B. Smith, Cowan, and Hoffman, *Rivers of Change*, 272–76, the introduction of maize to the southeast via the Caribbean is a possibility.

97. Prasanna, "Diversity in Global Maize Germplasm"; Ruiz Corral et al., "Climatic Adaptation and Ecological Descriptors." While Native varieties average three to six feet tall, certain modern varieties top thirteen feet. Many Native varieties are still grown today.

98. Research into the genetics of kernel color is ongoing. See Hanson et al., "Evolution of Anthocyanin Biosynthesis"; and Hu et al., "Characterization of Factors." Growers of native varieties recognize six types of maize: popcorn, flint, flour, dent, sweet, and pod corn. See Neff, "Types of Corn"; Will and Hyde, *Corn among the Indians*; and Theler and Boszhardt, *Twelve Millennia*, 142. For genetic links among native maize species in the Great Plains, see Moeller and Schaal, "Genetic Relationships."

99. Hatt, "Corn Mother."

100. Hatt, "Corn Mother," 861. Other stories show maize as a powerful, protective entity.

101. Gepts, "Origin and Evolution of Common Bean"; Larson et al., "Current Perspectives and the Future of Domestication Studies"; Bitocchi et al., "Mesoamerican Origin of the Common Bean." Although there are more than fifty species in the genus *Phaseolus*, only five are domesticated.

102. For growth habits, see Dale, "Some Effects of Alternating Temperature"; and Scully and Wallace, "Variation in and Relationship of Biomass." For nitrogen fixing, see Rondon et al., "Biological Nitrogen Fixation."

103. G. Wilson, *Uses of Plants by the Hidatsas*, 12–13; Munson-Scullin and Scullin, "Potential Productivity of Midwestern Native American Gardens," 20. Growing the Three Sisters together is not always beneficial and can create problems.

104. Milburn, "Indigenous Nutrition"; Postma and Lynch, "Complementarity in Root Architecture."

6. NATURE'S BOUNTY

Epigraph: Lois Ellen Frank, *Foods of the Southwest Indian Nations: Traditional and Contemporary Native American Recipes* (Berkeley CA: Ten Speed Press, 2002), introduction.

1. To learn how early people used the botanical wealth around them, I asked several student researchers to list the wild plants growing in the region and to indicate which ones Native peoples used. For plant distributions they consulted the maps in Barkley, *Atlas of the Flora of the Great Plains*, and information from the University of Manitoba Herbarium. The Native groups included the Anishinaabe (Chippewa, Ojibwa), Arikara, Assiniboine, Blackfoot, Cheyenne, Cree, Dakota (including Nakota and Lakota), Hidatsa, Ioway, Mandan, Menominee, Meskwaki, Omaha, Plains Ojibwa, Ponca, Potawatomi, Saulteaux, and Winnebago tribes. For plant uses the students consulted Moerman, *Native American Ethnobotany*; and Moerman, "Native American Ethnobotany" (database).

2. Whelan, "Archaeological and Ethnohistoric Evidence."

3. R. Whittaker, *Communities and Ecosystems*, 224; Leith, "Primary Productivity," 205; R. Whittaker and Likens, "Biosphere and Man," 306.

4. Passey et al., *Relationships between Soil, Plant Community, and Climate*, 25, 27; Harper and White, "Demography of Plants," 438; Abrahamson, "Reproductive Strategies in Dewberries"; Parciak, "Environmental Variation in Seed"; Parciak, "Seed Size, Number, and Habitat."

5. A. Murphy and Ehrenreich, "Fruit-Producing Trees and Shrubs," 500.

6. Funk, Koenig, and Knops, "Fire Effects on Acorn Production," 21.

7. Noyce and Coy, "Abundance and Productivity"; Karen Noyce, email to author, February 14, 2014.

8. Sherman and Dooley, *Sioux Chef's Indigenous Kitchen*, 178; Gabriel, "Tree Saps Expand the Range"; Farrell, "Tapping Walnut Trees." Birch sap has a lower sugar content than maple and a slightly tannic flavor. Walnut sap contains a pectin-like substance that requires multiple filterings, but the syrup tastes quite similar to maple.

9. Conger, "Comparative Analysis of Sugar Concentrations"; Ball, "Chemical Composition of Maple Syrup."

10. Holman, "Historic Documents and Prehistoric Sugaring"; Holman, "Identification of Late Woodland Maple Sugaring Sites"; C. I. Mason, "Maple Sugaring Again"; C. I. Mason, "Prehistoric Maple Sugaring"; Munson, "Contributions to Osage and Lakota Ethnobotany"; Turner et al., "Cultural Management of Living Trees."

11. Bastian and Mitchell, *Handbook of Native American Mythology*, 132.

12. Quoted in Densmore, *Chippewa Customs*, 122.

13. Quoted in Roufs, *When Everybody Called Me Gabe-bines*, chap. 7.

14. Near the end of the sugar-making season, the sap loses its sweetness. Some of this late-season sap might have been fermented into vinegar. Sherman and Dooley, *Sioux Chef's Indigenous Kitchen*, 179.

15. Sitting Bull, "The Spring," 20.

16. Risch, "Grammar of Time," 38.

17. Dunnell and Travers, "Shifts in the Flowering Phenology."

18. Gilmore, *Uses of Plants by the Indians of the Missouri River Region*, 19.

19. We know that the people of the Andean Altiplano harvest *Chenopodium pallidicaule*, known as cañihua, by pulling the plants out of the ground. D. Gade, "Ethnobotany of Cañihua." For the experimental harvesting of goosefoot in the northern plains, see Halwas, "Domesticating *Chenopodium*."

20. Laudan, "Pounding and Grinding." For more about grinding, see Laudan, *Cuisine and Empire*, 31–33.

21. Adair, "Great Plains Paleoethnobotany," 282; K. Wright, "Ground-Stone Tools."

22. For wooden mortars used by historic tribes, see VanStone, *Simms Collection of Southwestern Chippewa Material Culture*, i–iii, 1–17, 19–26. For hide mortars, see VanStone, *Ethnographic Collections from the Assiniboine and Yanktonia Sioux*, i–iv, 1–91. For descriptions of various pounding tools used, see Zarrillo and Kooyman, "Evidence for Berry and Maize Processing"; and Gilmore, *Uses of Plants by the Indians of the Missouri River Region*.

23. Gremillion, "Foraging Theory and Hypothesis Testing"; Bleiberg et al., "Duration of Activities."

24. Hungry Wolf, "Life in Harmony," 77.

25. G. Wilson, *Waheenee*, 101–3.

26. Quoted in Colby, McDonald, and Adkison, "Traditional Native American Foods," 69. Fred Ackley echoed this idea when describing the wild rice harvest: "One

thing about the resources I had to learn was, only take enough . . . for your own use." Ackley, *Ways, Manoomin.*

27. The succulent fruits of the genus *Fragaria* are enjoyed all over the world. As Izaak Walton wrote, "We may say of angling as Dr. Boteler said of strawberries: 'Doubtless God could have made a better berry, but doubtless God never did.'" Walton, *Compleat Angler,* 92.

28. Roufs, *When Everybody Called Me Gabe-bines,* chap. 10.

29. For chokecherry moon, see Gilmore, *Uses of Plants by the Indians of the Missouri River Region,* 36; and Palmer, *Dakota Peoples,* 31.

30. For distribution, see King and Graham, "Effects of Ecological and Paleoecological Patterns," 134; for use as a poultice, see Fielder, *Plant Medicine and Folklore,* 18; for red dye, see Lyford, *Ojibwa Crafts (Chippewa),* 153; for bows, see Lowie, *Indians of the Plains,* 73; for snowshoes, see Mandelbaum, *Plains Cree;* for sticks over fires, see Densmore, *Chippewa Customs;* for arrows, see Densmore, *Chippewa Customs;* and Kennedy, *Assiniboines;* for prayer sticks, see Lyon, *Encyclopedia of Native American Healing;* for fruit used in ceremonies, see Gilmore, *Uses of Plants by the Indians of the Missouri River Region,* 88–89; and for its role in the Sun Dance ceremony, see Liberty, "Northern Cheyenne Sun Dance."

31. Saboe-Wounded Head and Tiomanipi, "Drying Chokecherries."

32. Denig, *Five Indian Tribes of the Upper Missouri.*

33. Slaughter, *Leaves from Northwestern History,* 222–23; Colpitts, *Pemmican Empire.* Q. Jones and Earle, "Chemical Analyses of Seeds II," 138, lists the protein content of chokecherry seeds as 8.6 percent.

34. Kindscher, *Edible Wild Plants of the Prairie,* 185.

35. Snell, *Taste of Heritage,* 5. In one case it took a day of digging to collect half a bushel of turnips that, when peeled, yielded only about a quarter of a bushel of food. See Riggs, *Mary and I.*

36. G. Wilson, *Buffalo Bird Woman's Garden.* Will and Hyde, *Corn among the Indians,* 88, describes a Mandan digging stick as a "heavy ash pole about three and a half feet long and one and a half inches in diameter. The point was sharpened and hardened in the fire."

37. Gjesdahl, "Sauk and Mesquakie Food"; Sherman and Dooley, *Sioux Chef's Indigenous Kitchen,* 86. To me, the raw taproots are woody in texture and taste vaguely like garden peas. Others have said they taste like unroasted peanuts. This is logical, since breadroot belongs to the pea (legume) family.

38. Adapted from Snell, *Taste of Heritage,* 9.

39. Xu et al., "Phylogeny and Biogeography."

40. In recent times, the range of wild rice has shrunk, perhaps due to an increase in water pollution. See maps in Biota of North America Program, http://www .bonap.org.

41. Moyle, "Wild Rice in Minnesota"; Terrell et al., "Taxonomy of North American Species of *Zizania*."

42. Rickman et al., "Spatial and Temporal Analyses." Wild rice production experiences booms and busts in a cycle of about five years.

43. The statement by Paul Buffalo from Roufs, *When Everybody Called Me Gabebines*, chap. 13, is an example of traditional ecological knowledge among Native peoples well aware of natural resource cycles.

44. For archaeological finds beyond my own data, see Boyd et al., "Wild Rice (*Zizania* spp.)," 13; Crawford and Smith, "Paleoethnobotany in the Northeast"; and Elden Johnson, "Archaeological Evidence for Utilization of Wild Rice." For phytoliths, see Yost, Blinnikov, and Julius, "Detecting Ancient Wild Rice"; for pollen morphology, see Lee et al., "Identifying Fossil Wild Rice"; and for dating early use by people, see Sayers, Thompson, and Lusteck, "Phytoliths from Food Residues."

45. LaDuke, "Ricekeepers."

46. D. Hansen, "Natural Wild Rice"; Sherman and Dooley, *Sioux Chef's Indigenous Kitchen*, 79–80; Withycombe, Lindsay, and Stuiber, "Isolation and Identification of Volatile Components."

47. Vennum, *Wild Rice and the Ojibway*; Zedeño et al., *Traditional Ojibway Resources*, 50.

48. Quoted in D. Hansen, "Natural Wild Rice," 7.

49. Moerman, "Native American Ethnobotany" (database); Sherman and Dooley, *Sioux Chef's Indigenous Kitchen*, 169. Processed acorns taste like a cross between hazelnuts and sunflower seeds.

50. When spelled with an initial lowercase letter, the word *calorie* means the amount of energy needed to raise 1 gram of water 1 degree Celsius. When spelled with an uppercase C, the word *Calorie* signifies 1,000 calories. Nutritionists now use a standard measure of energy, the joule, and 1 Calorie equals 4,184 joules.

51. We based our estimates of energy expenditures on how much time and effort were spent in gathering. The resulting figures do not consider a food's taste or other nutrients; they offer only a rough idea of energy efficiency. We also used rather crude digging sticks that I had made from maple dowels—poor replicas of the well-crafted tools used by gatherers of old.

52. Kunec and Shay, *Effects of Military Activity on Native Mixed-Grass Prairie*.

53. This number was obtained by multiplying the time in minutes spent digging by the estimated amount of energy expended per minute. Energy estimates based upon figures in Passmore and Durnin, "Human Energy Expenditure."

54. Data also came from Schaefer, "Prehistoric Subsistence," for greens, wild plums, goosefoot, and knotweed seeds. For *Scirpus* rhizomes and cattail rhizomes, see Simms, "Acquisition Cost and Nutritional Data"; for *Scirpus* rhizomes, see Todt and Hannon, "Plant Food Resource Ranking"; for wild plums, see Reidhead, *Linear Programming Model of Prehistoric Subsistence Optimization*; for seeds, see Gremillion, "Seed Processing"; for hazelnuts, see Talalay, Keller, and Munson, "Hickory Nuts, Walnuts, Butternuts, and Hazelnuts"; and for cattail rhizomes, see K. Jones and Madsen, "Further Experiments in Native Food Procurement."

55. Gartner, "Raised Field Landscapes."

56. G. Wilson, *Buffalo Bird Woman's Garden*, 115.

57. G. Wilson, *Buffalo Bird Woman's Garden*, 16.

58. G. Wilson, *Buffalo Bird Woman's Garden*, 68.

59. G. Wilson, *Buffalo Bird Woman's Garden*, 82–83.

60. G. Wilson, *Buffalo Bird Woman's Garden*, 85.

61. Nickel, "Cultigens and Cultural Traditions."

62. G. Wilson, *Buffalo Bird Woman's Garden*; Will and Hyde, *Corn among the Indians*.

63. Catlin, *Letters and Notes*, 188.

64. G. Wilson, *Buffalo Bird Woman's Garden*, 43.

65. G. Wilson, *Buffalo Bird Woman's Garden*, 18–19. The sunflower seed's oil content actually increased if left in the field until after the first frost.

66. F. Schneider and M. Schneider, "Sunflowers and Native Americans," 145.

67. Unroasted wild onion bulbs pack a powerful punch, I once discovered to my chagrin. Others say that they are quite mild. In any case, chemical residues of onion, presumably wild onion, were found at a nine-hundred-year-old site in Winnipeg, Manitoba. See Cummings et al., "Ceramic, Protein, X-Ray Diffraction."

68. Thoms, "Rocks of Ages"; Black and Thoms, "Hunter-Gatherer Earth Ovens"; Wandsnider, "Roasted and the Boiled."

69. Danehy and Wolnak, "Maillard Technology."

70. Dion and Dempsey, *My Tribe, the Crees*, 3. For a discussion of early boiling techniques, see Speth, "When Did Humans Learn to Boil?" It is even possible to boil water or cook food in a flammable container directly over a fire if the flames never get higher than what is in the container.

71. Hohman-Caine and Syms, "Age of Brainerd Ceramics." Even though pottery was common, some cooks still stone-boiled food in animal stomachs (paunches) until the 1800s. Gregory, "Final Exhibit Text."

72. Rice, "On the Origins of Pottery," 8.

73. G. Wilson, *Buffalo Bird Woman's Garden*, 19–20.

74. Moerman, "Native American Ethnobotany" (database); Munson, "Contributions to Osage and Lakota Ethnobotany." For sage, see Hellson and Gadd, *Ethnobotany of the Blackfoot Indians*, 101. For chemical ingredients in culinary herbs, see Small, *Culinary Herbs*, 18–19. It should be noted that cedar berries are actually modified cones.

75. G. Wilson, *Buffalo Bird Woman's Garden*, 42; Sherman and Dooley, *Sioux Chef's Indigenous Kitchen*, 31.

76. Corn smut as a food has become so popular that even "gourmets crave its characteristic fungal umami taste while skeptics criticize its nutritional and safety status." See Patel, "Functional Food Corn Smut," 93.

77. Mandelbaum, *Plains Cree*, 203. According to María Nieves Zedeño and her coauthors, "The ever-present maple sugar is [still] used as an all-purpose seasoning, comparable to salt in the diet of Europeans." Zedeño et al., *Traditional Ojibway Resources*, 53.

78. Pehrsson et al., "Carotenoids and Folate Vitamers"; Fiedor and Burda, "Potential Role of Carotenoids," 466; Ferreira et al., "Traditional Elder's Anti-Aging Cornucopia," 5; Ruelle, "Plants and Foodways of the Standing Rock Nation," 123 (which notes that even turnip water was used medicinally); Kuhnlein and Turner, *Traditional Plant Foods*; Schauss, "Emerging Knowledge of the Bioactivity of Foods"; Green and Low, "Physicochemical Composition of Buffaloberry." For general information about antioxidants, see National Center for Complementary and Integrative Health, "Antioxidants"; Mazza, "Compositional and Functional Properties of Saskatoon Berry"; Valko et al., "Free Radicals and Antioxidants"; and Chen, Hu, and Wang, "Role of Antioxidants." Antioxidants remove potential disease-causing "free radicals" that enter the bloodstream. Left unchecked, those highly reactive molecules may trigger a number of human diseases. Lobo et al., "Free Radicals"; Phillips et al., "Nutrient Composition." For information about the dietary benefits of berry fruits, see Seeram, "Berry Fruits." For more about carotenoids, see E. J. Johnson, "Role of Carotenoids."

79. Sherman and Dooley, *Sioux Chef's Indigenous Kitchen*, 4.

Epigraph: Luther Standing Bear, *Land of the Spotted Eagle* (Lincoln: University of Nebraska Press, 2006), 277.

1. These biennial conferences offer a forum for prairie lovers—farmers, scientists, conservationists, and gardeners—to share their enthusiasm for this cherished ecosystem.

2. Wang, "On the Origin and Development of *Artemisia*." For the history of the Great Plains flora, see Axelrod, "Rise of the Grassland Biome," 170. Fossilized pollen was found in rocks near Kilgore, Nebraska.

3. Grimm, "Trends and Palaeoecological Problems," 59; Strong and Hills, "Late-Glacial and Holocene Palaeovegetation"; Yansa, "Timing and Nature of Late Quaternary Vegetation Changes," 274.

4. S. Mason, Hather, and Hillman, "Preliminary Investigation of the Plant Macro-Remains."

5. Some of these absinthe-influenced creatives included Charles Baudelaire, Oscar Wilde, W. B. Yeats, Pablo Picasso, Vincent van Gogh, Paul Gauguin, and Henri de Toulouse-Lautrec, who supposedly carried a specially designed hollow cane that held some two cups of the liqueur. One review suggests that it was the alcohol in absinthe that caused the so-called absinthism syndrome; see Padosch, Lachenmeier, and Kröner, "Absinthism."

6. The genus has about six hundred species and varieties. See Martkoplishvili and Kvavadze, "Some Popular Medicinal Plants"; and Vallès et al., "Biology, Genome Evolution." For the history of naming, see Coombes, *Dictionary of Plant Names*, 30; for Greek mythology, see Chandler-Ezell, "Artemisia"; for absinthe, see Baker, *Book of Absinthe*; for antimalarial uses, see Klayman, "Qinghaosu"; and White, "Malaria Medicine Chest"; for culinary and household uses, see Small, *Culinary Herbs*.

7. Seven wild species now grow in the northern plains region. To explore these seven, I reviewed fourteen published ecological surveys and found, in order of abundance: *Artemisia ludoviciana, A. biennis, A. dracunculus, A. frigida, A. campestris, A. cana,* and *A. longifolia*. I also ranked the species by the number of uses listed in Moerman, "Native American Ethnobotany" (database): *A. ludoviciana, A. dracunculus, A. frigida, A. campestris,* and *A. cana* but found no recorded uses for *A. biennis* and *A. longifolia. Artemisia dracunculus,* or wild tarragon, may have been introduced in parts of its present range; the popular herb cultivar is called French tarragon. From my understanding, the situation is complicated. I cannot

find an authoritative list of varieties, and I do not know whether the *A. dracunculus* listed in Moerman's "Native American Ethnobotany" (database) refers to the cultivar or the wild species. Nevertheless, sage plants are still widely used. See Morgan and Weedon, "Oglala Sioux Use of Medical Herbs."

8. Bucko, *Lakota Ritual of the Sweat Lodge*, 19; Savinelli, *Plants of Power*, 61.

9. G. Wilson, *Uses of Plants by the Hidatsas*, 256.

10. Cohen, *Honoring the Medicine*, 128–29.

11. C. Shay, "Medicinal Plant Remains."

12. Results from Utah reported in Varney, Puseman, and Cummings, *Pollen, Macrofloral, and Protein Residue*. For Wyoming and Oklahoma finds, see Adair, "Great Plains Paleoethnobotany," 280, 297.

13. Both chokecherry and red cedar possess disease-fighting antioxidants. For chokecherry, see Li et al., "Comparison of Antioxidant Capacity"; for eastern red cedar, see McCune and Johns, "Antioxidant Activity in Medicinal Plants." Wild mint, a popular flavoring, also contains antioxidants. Hussain et al., "Seasonal Variation."

14. Plant chemistry is a complex subject, so only highlights are included here. Various plant-derived chemicals are discussed in Cooper and Nicola, *Natural Products Chemistry*; Singer, Crowley, and Thompson, "Secondary Plant Metabolites," 123; and Arnason, Hebda, and Johns, "Use of Plants for Food and Medicine." For functional foods, see Aluko, *Functional Foods and Nutraceuticals*.

15. Tyler, Brady, and Robbers, *Pharmacognosy*, 77–81.

16. Thadani, *Medicinal and Pharmaceutical Uses*, 56; Yao et al., "Flavonoids in Food."

17. Modern aspirin is a semisynthetic product created by acetylation of salicylic acid. It does not occur naturally. Colin Wright, personal communication, January 2013; Pierpoint, "Natural History of Salicylic Acid."

18. W. Lewis and Elvin-Lewis, *Medical Botany*, 192; Tyler, Brady, and Robbers, *Pharmacognosy*. Warfarin, a drug that contains coumarins, is widely used as a blood thinner. Bairagi et al., "Medicinal Significance of Coumarins."

19. For the nicotine content and other alkaloids in tobacco species worldwide, see Saitoh, Noma, and Kawashima, "Alkaloid Contents." Nicotine occurs from trace amounts to more than 4 percent in various kinds of Native tobacco. For specific species, see J. Winter, *Tobacco Use*, 318–19, table 48.

20. Pomerleau, "Nicotine and the Central Nervous System"; Shepard, "Psychoactive Botanicals."

21. Different sources estimate numbers of terpenes ranging from 20,000 to 110,000.

22. For uses of alder and yarrow, see H. Smith, *Ethnobotany of the Menomini Indians*, 21, 24. Huron Smith notes the use of the bitter inner bark of hoary alder for poultices to reduce swelling and the astringent or "sharp" root bark as an infusion to reduce congestion or as a wash for sores. Smith also mentions rubbing the fresh tops of yarrow on skin as a treatment for eczema and the use of a yarrow poultice for children's skin rashes. For terpenes and other chemicals in *Artemisia*, see Abad et al., "*Artemisia* L. Genus." For the many uses of sweet flag, see Clavelle, "Ethnobotany of Two Cree Communities." In 1820 the first edition of the official *United States Pharmacopoeia* listed 170 indigenous plant cures; some of those are still included today. For more about the first edition, see Blouin, "Medicinal Use of Forest Trees and Shrubs." See also Dweck, "Ethnobotanical Use of Plants"; and Barsh, "Epistemology of Traditional Healing," 30, table 1. Information on the current pharmacopeia is from John McKenna, information center specialist at the United States Pharmacopeia, https://www.usp.org.

23. G. Wilson, *Buffalo Bird Woman's Garden*, 68; Lopes-Lutz et al., "Screening of Chemical Composition."

24. Pollen data from the Neotoma Paleoecology Database, https://www.neotomadb.org.

25. Plant selection has become a major topic in ethnobotanical theory. Gaoue et al., "Theories and Major Hypotheses."

26. Heinrich, "Ethnobotany and Natural Products"; Turner, "Food/Medicine/Poison Triangle."

27. W. Geniusz, *Our Knowledge Is Not Primitive*, 71. Over generations, healers may have learned which plants were most effective through such experimentation and then passed on their findings. For an example of cultural transmission in a village society, see Kline, Boyd, and Henrich, "Teaching and the Life History."

28. Asch, "Aboriginal Specialty-Plant Cultivation," 53.

29. B. Johnston, *Ojibway Heritage*, 83. For the Lakota pharmacopeia, see Moerman, "Native American Ethnobotany" (database). For trade of medicinal plants, see Asch, "Aboriginal Specialty-Plant Cultivation."

30. Obomsawin, *Traditional Medicine for Canada's First Peoples*, quoted in Coyhis and Simonelli, "Native American Healing Experience," 1934.

31. Peat, *Blackfoot Physics*, 128.

32. Ellerby, "Spirituality, Holism and Healing," 111–12.

33. Kindscher, *Echinacea*, 9.

34. Quoted in Ellerby, "Spirituality, Holism and Healing," 121.

35. Cohen, *Honoring the Medicine*; W. Geniusz, *Our Knowledge Is Not Primitive*; B. Johnston, *Ojibway Heritage*; Peat, *Blackfoot Physics*, 132–33.

36. Densmore, *Uses of Plants by the Chippewa Indians*, 326–27; C. Shay, "Medicinal Plant Remains."

37. N. Black Elk, *Sixth Grandfather*, 96; N. Black Elk, *Black Elk Speaks*, 30–31.

38. Because fire is so versatile and pervasive, I also deal with it in chapters 2, 3, 5, 6, and 8.

39. Benton-Banai, *Mishomis Book*, 18.

40. Cohen, *Honoring the Medicine*, 129; Jetter et al., "Characterization of Emissions from Burning Incense," 55; J. Winter, *Tobacco Use*, 9–58. A smudge bundle can burn for several hours.

41. N. Black Elk, *Sacred Pipe*, 32.

42. Bucko, *Lakota Ritual of the Sweat Lodge*, 4.

43. Curtis, *Teton Sioux*, 57; Bucko, *Lakota Ritual of the Sweat Lodge*, 275.

44. J. Walker, DeMallie, and Jahner, *Lakota Belief and Ritual*, 93, describes lining the floor of a sweat lodge during a sun dance. See also Rybak, Eastin, and Robbins, "Native American Healing"; and Cohen, *Honoring the Medicine*.

45. Tushingham and Eerkens, "Hunter-Gatherer Tobacco Smoking," 213–14; J. Winter, *Tobacco Use*, 71–84; Adair, "Great Plains Paleoethnobotany," 1. The earliest evidence of tobacco use in the northern plains consists of seeds from four Iowa archaeological sites dating from fourteen hundred to fifteen hundred years ago. For the antiquity of smoking tobacco, see "Cultivated Tobacco," https://archaeology.uiowa.edu/cultivated-tobacco.

46. Jassbi et al., "Ecological Roles," 12228; J. Winter, *Tobacco Use*, 305–30; Lowie, *Tobacco Society*, 101–200. One species occurs in Africa.

47. Eiffler, "Calumet Ceremony"; Kaiser, "Lakota Sacred Pipe," 1.

48. Holler, *Black Elk Reader*, 197.

49. Kaiser, "Lakota Sacred Pipe," 18. The arrival of the sacred pipe, known as the Sacred Calf Pipe Myth or the Coming of White Buffalo Calf Woman, begins a long history of sacred pipe rituals among the Lakotas.

50. For historical evidence of pipes on the plains, see Boszhardt and Gundersen, "X-Ray Powder Diffraction," 33. For information about catlinite use and trading, see Scott et al., *Archeological Inventory*, 68. References to red stone pipes used in trade date to as early as 1637. For more on pipes, see Godlaski, "Holy Smoke."

51. Scott et al., *Archeological Inventory*, 9.

52. Quoted in Scott et al., *Archeological Inventory*, 297.

53. Moerman, "Native American Ethnobotany" (database).

54. Gilmore, *Uses of Plants by the Indians of the Missouri River Region*, 60, 82–83, 106, 107.

55. B. Johnston, *Ojibway Heritage*, 8.

56. This text is adapted from Lacey, *Pawnee*, 6–10.

57. O'Brien, "Astronomy."

58. Keating, *Narrative of an Expedition*, 288–89.

59. Cowen, "Sacred Turnip."

60. This text is adapted from Gilmore, *Prairie Smoke*, 64–65.

61. Kimmerer, *Braiding Sweetgrass*, 229.

8. FROM TOOLS TO TOYS

Epigraph: Mary B. Anderson, quoted in Erica Oberndorfer, Nellie Winters, Carol Gear, Gita Ljubicic, and Jeremy Lundholm, "Plants in a 'Sea of Relationships': Networks of Plants and Fishing in Makkovik, Nunatsiavut (Labrador, Canada)," *Journal of Ethnobiology* 37, no. 3 (2017): 458, https://doi.org/10.2993/0278-0771-37.3.458.

1. W. Geniusz, *Our Knowledge Is Not Primitive*, 158. The red cedar is also revered as sacred.

2. M. Anderson, *Tending the Wild*, 55; Turner, "Roots of Reflection."

3. Cutting with stone tools requires careful, short strokes. I tried to get this idea across in archaeology courses when I asked students to whittle a tent peg from a piece of spruce using only a flake of obsidian. Some students quickly became skilled and managed to avoid cutting themselves on the razor-sharp stone.

4. The number of tree species in the region is based on the maps in Barkley's *Atlas of the Flora of the Great Plains* and information from the University of Manitoba Herbarium. I have extrapolated from these sources that the number before European contact was about the same.

5. On lack of trees in the northern plains, see Higgins, "Historical Occurrence of Woody Plants," 116–17; and Wells, "Scarp Woodlands." Trees were much more common and in greater variety in southern Minnesota and Iowa than in southwestern Saskatchewan or the western Dakotas. For a mapping of the number of trees and shrub species, see Barkley, *Atlas of the Flora of the Great Plains*.

6. Panshin, De Zeeuw, and Brown, *Textbook of Wood Technology*; R. Ross, *Wood Handbook*. Botanists also use cellular patterns to help identify charcoal fragments from archaeological sites.

7. The active transport cells are called sapwood. As the tree grows and new rings are added, sapwood turns into heartwood that no longer conducts nutrients but instead harbors tannins, gums, and resins.

8. Conifer trees, such as spruce and pine, are nonporous because water and nutrients are conducted through different kinds of cells.

9. For lists of fish most likely present in the Missouri River in the early 1800s, see D. Jones, *History of Nebraska's Fishery Resources*, 7. For fish traps, see Weitzner and Wilson, *Notes on the Hidatsa Indians*, 200; and Wissler, *Material Culture of the Blackfoot Indian*, 40.

10. Gilmore, *Prairie Smoke*, 92–93; Schambach, "Spiro and the Tunica," 182; J. Smith and Perino, "Osage Orange."

11. Cotterell and Kamminga, *Mechanics of Pre-Industrial Technology*; Laubin and Laubin, *American Indian Archery*.

12. Bohr, "Aboriginal Archery and European Firearms," 88–89.

13. Holland, "Pilot Study in the Thermal Properties of Buffalo Chips," 161.

14. Dion and Dempsey, *My Tribe, the Crees*, 3.

15. Denig, *Five Indian Tribes of the Upper Missouri*, 81.

16. Will and Spinden, *Mandans*, 128.

17. Cotterell and Kamminga, *Mechanics of Pre-Industrial Technology*, 68, table 3.1; Hoadley, *Understanding Wood*. For wood variables, see Mullins and McKnight, *Canadian Woods*. For buffalo chips, see Holland, "Pilot Study in the Thermal Properties of Buffalo Chips." Beginning in the 1980s, our small research group at the University of Manitoba wanted to find out which woods early peoples chose for fuel, so we analyzed six thousand pieces of charcoal from seventeen sites across the region. We found fifteen different kinds, but the top woods were ash, oak, elm, poplar, and willow, the last two virtually indistinguishable but both widely available. Ash and oak, the two that yield the most heat, made up a third of the total. Botany graduate student Janusz Zwiazek in our lab identified the charcoal.

18. Burk, "Puffball Usages," 55; Mails, *Mystic Warriors*, 536; Wissler, *Material Culture of the Blackfoot Indian*, 32.

19. A. Johnston, "Blackfoot Indian Utilization of the Flora," 303.

20. Coe, *Sacred Circles*, 161.

21. According to Edwin Tappan Adney and Howard Chapelle, "The bark canoes of the North American Indians, particularly those of birch bark, were among the most highly developed of manually propelled primitive watercraft. Built with Stone Age tools from materials available in the areas of their use, their design,

size, and appearance were varied so as to create boats suitable to the many and different requirements of their users. The great skill exhibited in their design and construction shows that a long period of development must have taken place before they became known to white men." Adney and Chapelle, *Bark Canoes and Skin Boats*, 3.

22. Densmore, *Chippewa Customs*, 151.

23. Denig, *Five Indian Tribes of the Upper Missouri*, 52.

24. Quote from Denig, *Five Indian Tribes of the Upper Missouri*, 52.

25. Denig, *Five Indian Tribes of the Upper Missouri*, 52.

26. Wissler, *Material Culture of the Blackfoot Indian*, 87.

27. The word *travois* is a pseudo-French spelling of *travoy*. It is linked to the French Canadian use of the word *travail*, referring to the shaft of a cart to which a horse is hitched. A dog travois consisted of two long poles arranged on the animal in a capital A shape, with a harness fixed near the apex. The long ends dragged on the ground, while a crossbar anchored a load on the frame. Crow story from Lowie, *Material Culture of the Crow Indians*, 220.

28. N. Henderson, "Replicating Dog Travois." Experiments with a dog travois pulled by a modern, short-haired distance husky showed that 27 kilograms (59.5 pounds) could be hauled for short distances. About half this weight could be pulled when covering longer distances over four days. The main problem encountered was the dog overheating.

29. Quoted in G. Smith, *Explorations of the La Vérendryes*, 50.

30. For tipi ring evidence, see Dyck, "Ancient Cold Weather Adaptations," 2023; and Kehoe, "Tipi Rings." For dating tipi rings, see Feathers et al., "Dating Stone Alignments." Their approach analyzes the luminescent properties of sediment directly below the stones that weighed down the edges of tipis to gauge when the soil last "saw" sunlight. Samples from sites in Montana and Wyoming estimate that some rings were more than two thousand years old, although the majority were calculated to be around six hundred years old.

31. Paraphrased from N. Black Elk, *Black Elk Speaks*, 198–200; M. Wilson, "Household as a Portable Mnemonic Landscape," 189.

32. E. Hansen, "Art of Tipi Living," 40.

33. Quoted in E. Hansen, *Memory and Vision*, 65.

34. Laubin and Laubin, *Indian Tipi*, 19.

35. Dyck, "Ancient Cold Weather Adaptations," 200–203; Laubin and Laubin, *Indian Tipi*, 182.

36. Quoted in E. Hansen, *Memory and Vision*, 65.

37. Quoted in E. Hansen, "Art of Tipi Living," 43.

38. Bales and Kvamme, "Geophysical Signatures of Earthlodges," 168, 171; Bamforth and Nepstad-Thornberry, "Shifting Social Landscape," 146; Lensink, "This Old Earthlodge Village," 147–48.

39. G. Wilson, *Hidatsa Earthlodge*, 336–420.

40. Roper and Pauls, *Plains Earthlodges*, 1–31.

41. E. Hansen, *Memory and Vision*, 66.

42. Quoted in G. Wilson, *Waheenee*, 45.

43. Quoted in E. Hansen, *Memory and Vision*, 66.

44. Blaine, *Ioway Indians*, 87; McKusick, "Reconstructing the Longhouse"; Office of the State Archaeologist, "House Types."

45. Lyford, *Ojibwa Crafts (Chippewa)*, 17–18.

46. Laubin and Laubin, *Indian Tipi*, 69; Weitzner and Wilson, *Notes on the Hidatsa Indians*, 266–67.

47. VanStone, *Material Culture of the Blackfoot*, 8; Weitzner and Wilson, *Notes on the Hidatsa Indians*, 266–67. For another description of a Blackfoot backrest, see Wissler, *Material Culture of the Blackfoot Indian*, 54–55.

48. M. Geniusz, *Plants Have So Much to Give Us*, 121; Kimmerer, *Braiding Sweetgrass*, 228.

49. Adovasio et al., "Perishable Fiber Artifacts"; Barber, *Women's Work*; Good, "Archaeological Textiles"; Petersen, *Most Indispensable Art*; M. Schneider, "Plains Indian Basketry." Some remains of woven clothing have been preserved due to their contact with copper plaques. See McKern, "Hopewell Type of Culture"; McKern, "Wisconsin Variant."

50. Bodros and Baley, "Study of the Tensile Properties of Stinging Nettle"; Bassett, Crompton, and Woodland, "Biology of Canadian Weeds." My research found nettle seeds in eleven of thirty-five archaeological sites in the region.

51. Lyford, *Ojibwa Crafts (Chippewa)*, 44; Whiteford, "Mystic and Decorative Art," 75–77.

52. Karoll, "Comparative Study of the Swennes Woven Nettle Bag."

53. Kimmerer, *Braiding Sweetgrass*, 256.

54. Adovasio, *Basketry Technology*; M. Schneider, "Investigation into the Origin," 268; M. Schneider, "Plains Indian Basketry." My team found no basket remains, but we did find the charred seeds of willow, nettle, and bulrush at several sites. Such plants make excellent baskets.

55. M. Schneider, "Investigation into the Origin," 266–71.

56. National Museum of the American Indian, *Language of Native American Baskets*.

57. Jolie, "Technomechanics of Plains Indian Coiled Gambling Baskets," 42.

58. Buffalo Bird Woman talks about Hidatsa dice baskets in G. Wilson, *Uses of Plants by the Hidatsas*, 402.

59. E. Hansen, *Memory and Vision*; Mails, *Mystic Warriors*, 8.

60. DeBoer, "Colors for a North American Past," 71; Parks, *Myths and Traditions*, 94; Irwin, *Dream Seekers*, 58. Color symbolism among people of the plains could fill many pages. See, for example, Eldridge, "Color and Number Patterns"; and Zedeño, "Art as the Road to Perfection." In a personal communication on May 3, 2020, dye specialist Anne Lindsay writes, "Meanings and symbolism, the complexity of how color is created as well as how it might be applied or deployed, and the relationships involved in doing so are complex, layered, and dynamic. In short, there is no simple way to convey the richness of this subject across individuals, communities, and time."

61. Gürses et al., "Dyes and Pigments"; R. Hill and Richter, "Anthraquinone Pigments."

62. Inorganic materials called mordants contain metal ions that create a chemical bond with a colorant and help fix the dye. For common mordants, see Beeman, *Bleaching of Pulp*; and Gordon, *Chemical Arts and Technologies*, 65–78. For a general discussion of mordants, see Dobelis, Dwyer, and Rattray, *Magic and Medicine of Plants*, 426; and Thresh and Thresh, *Introduction to Natural Dyeing*, 9. For metal ions forming molecular bridges, see Teague, *Textiles in Southwestern Prehistory*, 126, 128, 129. Some other organic materials, such as the tannins in acorns or tree bark, also have fixative properties. Kathryn Jakes, email to author, June 28, 2017.

63. For dye recipes, see Lyford, *Ojibwa Crafts (Chippewa)*, 153. For the effects of temperature on the composition of wood ash, see Misra, Ragland, and Baker, "Wood Ash Composition."

64. Gilmore, *Uses of Plants by the Indians of the Missouri River Region*, 101.

65. Jakes and Ericksen, "Prehistoric Use of Sumac and Bedstraw"; A. Thompson and Jakes, "Replication of Textile Dyeing." Sumac and bedstraw were good choices for these trials, as both occur as charred seeds in archaeological sites in the northern plains and across eastern North America. Another possible early dye plant was beeweed, chemical traces of which were found on pottery residues at a nine-hundred-year-old site in Winnipeg, Manitoba. Cummings et al., "Ceramic, Protein, X-Ray Diffraction." In addition, two charred seeds of beeweed were found at the Mitchell site in South Dakota in house remains of about the same age. See Benn, "Seed Analysis and Its Implications."

66. A. Thompson and Jakes, "Replication of Textile Dyeing," 254.

67. We did not test for color fastness, as this would have taken numerous washings. We also did not expose the dyed material to direct sunlight for any length of time, which is another test for color fastness.

68. Thanks to Anne Lindsay for her insights.

69. Penman, *Honor the Grandmothers*, 45.

70. Burk, "Puffball Usages"; Gilmore, *Uses of Plants by the Indians of the Missouri River Region*, 62.

71. Paget and Scott, *People of the Plains*, 121; G. Wilson, *Uses of Plants by the Hidatsas*, 219–21.

72. Red Shirt and Lone Woman, *Turtle Lung Woman's Granddaughter*, 116.

73. Lowie, *Indians of the Plains*, 42–43. A hoop at the top of the cradleboard protected the baby's head, much like a vehicle roll bar. E. Hansen, *Memory and Vision*. Exquisite decoration may have been one of the ways parents expressed love for their children, who, out of necessity, often spent much of their first two years in a baby carrier.

74. Hassrick, *Sioux*, 312.

75. Catlin, *Letters and Notes*, 596.

76. Gilmore, *Uses of Plants by the Indians of the Missouri River Region*, 30.

77. Linderman, *Pretty-Shield*, 27–28.

78. Culin, *Games of the North American Indians*, 758; G. Wilson, *Uses of Plants by the Hidatsas*, 203–6. Ethnologists are not certain that Native American children made popguns before European contact, but in what is now Peru archaeologists have found similar popguns that were made prior to contact.

79. Quoted in Weitzner and Wilson, *Notes on the Hidatsa Indians*, 154.

80. Carlisle, *Encyclopedia of Play*, 675. Archaeological evidence shows that even children of ancient Babylon and Egypt had tops.

81. Culin, *Games of the North American Indians*, 733–50, 775–76.

82. Quoted in G. Wilson, *Uses of Plants by the Hidatsas*, 206. They were probably made from soft-stem bulrush. Such a whistle was cut green, but even with frequent mouth-wetting it was too dry to blow after about a day.

83. Quoted in G. Wilson, *Uses of Plants by the Hidatsas*, 203.

84. Walters, *Spirit of Native America*, 36.

EPILOGUE

1. Although there are a number of small mammals in the prairie that eat seeds (granivores), the most common rodent by far is the deer mouse (*Peromyscus maniculatus*). Sharon Jansa, curator of mammals, Bell Museum of Natural History,

University of Minnesota, email to author, October 12, 2021. See also Maestas and Britten, "Flea and Small Mammal Species"; R. Murphy, Sweitzer, and Albertson, "Occurrences of Small Mammal Species."

2. Native Americans, along with their attitudes and actions with respect to the environment, have been portrayed in many ways: noble ecologists, desecrators of the land, greedy opportunists. Perhaps the best way to think about the people of the northern plains is to see them along a spectrum from totally "green" to totally "brown." This avoids simple stereotypes. See Nadasdy, "Transcending the Debate."

3. M. Schneider, "Regional Differences in Plains Indian Painting"; Kinsey, "Art."

4. Native writers are increasingly being heard: Vine Deloria Jr.'s *Custer Died for Your Sins: An Indian Manifesto* brought Indigenous issues to national attention. N. Scott Momaday's *House Made of Dawn* won a Pulitzer Prize for Fiction; Louise Erdrich won a National Book Award for Fiction for *The Round House*; and Gerald Vizenor won an American Book Award for his novella *Shrouds of White Earth*. Katherena Vermette is a Métis writer from Winnipeg, Manitoba, whose first book of poetry, *North End Love Songs*, won the 2013 Governor General's Literary Award for Poetry.

5. These were reported to be the last words of Crowfoot, a Blackfoot chief, in 1890. Quoted in Tibbits, *Aging in the Modern World*, 222.

BIBLIOGRAPHY

Abad, Maria José, Luis Miguel Bedoya, Luis Apaza, and Paulina Bermejo. "The *Artemisia* L. Genus: A Review of Bioactive Essential Oils." *Molecules* 17, no. 3 (2012): 2542–66.

Abrahamson, W. G. "Reproductive Strategies in Dewberries." *Ecology* 56, no. 3 (1975): 721–26.

Abrams, Marc D., and Gregory J. Nowacki. "Native Americans as Active and Passive Promoters of Mast and Fruit Trees in the Eastern USA." *The Holocene* 18, no. 7 (2008): 1123–37.

Ackley, Fred, Jr. *The Ways, Manoomin: Food That Grows on the Water*. Wisconsin Educational Communications Board, 2019. https://theways.org/story/manoomin.

Adair, Mary. "Great Plains Paleoethnobotany." In *People and Plants in Ancient North America*, edited by Paul Minnis, 258–346. Washington DC: Smithsonian Institution, 2003.

———. "Tobacco on the Plains: Historical Use, Ethnographic Accounts, and Archaeological Evidence." In *Tobacco Use by Native North Americans*, edited by Joseph C. Winter, 171–84. Norman: University of Oklahoma Press, 2000.

Adams, Karen R. "Little Barley Grass (*Hordeum pusillum* Nutt.): A Prehispanic New World Domesticate Lost to History." In *New Lives for Ancient and Extinct Crops*, edited by Paul E. Minnis, 139–79. Tucson: University of Arizona Press, 2014.

Adney, Edwin Tappan, and Howard I. Chapelle. *The Bark Canoes and Skin Boats of North America*. Washington DC: Smithsonian Institution, 1964.

Adovasio, J. M., O. Soffer, J. S. Illingworth, and D. C. Hyland. "Perishable Fiber Artifacts and Paleoindians: New Implications." *North American Archaeologist* 35, no. 4 (2014): 331–52.

Adovasio, James M. *Basketry Technology: A Guide to Identification and Analysis*. London: Routledge, 2016.

Agassiz, Louis. *Studies on Glaciers, Preceded by the Discourse of Neuchâtel.* Translated by Albert V. Carozzi. New York: Hafner, 1967. Originally published as *Études sur les glaciers* in Neuchâtel, Switzerland, 1840.

Ahler, Stanley A. "Plains Village Cultural Taxonomy for the Upper Knife-Heart Region." In *Phase I Archaeological Research Program for the Knife River Indian Villages National Historic Site, Part IV: Interpretation of the Archaeological Record,* edited by Thomas D. Thiessen. Lincoln NE: U.S. Department of the Interior, National Parks Service, Midwest Archeological Center, 1993.

Altena, Bas. "Observing Change in Glacier Flow by Using Optical Satellites." PhD diss., University of Oslo, 2018.

Aluko, Rotimi E. *Functional Foods and Nutraceuticals.* New York: Springer, 2012.

Anderson, Edgar. *Plants, Man and Life.* New York: Little, Brown, 1952.

Anderson, M. K. *Tending the Wild: Native American Knowledge and the Management of California's Natural Resources.* Berkeley: University of California Press, 2005.

Anderson, R. C. "The Eastern Prairie-Forest Transition—An Overview." In *Proceedings of the Eighth North American Prairie Conference,* edited by Richard Brewer, 86–92. Kalamazoo: Department of Biology, Western Michigan University, 1983.

Anfinson, John O. *The River We Have Wrought: A History of the Upper Mississippi.* Minneapolis: University of Minnesota Press, 2003.

Armstrong, Steven W. "Alder Complex Kitchens: Experimental Replication of Paleoindian Cooking Facilities." *Archaeology in Montana* 34, no. 2 (1993): 1–66.

Arnason, Thor, Richard J. Hebda, and Timothy Johns. "Use of Plants for Food and Medicine by Native Peoples of Eastern Canada." *Canadian Journal of Botany* 59, no. 11 (2011): 2189–325.

Asch, David L. "Aboriginal Specialty-Plant Cultivation in Eastern North America: Illinois Prehistory and a Post-Contact Perspective." In *Agricultural Origins and Development in the Midcontinent,* edited by William Green and Constance M. Arzigian, 25–86. Iowa City: Office of the State Archaeologist, University of Iowa, 1994.

Asch, David L., and John P. Hart. "Crop Domestication in Prehistoric Eastern North America." In *Encyclopedia of Plant and Crop Science,* edited by Robert M. Goodman, 314–19. New York: Marcel Dekker, 2004.

Axelrod, Daniel I. "Rise of the Grassland Biome, Central North America." *Botanical Review* 51, no. 2 (1985): 163–201.

Badertscher, P. M., L. J. Roberts, and S. L. Zoltai. *Hill of the Buffalo Chase: 1982 Excavations of the Stott Site, DlMa-1.* Papers in Manitoba Archaeology, no. 18. Winnipeg: Historic Resources Branch, Manitoba Culture, Heritage and Recreation, 1987.

Bairagi, Shriram H., Pooja P. Salaskar, Sonal D. Loke, Nilam N. Surve, Darshana V. Tandel, and Mitesh D. Dusara. "Medicinal Significance of Coumarins: A Review." *International Journal of Pharmaceutical Research* 4, no. 2 (2012): 16–19.

Baker, Phil. *The Book of Absinthe: A Cultural History*. New York: Grove Press, 2001.

Bales, Jennifer R., and Kenneth L. Kvamme. "Geophysical Signatures of Earthlodges in the Dakotas." In *Plains Earthlodges: Ethnographic and Archaeological Perspectives*, edited by Donna C. Roper and Elizabeth P. Pauls, 157–83. Tuscaloosa: University of Alabama Press, 2005.

Ball, David W. "The Chemical Composition of Maple Syrup." *Journal of Chemical Education* 84, no. 10 (2007): 1647–50.

Bamforth, Douglas B., and Curtis Nepstad-Thornberry. "The Shifting Social Landscape of the Fifteenth-Century Middle Missouri Region." In *Plains Village Archaeology: Bison-Hunting Farmers in the Central and Northern Plains*, edited by Stanley A. Ahler and Marvin Kay, 139–54. Salt Lake City: University of Utah Press, 2007.

Barber, Elizabeth Wayland. *Women's Work: The First 20,000 Years; Women, Cloth, and Society in Early Times*. New York: Norton, 1995.

Barkley, T. M., ed. *Atlas of the Flora of the Great Plains*. Ames: Iowa State University Press, 1977.

Barsh, Russel. "The Epistemology of Traditional Healing Systems." *Human Organization* 56, no. 1 (1997): 28–37.

Bassett, I. J., C. W. Crompton, and D. W. Woodland. "The Biology of Canadian Weeds. 21. *Urtica dioica* L." *Canadian Journal of Plant Science* 57, no. 2 (1977): 491–98. https://doi.org/10.4141/cjps77-072.

Bastian, Dawn E., and Judy K. Mitchell. *Handbook of Native American Mythology*. Santa Barbara CA: ABC-CLIO, 2004.

Bear, I. J., and Z. H. Kranz. "Fatty Acids from Exposed Rock Surfaces." *Australian Journal of Chemistry* 18, no. 6 (1965): 915–17.

Bear, I. J., and R. G. Thomas. "Nature of Argillaceous Odour." *Nature* 201, no. 4923 (March 7, 1964): 993–95.

———. "Petrichor and Plant Growth." *Nature* 207, no. 5004 (September 25, 1965): 1415–16.

Beeman, Lyman A. *The Bleaching of Pulp*. New York: Technical Association of the Pulp and Paper Industry, 1953.

Bellwood, Peter. *First Farmers: The Origins of Agricultural Societies*. Oxford: Blackwell, 2005.

Benn, David W. "Seed Analysis and Its Implications for an Initial Middle Missouri Site in South Dakota." *Plains Anthropologist* 19, no. 63 (1974): 55–72.

Benton-Banai, Edward. *The Mishomis Book: The Voice of the Ojibway*. St. Paul MN: Indian Country Press, 1979.

Benz, Bruce F. "Archaeological Evidence of Teosinte Domestication from Guilá Naquitz, Oaxaca." *Proceedings of the National Academy of Sciences* 98, no. 4 (2001): 2104–6.

Best, K. F. "The Biology of Canadian Weeds: 10. *Iva axillaris* Pursh." *Canadian Journal of Plant Science* 55, no. 1 (1975): 293–301.

Bickley, William B. "Paleoenvironmental Reconstruction of Late Quaternary Lacustrine Sediments (Seibold Site) in Southeastern North Dakota." Master's thesis, University of North Dakota, 1970.

Biota of North America Program (BONAP): North American Vascular Flora. http://bonap.org.

Bird, Ralph D. "Biotic Communities of the Aspen Parkland of Central Canada." *Ecology* 11, no. 2 (1930): 356–442.

———. *Ecology of the Aspen Parkland of Western Canada*. Ottawa: Research Branch, Canada Department of Agriculture, 1961.

———. "A Preliminary Ecological Survey of the District Surrounding the Entomological Station at Treesbank, Manitoba." *Ecology* 8, no. 2 (1927): 207–20.

Bischoff, Inge, Stefan Schröder, and Bernhard Misof. "Differentiation and Range Expansion of North American Squash Bee, *Peponapis pruinosa* (Apidae: Apiformes) Populations Assessed by Geometric Wing Morphometry." *Annals of the Entomological Society of America* 102, no. 1 (2009): 60–69.

Bitocchi, Elena, Laura Nanni, Elisa Bellucci, Monica Rossi, Alessandro Giardini, Pierluigi Spagnoletti Zeuli, Giuseppini Logozzo, et al. "Mesoamerican Origin of the Common Bean (*Phaseolus vulgaris* L.) Is Revealed by Sequence Data." *Proceedings of the National Academy of Sciences* 109, no. 14 (2012): E788–96.

Black, Stephen L., and Alston V. Thoms. "Hunter-Gatherer Earth Ovens in the Archaeological Record: Fundamental Concepts." *American Antiquity* 79, no. 2 (2015): 203–26.

Black Elk, Linda S., and Wilbur D. Flying By Sr. *Culturally Important Plants of the Lakota*. Fort Yates ND: Sitting Bull College, 1998.

Black Elk, Nicholas. *Black Elk Speaks: Being the Life Story of a Holy Man of the Oglala Sioux*. As told through John G. Neihardt. Annotated by Raymond J. DeMallie. Albany: Excelsior Editions, State University of New York Press, 2008. Originally published by William Morrow (New York), 1932.

———. *The Sacred Pipe: Black Elk's Account of the Seven Rites of the Oglala Sioux*. Recorded and edited by Joseph Epes Brown. [In English.] Norman: University of Oklahoma Press, 1989. First published by the University of Oklahoma Press, 1953.

———. *The Sixth Grandfather: Black Elk's Teachings Given to John G. Neihardt.* Edited by Raymond J. DeMallie. Lincoln: University of Nebraska Press, 1984.

Blaine, Martha Royce. *The Ioway Indians.* Norman: University of Oklahoma Press, 1995.

Blake, Leonard, and Hugh Carson Cutler. *Plants from the Past: Works of Leonard W. Blake and Hugh C. Cutler.* Tuscaloosa: University of Alabama Press, 2001.

Blake, Michael. "Dating the Initial Spread of *Zea mays.*" In *Histories of Maize: Multidisciplinary Approaches to the Prehistory, Linguistics, Biogeography, Domestication and Evolution of Maize,* edited by John Staller, Robert H. Tykot, and Bruce Benz, 55–72. Amsterdam: Elsevier, 2006.

Blake, Michael, B. Benz, D. Moreiras, L. Masur, N. Jakobsen, and R. Wallace. "Ancient Maize Map." Lab of Archaeology, University of British Columbia, Vancouver (2017). http://en.ancientmaize.com.

Bleiberg, Fanny M., Thierry A. Brun, Samuel Goihman, and Emile Gouba. "Duration of Activities and Energy Expenditure of Female Farmers in Dry and Rainy Seasons in Upper-Volta." *British Journal of Nutrition* 43, no. 1 (1980): 71–82.

Blouin, G. "Medicinal Use of Forest Trees and Shrubs by Indigenous People of Northeastern North America." In Proceedings of the Twelfth World Forestry Congress, September 21–28, 2003, Quebec City.

Bluemle, John P. *The Face of North Dakota.* 3rd ed. Grand Forks: North Dakota Geological Survey, 2000.

———. *North Dakota's Geologic Legacy: Our Land and How It Formed.* Fargo: North Dakota State University Press, 2016.

Bluemle, John P., and Bob Biek. "No Ordinary Plain: North Dakota's Physiography and Landforms." *North Dakota Geological Survey Notes,* no. 1 (2007). https://www.dmr.nd.gov/ndgs/ndnotes.

Bluemle, John P., and L. E. E. Clayton. "Large-Scale Glacial Thrusting and Related Processes in North Dakota." *Boreas* 13, no. 3 (1984): 279–99.

Bodros, Edwin, and Christophe Baley. "Study of the Tensile Properties of Stinging Nettle Fibres (*Urtica dioica*)." *Materials Letters* 62, no. 14 (May 15, 2008): 2143–45.

Boettcher, Susan E., and W. Carter Johnson. "Restoring the Pre-Settlement Landscape in Stanley County, South Dakota." *Great Plains Research* 7, no. 1 (1997): 27–40.

Bohr, Roland. "Aboriginal Archery and European Firearms on the Northern Great Plains and in the Central Subarctic: Survival and Adaptation, 1670–1870." PhD diss., University of Manitoba, 2005.

Boszhardt, Robert F., and James N. Gundersen. "X-Ray Powder Diffraction Analysis of Early and Middle Woodland Red Pipes from Wisconsin." *Midcontinental Journal of Archaeology* 28, no. 1 (2003): 33–48.

Bowman, David M. J. S., Jennifer K. Balch, Paulo Artaxo, William J. Bond, Jean M. Carlson, Mark A. Cochrane, Carla M. D'Antonio, et al. "Fire in the Earth System." *Science* 324, no. 5926 (April 24, 2009): 481–84.

Boyd, Matthew. "Identification of Anthropogenic Burning in the Paleoecological Record of the Northern Prairies: A New Approach." *Annals of the Association of American Geographers* 92, no. 3 (2002): 471–87.

Boyd, Matthew, Clarence Surette, Andrew Lints, and Scott Hamilton. "Wild Rice (*Zizania* spp.), the Three Sisters, and the Woodland Tradition in Western and Central Canada." In *Occasional Papers No. 1*, edited by M. Raviele and W. A. Lovis, 7–32. Champaign IL: Midwest Archaeological Conference, 2014.

Braun, Emma Lucy. *Deciduous Forests of Eastern North America*. Philadelphia: Blakiston, 1950.

Brink, J. W. "Fat Content in Leg Bones of *Bison bison*, and Applications to Archaeology." *Journal of Archaeological Science* 24, no. 3 (1997): 259–74.

Browman, David L. "Necrology: Hugh Carson Cutler." *Bulletin of the History of Archaeology* 9, no. 1 (1999): 1–6.

Brown, Douglass C., Veronica Cepeda-Cornejo, Peter J. Maughan, and Eric N. Jellen. "Characterization of the Granule-Bound Starch Synthase I Gene in Chenopodium." *Plant Genome* 8, no. 1 (2015). https://doi.org/10.3835/plantgenome2014.09.0051.

Brown, H. P., A. J. Panshin, and C. C. Forsaith. *Textbook of Wood Technology, Vol 1. Structure, Identification, Defects and Uses of the Commercial Woods of the United States*. New York: McGraw-Hill, 1949.

Brown, Peter M. "Climate Effects on Fire Regimes and Tree Recruitment in Black Hills Ponderosa Pine Forests." *Ecology* 87, no. 10 (2006): 2500–2510.

Brumley, John H. *Medicine Wheels on the Northern Plains: A Summary and Appraisal*. Archaeological Survey of Alberta Manuscript Series No. 12. Edmonton: Alberta Culture and Multiculturalism, Historical Resources Division, 1988.

Buchanan, Amanda Dawn. "Archaic Period Domestic Economy: Evidence from the Monday Creek Workshop Site (33H0413), Southeastern Ohio." Bachelor's thesis, Ohio University, 2016.

Bucko, Raymond A. *The Lakota Ritual of the Sweat Lodge: History and Contemporary Practice*. Lincoln: University of Nebraska Press, in cooperation with the American Indian Studies Research Institute, Indiana University, Bloomington, 1998.

Buell, Murray F., and John E. Cantlon. "A Study of Two Forest Stands in Minnesota with an Interpretation of the Prairie Forest Margin." *Ecology* 32, no. 2 (1951): 294–316.

Buell, Murray F., and Vera Facey. "Forest-Prairie Transition West of Itasca Park, Minnesota." *Bulletin of the Torrey Botanical Club* 87, no. 1 (1960): 46–58.

Bumsted, J. M., ed. *The Collected Writings of Lord Selkirk, 1810–1820*. Winnipeg: Manitoba Record Society, 1988.

——. *Floods of the Centuries: A History of Flood Disasters in the Red River Valley 1776–1997*. Winnipeg: Great Plains, 1997.

Burk, William R. "Puffball Usages among North American Indians." *Journal of Ethnobiology* 3, no. 1 (1983): 55–62.

Burstein, Ruth, Andy W. Coward, Wane E. Askew, Keren Carmel, Charles Irving, Ofer Shpilberg, Daniel Moran, Alon Pikarsky, Gad Ginot, Melcolm Sawyer, Rachel Golan, and Yoram Epstein. "Energy Expenditure Variations in Soldiers Performing Military Activities under Cold and Hot Climate Conditions." *Military Medicine* 161, no. 12 (1996): 750–54.

Cabrera, Leonardo, and Clint Jacobs. "Conversations about Fire in the Bkejwanong Territory: Building Community-Based Reflection and Capacity for Fire Management and Bio-Cultural Conservation." *Indigenous Peoples and Wildfire Research Newsletter*, March 2014, 2–3.

Carlisle, Rodney P., ed. *Encyclopedia of Play in Today's Society*. Vol. 1. Thousand Oaks CA: SAGE, 2009.

Carrington, Peter Howie. "The History, Taxonomic Status, and Nutritional Components of the Prehistoric American Indian Food Seed Plant *Iva annua*." PhD diss., Michigan State University, 2015.

Catlin, George. *Letters and Notes on the Manners, Customs, and Condition of the North American Indians*. 2 vols in one. Philadelphia: J. W. Bradley, 1859. First published by Wiley and Putnam, 1842.

Catling, Paul M., and Gisèle Mitrow. "The Recent Spread and Potential Distribution of *Phragmites australis* subsp. *australis* in Canada." *Canadian Field-Naturalist* 125, no. 2 (2011): 95–104.

Chandler, Kaitlyn Moore, Wendi Field Murray, María Nieves Zedeño, Samrat Miller Clements, and Robert James. *The Winged: An Upper Missouri River Ethno-Ornithology*. Tucson: University of Arizona Press, 2016.

Chandler-Ezell, Karol. "Artemisia: The Genus *Artemisia*; Medicinal and Aromatic Plants-Industrial Profiles, Vol. 18." *Economic Botany* 59, no. 1 (2005). https://doi.org/10.1663/0013-0001(2005)059[0092:ATGAMA]2.0.CO;2.

Chapman, Jefferson, and Patty Jo Watson. "The Archaic Period and the Flotation Revolution." In *Foraging and Farming in the Eastern Woodlands*, edited by C. Margaret Scarry, 27–38. Gainesville: University Press of Florida, 1993.

Chen, Lucy, Judy Y. Hu, and Steven Q. Wang. "The Role of Antioxidants in Photoprotection: A Critical Review." *Journal of the American Academy of Dermatology* 67, no. 5 (2012): 1013–24.

Christiansen, E. A. "The Wisconsinan Deglaciation of Southern Saskatchewan and Adjacent Areas." *Canadian Journal of Earth Sciences* 16, no. 4 (1979): 913–38.

Christiansen, Paul, and Mark J. Leoschke. *List of Flora*. Howard County IA: Hayden Prairie State Preserve, 1993.

Clark, William. "July 19, 1806." In *The Journals of the Lewis and Clark Expedition*, edited by Gary Moulton. Lincoln: University of Nebraska Press and University of Nebraska–Lincoln Libraries–Electronic Text Center, 2005. https://lewisandclarkjournals.unl.edu/item/lc.jrn.1806-07-19.

Clavelle, Christina Marie. "Ethnobotany of Two Cree Communities in the Southern Boreal Forest of Saskatchewan." Master's thesis, University of Saskatchewan, 1997.

Cochet, Jean Benoît Désiré. *La Seine-Inférieure historique et archéologique: Époques gauloise, romaine et Franque*. Paris: Librairie Historique et Archéologique de Derache, 1866.

Coe, Ralph T. *Sacred Circles: Two Thousand Years of North American Indian Art*. Kansas City MO: Nelson Gallery of Art and Atkins Museum of Fine Arts, 1977.

Cohen, Ken. *Honoring the Medicine: The Essential Guide to Native American Healing*. New York: Ballantine Books, 2003.

Colby, Sarah E., Leander R. McDonald, and Greg Adkison. "Traditional Native American Foods: Stories from Northern Plains Elders." *Journal of Ecological Anthropology* 15, no. 1 (2012): 65–73.

Colpitts, George. *Pemmican Empire: Food, Trade, and the Last Bison Hunts in the North American Plains, 1780–1882*. Cambridge: Cambridge University Press, 2014.

Conger, Andrew. "A Comparative Analysis of Sugar Concentrations in Various Maple Species on the St. Johns Campus." Collegeville MN: Saint John's University, 2007. https://employees.csbsju.edu/ssaupe/CV/conger_final_report.pdf.

Connolly, Declan A. J. "The Energy Expenditure of Snowshoeing in Packed vs. Unpacked Snow at Low-Level Walking Speeds." *Journal of Strength and Conditioning Research* 16, no. 4 (2002): 606–10.

Cook, E. R., and P. J. Krusic. *North American Summer PDSI Reconstructions*. IGBP PAGES/World Data Center for Paleoclimatology Data Contribution Series # 2004-045. Boulder CO: NOAA/NGDC Paleoclimatology Program, 2004.

Cook, E. R., R. Seager, R. R. Heim Jr., R. S. Vose, C. Herweijer, and C. Woodhouse. "Megadroughts in North America: Placing IPCC Projections of Hydroclimatic Change in a Long-Term Palaeoclimate Context." *Journal of Quaternary Science* 25 (December 2009): 48–61.

Coombes, Allen J. *Dictionary of Plant Names.* Portland OR: Timber Press, 1985.

Cooper, Raymond, and George Nicola. *Natural Products Chemistry: Sources, Separations and Structures.* Boca Raton FL: CRC Press, 2014.

Cortella, Alicia R., and Maria L. Pochettino. "Starch Grain Analysis as a Microscopic Diagnostic Feature in the Identification of Plant Material." *Economic Botany* 48, no. 2 (1994): 171–81.

Cotterell, Brian, and Johan Kamminga. *Mechanics of Pre-Industrial Technology: An Introduction to the Mechanics of Ancient and Traditional Material Culture.* Cambridge: Cambridge University Press, 1990.

Coupland, Robert T. "The Effects of Fluctuations in Weather upon the Grasslands of the Great Plains." *Botanical Review* 24, no. 5 (1958): 273–315.

Cowan, C. Wesley. "Evolutionary Changes Associated with the Domestication of *Cucurbita pepo*." In *People, Plants, and Landscapes: Studies in Paleoethnobotany,* edited by Kristen Gremillion, 63–85. Tuscaloosa: University of Alabama Press, 1997.

Cowen, Ron. "The Sacred Turnip: Dietary Clues Gleaned from Tuber Traditions." *Science News* 139, no. 20 (May 18, 1991): 316–17.

Coyhis, Don, and Richard Simonelli. "The Native American Healing Experience." *Substance Use and Misuse* 43, no. 12–13 (2008): 1927–49.

Crawford, G. W. *Paleobotany of the Kameda Peninsula Jomon.* Anthropological Papers No. 73. Ann Arbor MI: Museum of Anthropology, 1983.

Crawford, Gary W., and David G. Smith. "Paleoethnobotany in the Northeast." In *People and Plants in Ancient Eastern North America,* edited by Paul E. Minnis, 172–257. Washington DC: Smithsonian Institution Press, 2003.

Culin, Stewart. *Games of the North American Indians,* vol. 24. New York: Dover, 1975. First published 1907 as *24th Annual Report of the Bureau of American Ethnology.* Washington DC: Government Printing Office.

Cummings, Linda Scott, Chad Yost, Melissa K. Logan, and R. A. Varney. "Ceramic, Protein, X-Ray Diffraction (XRD), and Organic Residue (FTIR) Analysis of Samples from The Forks Site (DlLg-33/08A), Winnipeg, Manitoba." In *PaleoResearch Institute Technical Report 09-164.* Golden CO: PaleoResearch Institute, 2010.

Curtis, Edward S. *The Teton Sioux, the Yanktonai, the Assiniboin.* Vol. 3 of *The North American Indian,* edited by Frederick Webb Hodge. New York: J. P. Morgan, 1908.

Cuthbertson, E. G. "*Chondrilla juncea* in Australia: 4. Root Morphology and Regeneration from Root Fragments." *Australian Journal of Experimental Agriculture and Animal Husbandry* 12 (1972): 528–34.

Cvancara, Alan M., Lee Clayton, William B. Bickley Jr., Arthur F. Jacob, Allan C. Ashworth, John A. Brophy, C. T. Shay, L. Denis Delorme, and George E. Lammers. "Paleolimnology of Late Quaternary Deposits: Seibold Site, North Dakota." *Science* 171, no. 3967 (1971): 172–74.

Dale, J. E. "Some Effects of Alternating Temperature on the Growth of French Bean Plants." *Annals of Botany* 28, no. 1 (1964): 127–35.

Danehy, James P., and Bernard Wolnak. "Maillard Technology: Manufacturing Applications in Food Products." In *The Maillard Reaction in Foods and Nutrition*, edited by M. Joan Comstock, 303–15. Chicago: American Chemical Society, 1983.

Daubenmire, Rexford F. "The 'Big Woods' of Minnesota: Its Structure, and Relation to Climate, Fire, and Soils." *Ecological Monographs* 6, no. 2 (1936): 233–68.

De Beukelaar, Myrthe F. A., Gertrude G. Zeinstra, Jurriaan J. Mes, and Arnout R. H. Fischer. "Duckweed as Human Food: The Influence of Meal Context and Information on Duckweed Acceptability of Dutch Consumers." *Food and Quality Preference* 71 (January 2019): 76–86.

DeBoer, Warren R. "Colors for a North American Past." *World Archaeology* 37, no. 1 (2005): 66–91.

Denig, Edwin Thompson. *Five Indian Tribes of the Upper Missouri: Sioux, Arickaras, Assiniboines, Crees, Crow*. Norman: University of Oklahoma Press, 1961.

Denig, Edwin Thompson, and J. N. B. Hewitt. *The Assiniboine*. Norman: University of Oklahoma Press, 2000.

Densmore, Frances. *Chippewa Customs*. 2nd ed. St. Paul: Minnesota Historical Society Press, 1979. Originally published as Bulletin No. 86, by the Bureau of American Ethnology, Smithsonian Institution, 1929.

——. *Uses of Plants by the Chippewa Indians*. In *Forty-Fourth Annual Report of the Bureau of American Ethnology*, edited by Jesse Walter Fewkes, 273–379. Washington DC: Government Printing Office, 1928.

Deur, Douglas, and Nancy J. Turner, eds. *Keeping It Living: Traditions of Plant Use and Cultivation on the Northwest Coast of North America*. Seattle: University of Washington Press, 2005.

Dick, Everett N. *The Sod-House Frontier, 1854–1890: A Social History of the Northern Plains from the Creation of Kansas and Nebraska to the Admission of the Dakotas*. Lincoln NE: Johnsen, 1954.

Dion, Joseph E., and Hugh Aylmer Dempsey. *My Tribe, the Crees*. Glenbow: Alberta Institute, 1979.

Dobelis, Inge N., James Dwyer, and David Rattray, eds. *Magic and Medicine of Plants*. Pleasantville NY: Reader's Digest Association, 1986.

Doebley, John. "The Genetics of Maize Evolution." *Annual Review of Genetics* 38 (December 2004): 37–59.

——. "Teosinte as a Grain Crop." *Maize Genetics Cooperation Newsletter* 91 (2017).

Donovan, Josephine Barry. "Grasshopper Times." *The Palimpsest* 4, no. 6 (1923): 193–202.

Doran, Glen H., David N. Dickel, and Lee A. Newsom. "A 7,290-Year-Old Bottle Gourd from the Windover Site, Florida." *American Antiquity* 55, no. 2 (1990): 354–60.

Dorweiler, Jane E., and John Doebley. "Developmental Analysis of *Teosinte glume architecture1*: A Key Locus in the Evolution of Maize (Poaceae)." *American Journal of Botany* 84, no. 10 (1997): 1313–22.

Dunnell, Kelsey L., and Steven E. Travers. "Shifts in the Flowering Phenology of the Northern Great Plains: Patterns over 100 Years." *American Journal of Botany* 98, no. 6 (2011): 935–45.

Duval, Paul, Maurine Montagnat, Fanny Grennerat, Jerome Weiss, Jacques Meyssonnier, and Armelle Philip. "Creep and Plasticity of Glacier Ice: A Material Science Perspective." *Journal of Glaciology* 56, no. 200 (2010): 1059–67.

Dweck, Anthony C. "Ethnobotanical Use of Plants, Part 4: The American Continent." *Cosmetics and Toiletries* 112, no. 11 (1997).

Dyck, Ian. "Ancient Cold Weather Adaptations in the Northern Great Plains." *Revista de Arqueología Americana* 20 (November–December 2001): 189–231.

Egerton, Frank N. "History of the Ecological Sciences: Part 33, Naturalists Explore North America, Mid-1780s–Mid-1820s." *Bulletin of the Ecological Society of America* 90, no. 4 (Oct. 2009): 434–87.

Eiffler, Mark A. "Calumet Ceremony." In *Encyclopedia of the Great Plains*, edited by David J. Wishart. Lincoln: University of Nebraska, 2011. http://plainshumanities.unl.edu/encyclopedia/.

Eldridge, Pamela S. "Color and Number Patterns in the Symbolic Cosmologies of the Crow, Pawnee, Kiowa, and Cheyenne." Master's thesis, Wichita State University, 1999.

Ellerby, Jonathan H. "Spirituality, Holism and Healing among the Lakota Sioux: Towards an Understanding of Indigenous Medicine." Master's thesis, University of Manitoba, 2005.

Elson, John A. "Geology of Glacial Lake Agassiz." In *Life, Land and Water*, edited by William J. Mayer-Oakes, 37–94. Winnipeg: University of Manitoba Press, 1967.

Evans, David A., ed. *What the Tall Grass Says*. Sioux Falls SD: Center for Western Studies, 1982.

Farrell, Michael. "Tapping Walnut Trees for a Novel and Delicious Syrup." Small Farms Program, Cornell University, January 11, 2016. http://smallfarms.cornell .edu/2016/01/11/tapping-walnut-trees/.

Feathers, James K., María Nieves Zedeño, Lawrence C. Todd, and Stephen Aaberg. "Dating Stone Alignments by Luminescence." *Advances in Archaeological Practice* 3, no. 4 (2015): 378–96.

Ferreira, Maria Pontes, Jaclyn Palmer, Elder Betty McKenna, and Fidji Gendron. "A Traditional Elder's Anti-Aging Cornucopia of North American Plants." In *Foods and Dietary Supplements in the Prevention and Treatment of Disease in Older Adults*, edited by Ronald Ross Watson, 3–11. London: Elsevier, 2015.

Fiedor, Joanna, and Květoslava Burda. "Potential Role of Carotenoids as Antioxidants in Human Health and Disease." *Nutrients* 6, no. 2 (2014): 466–88.

Fielder, M. *Plant Medicine and Folklore*. New York: Winchester Press, 1975.

Finnigan, J. T. *Souris Basin Heritage Study: 1987 Heritage Investigations at the Rafferty and Alameda Reservoirs*. Saskatoon: Saskatchewan Research Council, 1988.

Fisk, Charles. "Minnesota Weather History 1820 to 1869." ClimateStations.com, March 13, 2010. https://www.climatestations.com/minnesota-weather-history -1820-to-1869/.

Flint-Garcia, Sherry A. "Kernel Evolution: From Teosinte to Maize." In *Maize Kernel Development*, edited by B. Larkins, 1–15. Wallingford, UK: Centre for Agriculture and Biosciences International (CABI), 2017.

Florin, Maj-Britt, and H. E. Wright Jr. "Diatom Evidence for the Persistence of Stagnant Ice in Minnesota." *Geological Society of America Bulletin* 80, no. 4 (1969): 695–704.

Ford, Richard I. "Ethnobotany in North America: An Historical Phytogeographic Perspective." *Canadian Journal of Botany* 59, no. 11 (1981): 2178–88.

———. "New Ideas about the Origin of Agriculture Based on 50 Years of Museum-Curated Plant Remains." *Annals of the New York Academy of Sciences* 376, no. 1 (1981): 345–56.

———. "Paleoethnobotany in American Archaeology." *Advances in Archaeological Method and Theory* 2 (1979): 285–336.

Foster, Lance M. "A Closing Circle: Musings on the Ioway Indians in Iowa." In *The Worlds between Two Rivers: Perspectives on American Indians in Iowa*, edited by

Gretchen M. Bataille, David Mayer Gradwohl, and Charles L. P. Silet. Iowa City: University of Iowa Press, 2000.

———. "Tanji na Che: Recovering the Landscape of the Ioway." In *Recovering the Prairie*, edited by Robert F. Sayre, 178–90. Madison: University of Wisconsin Press, 1999.

Fowler, Melvin L. "The Origin of Plant Cultivation in the Central Mississippi Valley: A Hypothesis." In *Prehistoric Agriculture*, edited by Stuart Struever, 122–28. New York: Natural History Press, 1971.

Frissell, Sidney S. "The Importance of Fire as a Natural Ecological Factor in Itasca State Park, Minnesota." *Quaternary Research* 3, no. 3 (1973): 397–407.

Fritz, Gayle J. "Eastern North America: An Independent Center of Agricultural Origins." In *Encyclopedia of Global Archaeology*, edited by Claire Smith, 2316–22. New York: Springer, 2014.

———. "Multiple Pathways to Farming in Precontact Eastern North America." *Journal of World Prehistory* 4, no. 4 (1990): 387–435.

Fritz, Gayle J., Maria C. Bruno, BrieAnna S. Langlie, Bruce D. Smith, and Logan Kistler. "Cultigen Chenopods in the Americas: A Hemispherical Perspective." In *Social Perspectives on Ancient Lives from Paleoethnobotanical Data*, edited by Matthew P. Sayre and Maria C. Bruno, 55–75. New York: Springer, 2017.

Fritz, Gayle J., and Bruce D. Smith. "Old Collections and New Technology: Documenting the Domestication of *Chenopodium* in Eastern North America." *Midcontinental Journal of Archaeology* 13, no. 1 (1988): 3–27.

Fuller, Wallace H. *Soils of the Desert Southwest*. Tucson: University of Arizona Press, 1975.

Funk, Kyle A., Walter D. Koenig, and Johannes M. H. Knops. "Fire Effects on Acorn Production Are Consistent with the Stored Resource Hypothesis for Masting Behavior." *Canadian Journal of Forest Research* 46, no. 1 (2015): 20–24.

Gabriel, Steve. "Tree Saps Expand the Range, Potential of Forest Farming." Farming the Woods, March 12, 2015. https://farmingthewoods.com/2015/03/12/tree-saps-expand-the-range-potential-of-forest-farming.

Gade, Daniel W. "Ethnobotany of Cañihua (*Chenopodium pallidicaule*), Rustic Seed Crop of the Altiplano." *Economic Botany* 24, no. 1 (1970): 55–61.

Gade, Gene. "Knife River Flint: Prized Knapping Stone of the Northern Plains." Vore Buffalo Jump. Accessed December 20, 2020. https://vorebuffalojump.org.

Gaertner, E. E. *Harvest without Planting: Eating and Nibbling Off the Land*. Pembroke ON: Donald F. Runge, 1967.

Gajewski, Konrad, Sam Muñoz, Matthew Peros, André Viau, R. Morlan, and Matthew Betts. "The Canadian Archaeological Radiocarbon Database (CARD): Archaeo-

logical 14c Dates in North America and Their Paleoenvironmental Context."
Radiocarbon 53, no. 2 (2011): 371–94.

Gaoue, Orou G., Michael A. Coe, Matthew Bond, Georgia Hart, Barnabas C. Seyler, and Heather McMillen. "Theories and Major Hypotheses in Ethnobotany." *Economic Botany* 71, no. 3 (2017): 269–87.

Gartner, William Gustav. "Raised Field Landscapes of Native North America." PhD diss., University of Wisconsin–Madison, 2003.

Geniusz, Mary Siisip. *Plants Have So Much to Give Us, All We Have to Do Is Ask: Anishinaabe Botanical Teachings.* Edited by Wendy Makoons Geniusz. Minneapolis: University of Minnesota Press, 2015.

Geniusz, Wendy Makoons. *Our Knowledge Is Not Primitive: Decolonizing Botanical Anishinaabe Teachings.* Syracuse NY: Syracuse University Press, 2009.

Gentry, C., P. M. Brown, S. Aldrich, J. Bauer, J. Kernan, R. Lusteck, R. McEwan, et al. "Reanalysis of the Fire History in *Pinus resinosa* Stands of the Mississippi Headwaters, Itasca State Park, Minnesota." Poster presentation, annual meeting of the Association of American Geographers, Denver, Colorado, April 5–9, 2005.

Gepts, Paul. "Origin and Evolution of Common Bean: Past Events and Recent Trends." *Horticultural Science* 33, no. 7 (1998): 1124–30.

Gerber, Nancy N. "Three Highly Odorous Metabolites from an Actinomycete: 2-Isopropyl-3-Methoxy-Pyrazine, Methylisoborneol, and Geosmin." *Journal of Chemical Ecology* 3, no. 4 (1977): 475–82.

Gibson, Terry, and Sabine Stratton. "In Search of the Individual in Prehistory: Analysing Fingerprints from Selkirk Pottery from Saskatchewan." Paper presented at the annual meeting of the Canadian Archaeological Association, Calgary, Alberta, April 22–26, 1987.

Gilman, Rhoda R., Carolyn Gilman, and Deborah M. Stultz. *The Red River Trails: Oxcart Routes between St. Paul and the Selkirk Settlement, 1820–1870.* St. Paul: Minnesota Historical Society, 1979.

Gilmore, Melvin R. *Prairie Smoke.* St. Paul: Minnesota Historical Society Press, 1987. First published by the author, 1922.

———. *Uses of Plants by the Indians of the Missouri River Region.* Lincoln: University of Nebraska Press, 1991. First published as *Thirty-Third Annual Report of the Bureau of American Ethnology, 1911–1912,* by the Smithsonian Institution, 1919.

———. "Vegetal Remains of the Ozark Bluff-Dweller Culture." *Michigan Academy of Science, Arts and Letters* 14 (1931): 83–102.

Gjesdahl, Jacob. "Sauk and Mesquakie Food Consumption in 1808." Grinnell College, April 26, 2009. https://www.grinnell.edu/sites/default/files/documents/gjesdahl_jacob_MesquakieFood1820.pdf.

Glynne-Jones, Tim. *The Pocket Book of Native American Wisdom*. London: Sirius, 2017.

Godlaski, Theodore M. "Holy Smoke: Tobacco Use among Native American Tribes in North America." *Substance Use and Misuse* 48, no. 1–2 (2013): 1–8.

Good, Irene. "Archaeological Textiles: A Review of Current Research." *Annual Review of Anthropology* 30, no. 1 (2001): 209–26.

Gordon, Burton Le Roy. *Chemical Arts and Technologies of Indigenous Americans*. Oxford: Archaeopress, 2009.

Gorrie, S., and J. M. Shay. "The Effects of Fire and Tank Traffic on Mixed-Grass Prairie at Shilo, Manitoba." In *2nd Annual Report to Department of National Defence Contract*, 66. Winnipeg: Department of Botany, University of Manitoba, 1988.

Gould, Roxanne, and Jim Rock. "Wakan Tipi and Indian Mounds Park: Reclaiming an Indigenous Feminine Sacred Site." *AlterNative: An International Journal of Indigenous Peoples* 12, no. 3 (2016): 224–36.

Green, Richard C., and Nicholas H. Low. "Physicochemical Composition of Buffaloberry (*Shepherdia argentea*), Chokecherry (*Prunus virginiana*) and Sea Buckthorn (*Hippophae rhamnoides*) Fruit Harvested in Saskatchewan, Canada." *Canadian Journal of Plant Science* 93, no. 6 (2013): 1143–53.

Gregory, Loris Sofia. "Final Exhibit Text." Jeffers Petroglyphs, Minnesota Historic Site, 1999.

Gremillion, Kristen J. *Food Production in Native North America: An Archaeological Perspective*. Washington DC: SAA Press, 2018.

———. "Foraging Theory and Hypothesis Testing in Archaeology: An Exploration of Methodological Problems and Solutions." *Journal of Anthropological Archaeology* 21, no. 2 (2002): 142–64.

———. "Paleoethnobotany." In *The Development of Southeastern Archaeology*, edited by Jay K. Johnson, 132–59. Tuscaloosa: University of Alabama Press, 1993.

———. "Seed Processing and the Origins of Food Production in Eastern North America." *American Antiquity* 69, no. 2 (2004): 215–33.

Grimm, Eric C. "Chronology and Dynamics of Vegetation Change in the Prairie-Woodland Region of Southern Minnesota, U.S.A." *New Phytologist* 93, no. 2 (1983): 311–50.

———. "Fire and Other Factors Controlling the Big Woods Vegetation of Minnesota in the Mid-Nineteenth Century." *Ecological Monographs* 54, no. 3 (1984): 291–311.

———. "Trends and Palaeoecological Problems in the Vegetation and Climate History of the Northern Great Plains, U.S.A." *Biology and Environment: Proceedings of the Royal Irish Academy* 101B, no. 1–2 (2001): 47–64.

Grove, Alfred Thomas, and Oliver Rackham. *The Nature of Mediterranean Europe: An Ecological History.* 2nd ed. New Haven CT: Yale University Press, 2003.

Gürses, Ahmet, Metin Açikyildiz, Kübra Güneş, and M. Sadi Gürses. "Dyes and Pigments: Their Structure and Properties." In *Dyes and Pigments*, by Ahmet Gürses, Metin Açikyildiz, Kübra Güneş, and M. Gürses, 13–29. New York: Springer International, 2016.

Haas, Randall, James Watson, Tammy Buonasera, John Southon, Jennifer C. Chen, Sarah Noe, Kevin Smith, Carlos Viviano Llave, Jelmer Eerkens, and Glendon Parker. "Female Hunters of the Early Americas." *Science Advances* 6, no. 45 (2020): EABD0310. https://www.doi.org/10.1126/sciadv.abd0310.

Hall, Joan. "Gardening Nettle-Leaf Goosefoot: A Nutritious Edible Weed." Dengarden .com, June 21, 2021. https://dengarden.com/gardening/chenopodium-murale.

Halwas, Sara Jane. "Domesticating *Chenopodium*: Applying Genetic Techniques and Archaeological Data to Understanding Pre-Contact Plant Use in Southern Manitoba (AD 1000–1500)." PhD diss., University of Manitoba, 2017.

Hamilton, Paula, and Linda Shopes, eds. *Oral History and Public Memories.* Philadelphia: Temple University Press, 2009.

Hansen, David. "Natural Wild Rice in Minnesota." Minnesota Department of Natural Resources, 2008. https://www.leg.state.mn.us/docs/2008/mandated/080235.pdf.

Hansen, Emma I. "The Art of Tipi Living." In *Tipi: Heritage of the Great Plains*, edited by Nancy B. Rosoff and Susan Kennedy Zeller, 39–56. Seattle: University of Washington Press, 2011.

———. *Memory and Vision: Arts, Cultures, and Lives of Plains Indian Peoples.* Seattle: University of Washington Press, 2007.

Hanson, Michael A., Brandon S. Gaut, Adrian O. Stec, Susan I. Fuerstenberg, Major M. Goodman, Edward H. Coe, and John F. Doebley. "Evolution of Anthocyanin Biosynthesis in Maize Kernels: The Role of Regulatory and Enzymatic Loci." *Genetics* 143, no. 3 (1996): 1395–407.

Hanuta, Irene. "Mapping Pre-Settlement Landscape in Southern Manitoba, Canada." *Prairie Perspectives* 4 (October 2001): 299–315.

Harms, Vernon L. "Bur Oak—An Uncommon Native Tree in Saskatchewan." *Blue Jay* 60, no. 2 (2002). https://www.doi.org/10.29173/bluejay5683.

Harper, J. L., and J. White. "The Demography of Plants." *Annual Review of Ecology and Systematics* 5 (November 1974): 419–64.

Harrington, Mark Raymond. *The Ozark Bluff-Dwellers*. New York: Museum of the American Indian, Heye Foundation, 1960.

Hart, Jeffrey A. "The Ethnobotany of the Northern Cheyenne Indians of Montana." *Journal of Ethnopharmacology* 4, no. 1 (1981): 1–55.

Hart, John P. "Can *Cucurbita pepo* Gourd Seeds Be Made Edible?" *Journal of Archaeological Science* 31, no. 11 (2004): 1631–33.

Hassrick, Royal B. *The Sioux: Life and Customs of a Warrior Society*. Norman: University of Oklahoma Press, 2012.

Hastorf, C., and S. Archer. "Paleoethnobotany." In *Encyclopedia of Archaeology*, 1790–95. Amsterdam: Elsevier Science and Technology, 2008.

Hatt, Gudmund. "The Corn Mother in America and in Indonesia." *Anthropos* 46, no. 5–6 (1951): 853–914.

Hawkes, Kristen, James O'Connell, and Nicholas Blurton Jones. "Hunter-Gatherer Studies and Human Evolution: A Very Selective Review." *American Journal of Physical Anthropology* 165, no. 4 (2018): 777–800.

Hayden, Ferdinand Vandeveer. *Report of the United States Geological Survey of the Territories*. Vol. 7. Washington DC: Government Printing Office, 1878.

Heddinghaus, Thomas R., and Paul Sabol. "A Review of the Palmer Drought Severity Index and Where Do We Go from Here." In *Seventh Conference on Applied Climatology, September 10–13, 1991, Salt Lake City, Utah*, 242–46. Boston MA: American Meteorological Society, 1991.

Heinrich, Michael. "Ethnobotany and Natural Products: The Search for New Molecules, New Treatments of Old Diseases or a Better Understanding of Indigenous Cultures?" *Current Topics in Medicinal Chemistry* 3, no. 2 (2003): 141–54.

Heiser, Charles B. *Of Plants and People*. Norman: University of Oklahoma Press, 1985.

———. "The Sunflower among the North American Indians." *Proceedings of the American Philosophical Society* 95, no. 4 (1951): 432–48.

Hellborg, R., and G. Skog. "Accelerator Mass Spectrometry." *Mass Spectrometry Reviews* 27, no. 5 (2008): 398–427.

Hellson, J. C., and M. Gadd. *Ethnobotany of the Blackfoot Indians*. Ottawa: National Museum of Canada, 1974.

Henderson, N., E. Hogg, E. Barrow, and B. Dolter. *Climate Change Impacts on the Island Forests of the Great Plains and the Implications for Nature Conservation Policy: The Outlook for Sweet Grass Hills (Montana), Cypress Hills (Alberta–Saskatchewan), Moose Mountain (Saskatchewan), Spruce Woods (Manitoba) and Turtle Mountain (Manitoba–North Dakota)*. Saskatchewan: Prairie Adaptation and Research Collaborative, University of Regina, 2002.

Henderson, Norman. "Replicating Dog Travois Travel on the Northern Plains." *Plains Anthropologist* 39, no. 148 (1994): 145–59.

Henderson, Richard. "Oak Savanna Communities." In *Wisconsin's Biodiversity as a Management Issue: A Report to the Department of National Resources Managers*, edited by James Addis et al., 88–96. Madison: Wisconsin Department of Natural Resources, May 1995.

Heron, Francis. "Journal of Occurrences by Francis Heron Kept at Fort Garry, 1 January 1825 to 31 July 1826." B235/a/7, folios 32d–46. Hudson's Bay Company Archives, Winnipeg, Manitoba.

Hewes, Leslie. "The Northern Wet Prairie of the United States: Nature, Sources of Information, and Extent." *Annals of the Association of American Geographers* 41, no. 4 (1951): 307–23.

Hicks, Sheila, Heather Tinsley, Antti Huusko, Christin Jensen, Martina Hättestrand, Achilles Gerasimides, and Eliso Kvavadze. "Some Comments on Spatial Variation in Arboreal Pollen Deposition: First Records from the Pollen Monitoring Programme (PMP)." *Review of Palaeobotany and Palynology* 117, no. 1 (2001): 183–94.

Higgins, Kenneth F. "Evidence of the Historical Occurrence of Woody Plants in Areas of North Dakota Grasslands." In *Proceedings of the Ninth North American Prairie Conference*, edited by Gary K. Clambey and Richard H. Pemble, 115–17. Fargo ND and Moorhead MN: Tri-College University Center for Environmental Studies, 1986.

Hill, Matthew E., Jr. "Variation in Paleoindian Fauna Use on the Great Plains and Rocky Mountains of North America." *Quaternary International* 191, no. 1 (2008): 34–52.

Hill, Robert, and Derek Richter. "Anthraquinone Pigments in *Galium*." *Proceedings of the Royal Society of London*, Series B, Biological Sciences, 121, no. 825 (February 1937): 547–60.

Hind, Henry Youle. *Narrative of the Canadian Red River Exploring Expedition of 1857 and of the Assiniboine and Saskatchewan Exploring Expedition of 1858*. 2 vols. Edmonton: M. G. Hurtig, 1971. First published by Longman, Green (London), 1860.

Hitchcock, Albert Spear. *Manual of the Grasses of the United States*. Publication No. 200. 2nd ed. Washington DC: U.S. Department of Agriculture, 1950.

Hoadley, R. B. *Understanding Wood: A Craftsman's Guide to Wood Technology*. Newtown CT: Taunton Press, 1980.

Hoffman, Walter James. "The Menomini Indians." In *Annual Report of the Bureau of American Ethnology*. Vol. 14, part 1. Washington DC: Government Printing Office, 1896.

Hohman-Caine, Christy A., and E. Leigh Syms. "The Age of Brainerd Ceramics." In *Statewide Survey of Historical and Archaeological Sites*. Minnesota Historical Society, 2012. https://mn.gov/admin/assets/2012-The-Age-of-Brainerd-Ceramics_tcm36-187341.pdf.

Holland, Thomas D. "A Pilot Study in the Thermal Properties of Buffalo Chips." *Plains Anthropologist* 29, no. 104 (1984): 161–65.

Hollenbach, Kandace D. *Foraging in the Tennessee River Valley: 12,500 to 8,000 Years Ago*. Tuscaloosa: University of Alabama Press, 2009.

Hollenbach, Kandace D., and Stephen B. Carmody. "Agricultural Innovation and Dispersal in Eastern North America." In *Oxford Research Encyclopedia of Environmental Science*, February 25, 2019. https://oxfordre.com/environmentalscience.

Hollenbach, Kandace D., and Renee B. Walker. "Documenting Subsistence Change during the Pleistocene/Holocene Transition: Investigations of Paleoethnobotanical Zooarchaeological Data from Dust Cave, Alabama." In *Integrating Zooarchaeology and Paleoethnobotany*, edited by Amber VanDerwarker and Tanya M. Peres, 227–44. New York: Springer, 2010.

Holler, Clyde. *The Black Elk Reader*. Syracuse NY: Syracuse University Press, 2000.

Holm, Leroy G., Donald L. Plucknett, Juan V. Pancho, and James P. Herberger. *The World's Worst Weeds*. Honolulu: East-West Center, University Press of Hawaii, 1977.

Holman, Margaret B. "Historic Documents and Prehistoric Sugaring: A Matter of Cultural Context." *Midcontinental Journal of Archaeology* 11, no. 1 (1986): 125–31.

———. "The Identification of Late Woodland Maple Sugaring Sites in the Upper Great Lakes." *Midcontinental Journal of Archaeology* 9, no. 1 (1984): 63–89.

Homsey, Lara K., Renee B. Walker, and Kandace D. Hollenbach. "What's for Dinner? Investigating Food-Processing Technologies at Dust Cave, Alabama." *Southeastern Archaeology* 29, no. 1 (2010): 182–96.

Horton, Elizabeth Temple. "The Ties That Bind: Fabric Traditions and Fiber Use in the Ozark Plateau." PhD diss., Washington University, 2010.

Howard, James H. "Yanktonai Ethnohistory and the John K. Bear Winter Count." *Plains Anthropologist* 21, no. 73 (1976): 1–45.

Hoyt, C. A. "Pollen Signatures of the Arid to Humid Grasslands of North America." *Journal of Biogeography* 27, no. 3 (2000): 687–96.

Hu, Chaoyang, Quanlin Li, Xuefang Shen, Sheng Quan, Hong Lin, Lei Duan, Yifa Want, et al. "Characterization of Factors Underlying the Metabolic Shifts in Developing Kernels of Colored Maize." *Scientific Reports* 6 (October 2016): 35479. https://doi.org/10.1038/srep35479.

Hugenholtz, Chris H., and Stephen A. Wolfe. "Recent Stabilization of Active Sand Dunes on the Canadian Prairies and Relation to Recent Climate Variations." *Geomorphology* 68, no. 1–2 (2005): 131–47.

Hungry Wolf, Beverly. "Life in Harmony with Nature." In *Women of the First Nations: Power, Wisdom, and Strength,* edited by Christine Miller and Patricia Chuchryk, 77–82. Winnipeg: University of Manitoba Press, 1996.

Hunt, Melany L., and Nathalie M. Vriend. "Booming Sand Dunes." *Annual Review of Earth and Planetary Sciences* 38 (May 2010): 281–301.

Hussain, Abdullah I., Farooq Anwar, Poonam S. Nigam, Muhammad Ashraf, and Anwarul H. Gilani. "Seasonal Variation in Content, Chemical Composition and Antimicrobial and Cytotoxic Activities of Essential Oils from Four Mentha Species." *Journal of the Science of Food and Agriculture* 90, no. 11 (2010): 1827–36.

Hyde, George E. *Spotted Tail's Folk: A History of the Brulé Sioux.* 2nd ed. Norman: University of Oklahoma Press, 1974.

Irwin, Lee. *The Dream Seekers: Native American Visionary Traditions of the Great Plains.* Norman: University of Oklahoma Press, 1994.

Jackson, William Turrentine. *Wagon Roads West: A Study of Federal Road Surveys and Construction in the Trans-Mississippi West, 1846–1869.* Berkeley: University of California Press, 1952.

Jakes, Kathryn A., and Annette G. Ericksen. "Prehistoric Use of Sumac and Bedstraw as Dye Plants in Eastern North America." *Southeastern Archaeology* 20, no. 1 (2001): 56–66.

Jarman, H. N., A. J. Legge, and J. A. Charles. "Retrieval of Plant Remains from Archaeological Sites by Froth Flotation." In *Papers in Economic Prehistory,* edited by E. S. Higgs, 39–48. Cambridge: Cambridge University Press, 1972.

Jassbi, Amir Reza, Somayeh Zare, Mojtaba Asadollahi, and Meredith C. Schuman. "Ecological Roles and Biological Activities of Specialized Metabolites from the Genus *Nicotiana.*" *Chemical Reviews* 117, no. 19 (2017): 12227–80.

Jellen, Eric N., Bozena A. Kolano, Maria C. Sederberg, Alejandro Bonifacio, and Peter J. Maughan. "Chenopodium." In *Wild Crop Relatives: Genomic and Breeding Resources,* edited by Chittaranjan Kole, 35–61. Berlin: Springer-Verlag, 2011.

Jenks, Albert. "A Minnesota Kitchen Midden with Fossil Bison." *Science* 86, no. 2228 (September 10, 1937): 243–44.

Jennings, Carrie E. "Terrestrial Ice Streams—A View from the Lobe." *Geomorphology* 75, no. 1–2 (2006): 100–124.

Jetter, James J., Zhishi Guo, Jenia A. McBrian, and Michael R. Flynn. "Characterization of Emissions from Burning Incense." *Science of the Total Environment* 295, no. 1–3 (2002): 51–67.

Johnson, Elden. "Archaeological Evidence for Utilization of Wild Rice." *Science* 163, no. 3864 (January 17, 1969): 276–77.

———. "The Prehistory of the Red River Valley." *Minnesota History* 38, no. 4 (1962): 157–65.

Johnson, Elizabeth J. "The Role of Carotenoids in Human Health." *Nutrition in Clinical Care* 5, no. 2 (2002): 56–65.

Johnson, W. Carter, and Karen A. Poiani. "Climate Change Effects on Prairie Pothole Wetlands: Findings from a Twenty-Five-Year Numerical Modeling Project." *Wetlands* 36, no. 2 (2016): 273–85.

Johnston, Alex. "Blackfoot Indian Utilization of the Flora of the Northwestern Great Plains." *Economic Botany* 24, no. 3 (1970): 301–24.

Johnston, Basil. *Honour Earth Mother.* Lincoln: University of Nebraska Press, 2004.

———. *Ojibway Heritage.* Lincoln: University of Nebraska Press, 1990. Originally published by McClelland & Stewart (Toronto), 1976.

Jolie, Edward A. "The Technomechanics of Plains Indian Coiled Gambling Baskets." *Plains Anthropologist* 51, no. 197 (2006): 17–49.

Jones, David J. *A History of Nebraska's Fishery Resources.* Lincoln: Nebraska Game, Forestation and Parks Commission, 1963. https://digitalcommons.unl.edu/nebgamepubs/31.

Jones, Kevin T., and David B. Madsen. "Further Experiments in Native Food Procurement." *Utah Archaeology* 4, no. 1 (1991): 68–77.

Jones, Quentin, and F. R. Earle. "Chemical Analyses of Seeds II: Oil and Protein Content of 759 Species." *Economic Botany* 20, no. 2 (1966): 127–55.

Jones, Volney H. "The Vegetal Remains of Newt Kash Hollow Shelter." In *Rock Shelters in Menifee County, Kentucky,* edited by W. S. Webb and W. D. Funkhouser, 147–65. Lexington: University of Kentucky, 1936.

Kaiser, Patricia L. "The Lakota Sacred Pipe: Its Tribal Use and Religious Philosophy." *American Indian Culture and Research Journal* 8, no. 3 (1984): 1–26.

Kantrud, Harold A., and Wesley E. Newton. "A Test of Vegetation-Related Indicators of Wetland Quality in the Prairie Pothole Region." *Journal of Aquatic Ecosystem Health* 5, no. 3 (1996): 177–91.

Karoll, Amy B. "A Comparative Study of the Swennes Woven Nettle Bag and Weaving Techniques." *University of Wisconsin-LaCrosse Journal of Undergraduate Research* 12 (2009): 1–28.

Karp, Allison T., Anna K. Behrensmeyer, and Katherine H. Freeman. "Grassland Fire Ecology Has Roots in the Late Miocene." *Proceedings of the National Academy of Sciences* 115, no. 48 (2018): 12130–35.

Kates, Heather R., Pamela S. Soltis, and Douglas E. Soltis. "Evolutionary and Domestication History of Cucurbita (Pumpkin and Squash) Species Inferred from 44 Nuclear Loci." *Molecular Phylogenetics and Evolution* 111, no. 1 (2017): 98–109.

Katinas, Liliana, Jorge V. Crisci, Peter Hoch, Maria C. Tellería, and María J. Apodaca. "Trans-Oceanic Dispersal and Evolution of Early Composites (Asteraceae)." *Perspectives in Plant Ecology, Evolution and Systematics* 15, no. 5 (2013): 269–80.

Keating, William H. *Narrative of an Expedition to the Source of St. Peter's River, Lake Winnepeek, Lake of the Woods, etc., Performed in the Year 1823.* Minneapolis: Ross & Haines, 1959. First published by H. C. Carey & I. Lea (Philadelphia), 1824.

Kehew, Alan E. "Catastrophic Flood Hypothesis for the Origin of the Souris Spillway, Saskatchewan and North Dakota." *Geological Society of America Bulletin* 93, no. 10 (1982): 1051–58.

Kehew, Alan E., and Mark L. Lord. "Origin and Large-Scale Erosional Features of Glacial-Lake Spillways in the Northern Great Plains." *Geological Society of America Bulletin* 97, no. 2 (1986): 162–77.

Kehew, Alan E., and James T. Teller. "History of Late Glacial Runoff along the Southwestern Margin of the Laurentide Ice Sheet." *Quaternary Science Reviews* 13, no. 9–10 (1994): 859–77.

Kehoe, Thomas F. "Tipi Rings: The 'Direct Ethnological' Approach Applied to an Archeological Problem." *American Anthropologist* 60, no. 5 (1958): 861–73.

Kehoe, Thomas F., and Alice B. Kehoe. "Stones, Solstices, and Sun Dance Structures." *Plains Anthropologist* 22, no. 76 (1977): 85–95.

Kelly, Fanny. *My Captivity among the Sioux Indians.* Hartford CT: Mutual, 1871.

Kelly, Robert L., and David Hurst Thomas. *Archaeology: Down to Earth.* 4th ed. Boston: Cengage Learning, 2011.

Kennedy, M. S. *The Assiniboines.* Norman: University of Oklahoma Press, 1961.

Kiel, William H., Jr., Arthur S. Hawkins, and Nolan G. Perret. *Waterfowl Habitat Trends in the Aspen Parkland of Manitoba.* Canadian Wildlife Service, Report Series No. 18 (1972).

Kimmerer, Robin Wall. *Braiding Sweetgrass: Indigenous Wisdom, Scientific Knowledge and the Teachings of Plants.* Minneapolis: Milkweed Editions, 2013.

Kindscher, Kelly, ed. *Echinacea: Herbal Medicine with a Wild History.* New York: Springer, 2016.

————. *Edible Wild Plants of the Prairie: An Ethnobotanical Guide.* Lawrence: University Press of Kansas, 1987.

King, F. B., and R. W. Graham. "Effects of Ecological and Paleoecological Patterns in Subsistence and Paleoenvironmental Reconstructions." *American Antiquity* 46, no. 1 (1981): 128–42.

Kinsey, Joni L. "Art." In *Encyclopedia of the Great Plains*, edited by David J. Wishart, 103–10. Lincoln: University of Nebraska Press, 2004.

Kirschman, J. C., and R. L. Suber. "Recent Food Poisonings from Cucurbitacin in Traditionally Bred Squash." *Food and Chemical Toxicology* 27, no. 8 (1989): 555–56.

Kistler, Logan, Álvaro Montenegro, Bruce D. Smith, John A. Gifford, Richard E. Green, Lee A. Newsom, and Beth Shapiro. "Transoceanic Drift and the Domestication of African Bottle Gourds in the Americas." *Proceedings of the National Academy of Sciences* 111, no. 8 (Feb. 2014): 2937–41.

Kistler, Logan, Lee A. Newsom, Timothy M. Ryan, Andrew C. Clarke, Bruce D. Smith, and George Perry. "Gourds and Squashes (*Cucurbita* spp.) Adapted to Megafaunal Extinction and Ecological Anachronism through Domestication." *Proceedings of the National Academy of Sciences* 112, no. 49 (2015): 15107–12.

Kistler, Logan, and Beth Shapiro. "Ancient DNA Confirms a Local Origin of Domesticated Chenopod in Eastern North America." *Journal of Archaeological Science* 38, no. 12 (2011): 3549–54.

Klassen, R. W. "Quaternary Geology of the Southern Canadian Interior Plains." In *Quaternary Geology of Canada and Greenland*, edited by R. J. Fulton, 138–74. Ottawa: Geological Survey of Canada, 1989.

————. "Wisconsin Events and the Assiniboine and Qu'Appelle Valleys of Manitoba and Saskatchewan." *Canadian Journal of Earth Sciences* 9, no. 5 (1972): 544–60.

Klayman, D. L. "Qinghaosu (arteminsinin): An Antimalarial Drug from China." *Science* 228, no. 4703 (May 31, 1985): 1049–55.

Klein, Richard M. *The Green World: An Introduction to Plants and People.* New York: Harper and Row, 1987.

Kline, Michelle A., Robert Boyd, and Joseph Henrich. "Teaching and the Life History of Cultural Transmission in Fijian Villages." *Human Nature* 24, no. 4 (2013): 351–74.

Klug, Aaron. "The Discovery of the DNA Double Helix." *Journal of Molecular Biology* 335, no. 1 (2004): 3–26.

Kornfeld, Marcel, and Mary L. Larson. "Bonebeds and Other Myths: Paleoindian to Archaic Transition on North American Great Plains and Rocky Mountains." *Quaternary International* 191, no. 1 (2008): 18–33.

Kroker, Sid, Barry B. Greco, and Kate Peach. *1991 Investigations at Fort Gibraltar I: The Forks Public Archaeology Project*. Winnipeg MB: Forks Public Archaeological Association, 1992.

Krozser, Kit. "The Late Prehistoric Period at the Turn in Kingsway Park, Moose Jaw, Saskatchewan." Master's thesis, University of Saskatchewan, 1989.

Küchler, A. W. *Potential Natural Vegetation of the Conterminous United States*. New York: American Geographical Society, 1975.

Kuhnlein, H. V., and M. M. Humphries. "Traditional Animal Foods of Indigenous Peoples of Northern North America." Center for Indigenous Peoples' Nutrition and Environment, McGill University, 2017. http://traditionalanimalfoods.org/.

Kuhnlein, H. V., and N. J. Turner. *Traditional Plant Foods of Canadian Indigenous Peoples: Nutrition, Botany and Use*. Vol. 8. Philadelphia: Gordon and Breach Science, 1991.

Kunec, Diane L., and Jennifer M. Shay. *The Effects of Military Activity on Native Mixed-Grass Prairie C.F.B. Shilo: Supplementary Report, March, 1990*. Winnipeg: Department of Botany, University of Manitoba, 1990.

Lacey, Theresa Jensen. *The Pawnee*. New York: Infobase, 2009.

Ladd, Doug, and Frank Oberle. *Tallgrass Prairie Wildflowers: A Field Guide*. Helena MT: Falcon, 1995.

LaDuke, Winona. *Recovering the Sacred: The Power of Naming and Claiming*. Boston: South End Press, 2005.

———. "Ricekeepers." *Orion Magazine* 26, no. 4 (2007). https://orionmagazine.org/article/ricekeepers/.

Larson, Greger, Dolores R. Piperno, Robin G. Allaby, et al. "Current Perspectives and the Future of Domestication Studies." *Proceedings of the National Academy of Sciences* 111, no. 17 (2014): 6139–46.

Laubin, Reginald, and Gladys Laubin. *American Indian Archery*. Norman: University of Oklahoma Press, 1980.

———. *The Indian Tipi: Its History, Construction, and Use*. Norman: University of Oklahoma Press, 1957.

Laudan, Rachel. *Cuisine and Empire: Cooking in World History*. Berkeley: University of California Press, 2015.

———. "Pounding and Grinding." *Rachel Laudan: A Historian's Take on Food and Food Politics* (blog), November 22, 2009. https://www.rachellaudan.com/2009/11/pounding-and-grinding.html.

Lee, Gyoung-Ah, Anthony M. Davis, David G. Smith, and John H. McAndrews. "Identifying Fossil Wild Rice (*Zizania*) Pollen from Cootes Paradise, Ontario:

A New Approach Using Scanning Electron Microscopy." *Journal of Archaeological Science* 31, no. 4 (2004): 411–21.

Leichty, Reid J., Steven H. Emerman, Lyndon R. Hawkins, and Michael J. Tiano. "Pre-Settlement Vegetation at Casey's Paha State Preserve, Iowa." *Journal of the Iowa Academy of Science* 115, no. 1–4 (2008): 12–16.

Leith, Helmut. "Primary Productivity of the Major Vegetation Units of the World." In *Primary Productivity of the Biosphere*, edited by H. Leith and R. H. Whittaker, 203–15. New York: Springer-Verlag, 1975.

Lensink, Stephen C. "This Old Earthlodge Village: How Long Were Sites of the Middle Missouri Tradition Occupied?" In *Plains Earthlodges: Ethnographic and Archaeological Perspectives*, edited by Donna C. Roper and Elizabeth P. Pauls, 133–56. Tuscaloosa: University of Alabama Press, 2005.

Lentz, David L., Mary DeLand Pohl, José Luis Alvarado, Somayeh Tarighat, and Robert Bye. "Sunflower (*Helianthus annuus* L.) as a Pre-Columbian Domesticate in Mexico." *Proceedings of the National Academy of Sciences* 105, no. 17 (April 29, 2008): 6232–37.

Leopold, Aldo. *A Sand County Almanac: With Other Essays on Conservation from Round River*. New York: Ballantine Books, 1966. Originally published by Oxford University Press (New York), 1949.

Lev, Efraim, Mordechai E. Kislev, and Ofer Bar-Yosef. "Mousterian Vegetal Food in Kebara Cave, Mt. Carmel." *Journal of Archaeological Science* 32, no. 3 (2005): 475–84.

Lewis, Deborah Q. "Ada Hayden: Champion of Iowa Prairies." In *Proceedings of the 17th North American Prairie Conference*, edited by N. Berstein and L. J. Ostrander. Mason City: Northern Iowa Area Community College, 2001.

Lewis, Meriwether, and William Clark. *History of the Expedition under the Command of Captains Lewis and Clark*. Reissued ed. 4 vols. New York: Francis P. Harper, 1893.

Lewis, Walter H., and Memory P. F. Elvin-Lewis. *Medical Botany: Plants Affecting Man's Health*. Toronto: Wiley-Interscience, 1977.

Li, Wende, Arnold W. Hydamaka, Lynda Lowry, and Trust Beta. "Comparison of Antioxidant Capacity and Phenolic Compounds of Berries, Chokecherry and Seabuckthorn." *Central European Journal of Biology* 4, no. 4 (2009): 499–506.

Liberty, Margot. "The Northern Cheyenne Sun Dance and the Opening of the Sacred Medicine Hat 1959." *Plains Anthropologist* 12, no. 38 (1967): 367–85.

Linderman, Frank Bird. *Pretty-Shield, Medicine Woman of the Crows*. New York: John Day, 1972. Originally published as *Red Mother* by John Day (New York), 1932.

Lindgren, C. J., and K. De Smet. "Community Conservation Plan for the Southwestern Manitoba Mixed-Grass Prairie Important Bird Area." Canadian Nature

Federation, Bird Studies Canada, Bird Life International and Manitoba Naturalists Society, 2001.

Lints, Andrew. "Early Evidence of Maize (*Zea mays* ssp. *mays*) and Beans (*Phaseolus vulgaris*) on the Northern Plains: An Examination of Avonlea Cultural Materials (AD 300–1100)." Master's thesis, Lakehead University, 2013.

Liu, Yao, Jennifer A. Andersen, John W. Williams, and Stephen T. Jackson. "Vegetation History in Central Kentucky and Tennessee (USA) during the Last Glacial and Deglacial Periods." *Quaternary Research* 79, no. 2 (2013): 189–98.

Livingstone, Stephen J., and Chris D. Clark. "Morphological Properties of Tunnel Valleys of the Southern Sector of the Laurentide Ice Sheet and Implications for Their Formation." *Earth Surface Dynamics* 4 (July 2016): 567–89.

Lobo, Vijaya, Avinash Patil, A. Phatak, and Naresh Chandra. "Free Radicals, Antioxidants and Functional Foods: Impact on Human Health." *Pharmacognosy Reviews* 4, no. 8 (2010): 118–26.

Lockwood, Jeffrey A. "The Fate of the Rocky Mountain Locust, *Melanoplus spretus* Walsh: Implications for Conservation Biology." *Terrestrial Arthropod Reviews* 3, no. 2 (2010): 129–60.

———. "Voices from the Past: What We Can Learn from the Rocky Mountain Locust." *American Entomologist* 47, no. 4 (2001): 208–15.

Lockwood, Jeffrey A., Scott P. Schell, James K. Wangberg, Larry D. DeBrey, William G. DeBrey, and Charles R. Bomar. "Preserved Insects and Physical Condition of Grasshopper Glacier, Carbon County, Montana, USA." *Arctic and Alpine Research* 24, no. 3 (1992): 229–32.

Lopes-Lutz, Daíse, Daniela S. Alviano, Celuta S. Alviano, and Paul P. Kolodziejczyk. "Screening of Chemical Composition, Antimicrobial and Antioxidant Activities of *Artemisia* Essential Oils." *Phytochemistry* 69, no. 8 (2008): 1732–38.

Lorant, Anne, Sarah Pedersen, Irene Holst, Matthew B. Hufford, Klaus Winter, Dolores Piperno, and Jeffrey Ross-Ibarra. "The Potential Role of Genetic Assimilation during Maize Domestication." *PLOS One* 12, no. 9 (2017): e0184202. https://doi.org/10.1371/journal.pone.0184202.

Lowie, Robert H. *Indians of the Plains*. New York: McGraw-Hill, 1954.

———. *The Material Culture of the Crow Indians*. New York: American Museum of Natural History, 1922.

———. *The Tobacco Society of the Crow Indians*. New York: American Museum of Natural History, 1919.

Luckett, Hubert P. "PS What's News." *Popular Science* 214, no. 6 (1979): 71.

Lyford, Carrie A. *Ojibwa Crafts (Chippewa)*. Lawrence KS: Bureau of Indian Affairs, U.S. Department of the Interior, 1953.

Lyon, William S. *Encyclopedia of Native American Healing*. New York: Norton, 1996.

Maestas, Lauren P., and Hugh B. Britten. "Flea and Small Mammal Species Composition in Mixed-Grass Prairies: Implications for the Maintenance of *Yersinia pestis*." *Vector-Borne and Zoonotic Diseases* 17, no. 7 (2017): 467–74.

Magilligan, Francis J., E. M. Buraas, and C. E. Renshaw. "The Efficacy of Stream Power and Flow Duration on Geomorphic Responses to Catastrophic Flooding." *Geomorphology* 228 (January 2015): 175–88.

Mails, Thomas E. *The Mystic Warriors of the Plains*. New York: Marlowe, 1995.

Malainey, M. E., R. Przybylski, and B. L. Sherriff. "Identifying the Former Contents of Late Precontact Period Pottery Vessels from Western Canada Using Gas Chromatography." *Journal of Archaeological Science* 26, no. 4 (1999): 425–38.

Mandelbaum, David G. *The Plains Cree: An Ethnographic, Historical and Comparative Study*. Regina SK: University of Regina Press, 1979. Originally published as vol. 37, part 2, Anthropological Papers of the American Museum of Natural History (New York), 1940.

Margold, Martin, Chris R. Stokes, and Chris D. Clark. "Ice Streams in the Laurentide Ice Sheet: Identification, Characteristics and Comparison to Modern Ice Sheets." *Earth-Science Reviews* 143 (April 2015): 117–46.

Marshall, John, and R. Alan Plumb. *Atmosphere, Ocean, and Climate Dynamics: An Introductory Text*. Cambridge MA: Academic Press, 2016.

Martkoplishvili, Inga, and Eliso Kvavadze. "Some Popular Medicinal Plants and Diseases of the Upper Palaeolithic in Western Georgia." *Journal of Ethnopharmacology* 166, no. 1 (2015): 42–52.

Marzano, Mariella, and Norman Dandy. "Recreationist Behaviour in Forests and the Disturbance of Wildlife." *Biodiversity and Conservation* 21, no. 11 (2012): 2967–86.

Mason, Carol I. "Maple Sugaring Again; or the Dog That Did Nothing in the Night." *Canadian Journal of Archaeology* 11 (1987): 99–107.

———. "Prehistoric Maple Sugaring: A Sticky Subject." *North American Archaeologist* 7, no. 4 (1987): 305–11.

Mason, Christopher F. *Decomposition*. London: Edward Arnold, 1977.

Mason, Sarah L. R., Jon G. Hather, and Gordon C. Hillman. "Preliminary Investigation of the Plant Macro-Remains from Dolní Věstonice II, and Its Implications for the Role of Plant Foods in Palaeolithic and Mesolithic Europe." *Antiquity* 68, no. 258 (1994): 48–57.

Mather, Katelyn R. "Situating the Pot and Potter: Ceramic Production and Use at the Silvercreek Sites, Two Early-Late Woodland Sites in Elgin County, Ontario." Master's thesis, University of Western Ontario, 2015.

Mazza, G. "Compositional and Functional Properties of Saskatoon Berry and Blueberry." *International Journal of Fruit Science* 5, no. 3 (2008): 101–20.

McAndrews, John H. "Holocene Environment of a Fossil Bison from Kenora, Ontario." *Ontario Archaeology* 37 (1982): 41–51.

McCune, Letitia M., and Timothy Johns. "Antioxidant Activity in Medicinal Plants Associated with the Symptoms of Diabetes Mellitus Used by the Indigenous Peoples of the North American Boreal Forest." *Journal of Ethnopharmacology* 82, no. 2–3 (2002): 197–205.

McKay, S. P., D. Meslemani, R. J. Stachler, and J. H. Krouse. "Intradermal Positivity after Negative Prick Testing for Inhalants." *Otolaryngology–Head and Neck Surgery* 135, no. 2 (2006): 232–35.

McKern, W. C. "A Hopewell Type of Culture in Wisconsin." *American Antiquities* 31, no. 2 (1929): 307–12.

———. "A Wisconsin Variant of the Hopewell Culture." *Bulletin of the Public Museum of the City of Milwaukee* 10, no. 2 (1931): 185–328.

McKusick, Marshall. "Reconstructing the Longhouse Village Settlement Patterns." *Plains Anthropologist* 19, no. 65 (1974): 197–210.

McLeod, Sheldon. *The Sands of the Assiniboine Delta: A Visitor's Guide.* Winnipeg MB: printed by the author, 2019.

McNab, W. Henry, and Peter E. Avers. "Eastern Broadleaf Forest (Oceanic)." In *Ecological Subregions of the United States, Section Descriptions*, chap. 16. Washington DC: National Forest Service, U.S. Department of Agriculture, 1994.

Messner, Timothy C. *Acorns and Bitter Roots: Starch Grain Research in the Prehistoric Eastern Woodlands.* Tuscaloosa: University of Alabama Press, 2011.

Metcalf, Fay. "Knife River: Early Village Life on the Plains." *OAH Magazine of History* 9, no. 1 (1994): 34–47.

Meyer, David, and Dale Russell. "'Through the Woods Whare Thare Ware Now Track Ways': Kelsey, Henday and Trails in East Central Saskatchewan." *Canadian Journal of Archaeology* 31, no. 3 (2007): 163–97.

Milburn, Michael P. "Indigenous Nutrition: Using Traditional Food Knowledge to Solve Contemporary Health Problems." *American Indian Quarterly* 28, no. 3–4 (2004): 411–34.

Miller, D. S. *From Colonization to Domestication: Population, Environment, and the Origins of Agriculture in Eastern North America.* Salt Lake City: University of Utah Press, 2018.

Millett, Bruce, W. Carter Johnson, and Glenn Guntenspergen. "Climate Trends of the North American Prairie Pothole Region 1906–2000." *Climatic Change* 93, no. 1–2 (2009): 243–67.

Misra, Mahendra K., Kenneth W. Ragland, and Andrew J. Baker. "Wood Ash Composition as a Function of Furnace Temperature." *Biomass and Bioenergy* 4, no. 2 (1993): 103–16.

Mock, Cary J. "Rainfall in the Garden of the United States Great Plains, 1870–1889." *Climatic Change* 44, no. 1–2 (2000): 173–95.

Moeller, D. A., and B. A. Schaal. "Genetic Relationships among Native American Maize Accessions of the Great Plains Assessed by RAPDS." *Theoretical and Applied Genetics* 99, no. 6 (1999): 1061–67.

Moerman, Daniel E. "Native American Ethnobotany: A Database of Foods, Drugs, Dyes and Fibers of Native American Peoples, Derived from Plants." http://naeb.brit.org.

———. *Native American Ethnobotany.* Portland OR: Timber Press, 1998.

Monaghan, G. William, William A. Lovis, and Kathryn C. Egan-Bruhy. "Earliest Cucurbita from the Great Lakes, Northern USA." *Quaternary Research* 65, no. 2 (2006): 216–22.

Morgan, George Robert, and Ronald R. Weedon. "Oglala Sioux Use of Medical Herbs." *Great Plains Quarterly* 10 (Winter 1990): 18–35.

Morton, W. L. *Manitoba: A History.* Toronto: University of Toronto Press, 1967.

Moyle, John B. "Wild Rice in Minnesota." *Journal of Wildlife Management* 8, no. 3 (1944): 177–84.

Mueller, Natalie G. "An Extinct Domesticated Subspecies of Erect Knotweed in Eastern North America: *Polygonum erectum* subsp. *watsoniae* (Polygonaceae)." *Novon: A Journal for Botanical Nomenclature* 25, no. 2 (2017): 166–80.

———. *Mound Centers and Seed Security: A Comparative Analysis of Botanical Assemblages from Middle Woodland Sites in the Lower Illinois Valley.* New York: Springer, 2013.

———. "Seeds as Artifacts of Communities of Practice: The Domestication of Erect Knotweed in Eastern North America." PhD diss., Washington University, 2017.

Mueller, Natalie G., Gayle J. Fritz, Paul Patton, Stephen Carmody, and Elizabeth T. Horton. "Growing the Lost Crops of Eastern North America's Original Agricultural System." *Nature Plants* 3, no. 7 (2017): 1–5.

Muhs, Daniel R., and E. Arthur Bettis. "Geochemical Variations in Peoria Loess of Western Iowa Indicate Paleowinds of Midcontinental North America during Last Glaciation." *Quaternary Research* 53, no. 1 (2000): 49–61.

Muhs, Daniel R., E. Arthur Bettis, J. Been, and J. P. McGeehin. "Impact of Climate and Parent Material on Chemical Weathering in Loess-Derived Soils of the Mississippi River Valley." *Soil Science Society of America Journal* 65 (November–December 2001): 1761–77.

Muller, Richard A. "Radioisotope Dating with a Cyclotron." *Science* 196, no. 4289 (1977): 489–94.

Mullins, E. J., and T. S. McKnight, eds. *Canadian Woods: Their Properties and Uses.* 3rd ed. Toronto: University of Toronto Press, 1981.

Munson, Patrick J. "Contributions to Osage and Lakota Ethnobotany." *Plains Anthropologist* 26, no. 93 (1981): 229–40.

Munson-Scullin, Wendy, and Michael Scullin. "Potential Productivity of Midwestern Native American Gardens." *Plains Anthropologist* 50, no. 193 (2005): 9–21.

Murphy, A., and John H. Ehrenreich. "Fruit-Producing Trees and Shrubs in Missouri's Ozark Forests." *Journal of Wildlife Management* 29, no. 3 (1965): 497–503.

Murphy, Robert K., Richard A. Sweitzer, and John D. Albertson. "Occurrences of Small Mammal Species in a Mixedgrass Prairie in Northwestern North Dakota." *Prairie Naturalist* 39, no. 2 (2007): 91–95.

Mushet, David M., and Ned H. Euliss Jr. "The Cottonwood Lake Study Area, a Long-Term Wetland Ecosystem Monitoring Site." U.S. Geological Survey Fact Sheet 2012-3040, 2012.

Mutel, Cornelia F. *Fragile Giants: A Natural History of the Loess Hills.* Iowa City: University of Iowa Press, 1989.

Nabhan, Gary Paul. *Gathering the Desert.* Tucson: University of Arizona Press, 1985.

———. "Restoring and Re-storying the Landscape." *Ecological Restoration* 9, no. 1 (1991): 3–4.

Nadasdy, Paul. "Transcending the Debate over the Ecologically Noble Indian: Indigenous Peoples and Environmentalism." *Ethnohistory* 52, no. 2 (2005): 291–331.

Nansen, Fridtjof. *Farthest North: Being the Record of a Voyage of Exploration of the Ship "Fram" 1893–96 and of a Fifteen Months' Sleigh Journey.* New York: Harper & Brothers, 1897.

National Center for Complementary and Integrative Health. "Antioxidants: In-Depth." National Institutes of Health, U.S. Department of Health and Human Services, update of November 2013. https://nccih.nih.gov/health/antioxidants.

National Museum of the American Indian. *The Language of Native American Baskets from the Weaver's View*. Washington DC: Smithsonian Institution, 2003.

Neff, Laura. "Types of Corn." *Native Seeds/SEARCH* (blog), June 12, 2018. Accessed October 1, 2021. https://www.nativeseeds.org/blogs/blog-news/types-of-corn#.

Nelson, John C., Richard E. Sparks, Lynne DeHaan, and Larry Robinson. "Presettlement and Contemporary Vegetation Patterns along Two Navigational Reaches of the Upper Mississippi River." In *Perspectives on the Land-Use History of North America: A Context for Understanding Our Changing Environment*, 51–60. Washington DC: U.S. Geological Survey, Biological Resources Division, 1998.

Nelson, Paul. *St. Paul's Indian Burial Grounds*. St. Paul MN: Macalester College Institute for Global Citizenship, 2008.

Newbrey, Michael G., and Allan C. Ashworth. "A Fossil Record of Colonization and Response of Lacustrine Fish Populations to Climate Change." *Canadian Journal of Fisheries and Aquatic Sciences* 61, no. 10 (2004): 1807–16.

Nicholson, Beverley A., David Meyer, Sylvia Nicholson, and Scott Hamilton. "The Function of Ice-Gliders and Their Distribution in Time and Space across the Northern Plains and Parklands." *Plains Anthropologist* 48, no. 186 (2003): 121–31.

Nickel, Robert K. "Cultigens and Cultural Traditions in the Middle Missouri." In *Plains Village Archaeology: Bison Hunting Farmers in the Central and Northern Plains*, edited by Stanley A. Ahler and Marvin Kay, 126–36. Salt Lake City: University of Utah Press, 2007.

Noyce, Karen V., and Pamela L. Coy. "Abundance and Productivity of Bear Food Species in Different Forest Types of Northcentral Minnesota." In *Bears: Their Biology and Management*. 8 (1990): 169–81. https://www.doi.org/10.2307/3872917.

Obomsawin, Raymond. *Traditional Medicine for Canada's First Peoples*. Ottawa: National Aboriginal Health Organization, 2007.

O'Brien, Patricia J. "Astronomy." In *Encyclopedia of the Great Plains*, edited by D. J. Wishart. Lincoln: University of Nebraska, 2011. http://plainshumanities.unl.edu/encyclopedia/.

Office of the State Archaeologist. "House Types." In *Maps, Material Culture, and Memory: On the Trail of the Ioway*. Iowa City: University of Iowa, 2007.

Osborn, Alan J. "Adaptive Responses of Paleoindians to Cold Stress on the Periglacial Northern Great Plains." In *Hunters and Gatherers in Theory and Archaeology*, edited by George M. Crothers, 10–47. Carbondale: Southern Illinois University Press, 2004.

Östlund, Lars, Lisa Ahlberg, Olle Zackrisson, Ingela Bergman, and Steve Arno. "Bark-Peeling, Food Stress and Tree Spirits: The Use of Pine Inner Bark for Food in Scandinavia and North America." *Journal of Ethnobiology* 29, no. 1 (2009): 94–112.

Padosch, Stephan A., Dirk W. Lachenmeier, and Lars U. Kröner. "Absinthism: A Fictitious 19th Century Syndrome with Present Impact." *Substance Abuse Treatment, Prevention, and Policy* 1, no. 1 (2006): 1–14.

Paget, Amelia M., and Duncan Campbell Scott. *The People of the Plains.* Toronto: W. Briggs, 1909.

Palmer, Jessica Dawn. *The Dakota Peoples: A History of the Dakota, Lakota and Nakota through 1863.* Jefferson NC: McFarland, 2011.

Panshin, Alexis John, C. de Zeeuw, and Harry Philip Brown. *Textbook of Wood Technology: Structure, Identification, Uses, and Properties of the Commercial Woods of the United States and Canada.* Vol. 1. New York: McGraw-Hill, 1970.

Parciak, Wendy. "Environmental Variation in Seed Number, Size, and Dispersal of a Fleshy-Fruited Plant." *Ecology* 83, no. 3 (2002): 780–93.

———. "Seed Size, Number, and Habitat of a Fleshy-Fruited Plant: Consequences for Seedling Establishment." *Ecology* 83, no. 3 (2002): 794–808.

Parks, Douglas R., ed. *Myths and Traditions of the Arikara Indians.* Lincoln: University of Nebraska Press, 1991.

Partap, Tej, and Promila Kapoor. "The Himalayan Grain Chenopods: I. Distribution and Ethnobotany." *Agriculture, Ecosystems and Environment* 14, no. 3–4 (1985): 185–99.

Passey, Howard B., Vern K. Hugie, E. W. Williams, and D. E. Ball. *Relationships between Soil, Plant Community, and Climate on Rangelands of the Intermountain West.* Technical Bulletin No. 1669. Washington DC: U.S. Department of Agriculture, 1982.

Passmore, R., and J. V. G. A. Durnin. "Human Energy Expenditure." *Physiological Reviews* 35, no. 4 (1955): 801–40.

Patel, Seema. "Nutrition, Safety, Market Status Quo Appraisal of Emerging Functional Food Corn Smut (Huitlacoche)." *Trends in Food Science and Technology* 57, part A (November 2016): 93–102.

Patterson, Carrie J. "Southern Laurentide Ice Lobes Were Created by Ice Streams: Des Moines Lobe in Minnesota, USA." *Sedimentary Geology* 111, no. 1–4 (1997): 249–61.

Patton, Paul E. "People, Places, and Plants: An Appraisal of Subsistence, Technology and Sedentism in the Eastern Woodlands." PhD diss., Ohio State University, 2013.

Patton, Paul E., and Sabrina Curran. "Archaic Period Domesticated Plants in the Mid-Ohio Valley: Archaeobotanical Remains from the County Home Site (33at40),

Southeastern Ohio." *Midcontinental Journal of Archaeology* 41, no. 2 (2016): 127–58. https//www.doi.org/10.1080/01461109.2016.1153180.

Peach, K. "Ph.D. Abstract: Faunal Exploitation at the Forks; 3000 BP to 1860 AD." *Canadian Zooarchaeology* 14 (Autumn 1998): 3–4.

Pearl, Jessie K., John R. Keck, William Tintor, Liliana Siekacz, Hannah M. Herrick, Matthew D. Meko, and Charlotte L. Pearson. "New Frontiers in Tree-Ring Research." *The Holocene* 30, no. 6 (2020): 923–41.

Peat, F. David. *Blackfoot Physics*. Boston: Weiser Books, 2005.

Pehrsson, Pamela, Angela Scheet, Katherine Phillips, Kristine Patterson, and Henry Lukaski. "Carotenoids and Folate Vitamers in Indigenous Plants Consumed by Northern Plains American Indians." *FASEB Journal* 25, no. 1 (2011): supplement 609.5.

Penman, Sarah, ed. *Honor the Grandmothers: Dakota and Lakota Women Tell Their Stories*. St. Paul: Minnesota Historical Society Press, 2000.

Perrot, Nicolas, Morrell Marston, and Thomas Forsyth. *The Indian Tribes of the Upper Mississippi Valley and Region of the Great Lakes as Described by Nicolas Perrot*. Translated by Emma Helen Blair. Vol. 1. Cleveland: Arthur H. Clark, 1911.

Petersen, James B. *A Most Indispensable Art: Native Fiber Industries from Eastern North America*. Knoxville: University of Tennessee Press, 1996.

Peterson, E. B., and N. M. Peterson. *Ecology, Management and Use of Aspen and Balsam Poplar in the Prairie Provinces: Northwest Region Special Report 1*. Edmonton AB: Northern Forestry Centre, 1992.

Pettipas, Leo F. "Introducing Manitoba Prehistory." In *Papers in Manitoba Archaeology, Popular Series 4*, edited by Leo F. Pettipas. Winnipeg: Manitoba Department of Cultural Affairs and Historical Resources, 1983.

Phillips, Katherine M., Pamela R. Pehrsson, Wanda W. Agnew, Angela J. Scheett, Jennifer R. Follett, Henry C. Lukaski, and Kristine Y. Patterson. "Nutrient Composition of Selected Traditional United States Northern Plains Native American Plant Foods." *Journal of Food Composition and Analysis* 34, no. 2 (2014): 136–52.

Pierpoint, W. S. "The Natural History of Salicylic Acid Plant Product and Mammalian Medicine." *Interdisciplinary Science Reviews* 22, no. 1 (1997): 45–52.

Pinter, Nicholas, Stuart Fiedel, and Jon E. Keeley. "Fire and Vegetation Shifts in the Americas at the Vanguard of Paleoindian Migration." *Quaternary Science Reviews* 30, no. 3–4 (2011): 269–72.

Piperno, Dolores R. *Phytoliths: A Comprehensive Guide for Archaeologists and Paleoecologists*. Lanham MD: Altamira Press, 2006.

Piperno, Dolores R., and Kent V. Flannery. "The Earliest Archaeological Maize (*Zea mays* L.) from Highland Mexico: New Accelerator Mass Spectrometry Dates and Their Implications." *Proceedings of the National Academy of Sciences* 98, no. 4 (2001): 2101–3.

Podolskiy, Evgeny A., and Fabian Walter. "Cryoseismology." *Reviews of Geophysics* 54, no. 4 (2016): 708–58.

Pollan, Michael. *The Botany of Desire: A Plant's-Eye View of the World*. New York: Random House, 2001.

Polo, Marco. *The Travels of Marco Polo the Venetian*. New York: Dutton, 1908.

Pomerleau, Ovide F. "Nicotine and the Central Nervous System: Biobehavioral Effects of Cigarette Smoking." *American Journal of Medicine* 93, no. 1 (1992): S2–S7.

Postma, Johannes A., and Jonathan P. Lynch. "Complementarity in Root Architecture for Nutrient Uptake in Ancient Maize/Bean and Maize/Bean/Squash Polycultures." *Annals of Botany* 110, no. 2 (2012): 521–34.

Prasanna, B. M. "Diversity in Global Maize Germplasm: Characterization and Utilization." *Journal of Biosciences* 37, no. 5 (2012): 843–55.

Pybus, Nani Suzette. "Whirlwind Woman: Native American Tornado Mythology and Global Parallels." PhD diss., Oklahoma State University, 2009.

Quimby, George. "The Possibility of an Independent Agricultural Complex in the Southeastern United States." In *Human Origins: An Introductory General Course in Anthropology; Selected Readings, Series 31*, 206–10. Chicago: University of Chicago Press, 1946.

Rasse, Daniel P., Cornelia Rumpel, and Marie-France Dignac. "Is Soil Carbon Mostly Root Carbon? Mechanisms for a Specific Stabilisation." *Plant and Soil* 269, no. 1–2 (2005): 341–56.

Red Shirt, Delphine, and Lone Woman. *Turtle Lung Woman's Granddaughter*. Lincoln: University of Nebraska Press, 2002.

Redekop, Bill. *Lake Agassiz: The Rise and Demise of the World's Greatest Lake*. Winnipeg MB: Heartland Associates, 2017.

Reidhead, Van A. *A Linear Programming Model of Prehistoric Subsistence Optimization: A Southeastern Indiana Example*. Indianapolis: Indiana Historical Society, 1981.

Rhindos, David. *The Origins of Agriculture: An Evolutionary Perspective*. Cambridge MA: Academic Press, 1984.

Rice, Prudence M. "On the Origins of Pottery." *Journal of Archaeological Method and Theory* 6, no. 1 (1999): 1–54.

Rickman, Douglas L., Wayne Greensky, M. Z. Al-Hamdan, M. G. Estes, W. L. Crosson, and Sue M. Estes. "Spatial and Temporal Analyses of Environmental Affects [*sic*] on *Zizania palustris* and Its Natural Cycles." NASA STI Technical Memorandum, October 2017.

Riggs, Rev. S. R. *Mary and I, or Forty Years with the Sioux.* Williamstown MA: Corner House, 1971. Originally published by W. G. Holmes (Chicago), 1880.

Riley, Thomas J., Richard Edging, Jack Rossen, George F. Carter, Gregory Knapp, Michael J. O'Brien, and Karl H. Scherwin. "Cultigens in Prehistoric Eastern North America: Changing Paradigms [with comments and replies]." *Current Anthropology* 31, no. 5 (1990): 525–41.

Ripple, William J., and Robert L. Beschta. "Hardwood Tree Decline Following Large Carnivore Loss on the Great Plains, USA." *Frontiers in Ecology and the Environment* 5, no. 5 (2007): 241–46.

Risch, Barbara. "A Grammar of Time: Lakota Winter Counts, 1700–1900." *American Indian Culture and Research Journal* 24, no. 2 (2000): 23–48.

Ritchie, J. C. "The Late-Quaternary Vegetational History of the Western Interior of Canada." *Canadian Journal of Botany* 54, no. 15 (1976): 1793–1818.

———. "The Vegetation of Northern Manitoba[:] V. Establishing the Major Zonation." *Arctic* 13, no. 4 (1960): 209–29.

Roberts, Neil. *The Holocene: An Environmental History.* New York: John Wiley & Sons, 2013.

Rondon, Marco A., Johannes Lehmann, Juan Ramírez, and Maria Hurtado. "Biological Nitrogen Fixation by Common Beans (*Phaseolus vulgaris* L.) Increases with Bio-Char Additions." *Biology and Fertility of Soils* 43, no. 6 (2007): 699–708.

Roos, Christopher I., and Kevin C. Nolan. "Phosphates, Plowzones, and Plazas: A Minimally Invasive Approach to Settlement Structure of Plowed Village Sites." *Journal of Archaeological Science* 39, no. 1 (2012): 23–32.

Roper, Donna C., and Elizabeth P. Pauls, eds. *Plains Earthlodges: Ethnographic and Archaeological Perspectives.* Tuscaloosa: University of Alabama Press, 2005.

Ross, Alexander. "Red River Flood—1826." *Manitoba Pageant* 11, no. 3 (1966). http://www.mhs.mb.ca/docs/pageant/11/redriverflood1826.shtml.

Ross, Robert J. *Wood Handbook: Wood as an Engineering Material.* General Technical Report FPL-GTR-190. Madison WI: U.S. Department of Agriculture, Forest Service, Forest Products Laboratory, 2010.

Roth, Barbara J. "The Role of Gender in the Adoption of Agriculture in the Southern Southwest." *Journal of Anthropological Research* 62, no. 4 (2006): 513–38.

Roufs, Timothy G. *When Everybody Called Me Gabe-bines, "Forever-Flying-Bird": Teachings from Paul Buffalo.* Vol. 1. Duluth: University of Minnesota, 2014. https://www.d.umn.edu/cla/faculty/troufs/Buffalo/pbwww.html.

Rowe, John Stanley. *Forest Regions of Canada*. Ottawa: Fisheries and Environment Canada, Canadian Forest Service, 1972.

Ruelle, Morgan. "Plants and Foodways of the Standing Rock Nation: Diversity, Knowledge, and Sovereignty." Master's thesis, Cornell University, 2011.

Ruiz Corral, José Ariel, Noé Durán Puga, José de Jesús Sánchez González, José Ron Parra, Diego Raymundo Gonzalez Eguiarte, J. B. Holland, and Guillermo Medina García. "Climatic Adaptation and Ecological Descriptors of 42 Mexican Maize Races." *Crop Science* 48, no. 4 (2008): 1502–12.

Rybak, Christopher J., Carol Lakota Eastin, and Irma Robbins. "Native American Healing Practices and Counseling." *Journal of Humanistic Counseling* 43, no. 1 (2004): 25–32.

Rychlo, Jennifer. "The Camp Rayner Site: Terminal/Late Paleoindian and Early Middle Period Transitions on the Northern Plains." Master's thesis, University of Saskatchewan, 2016.

Saboe-Wounded Head, Lorna, and Gabrielle Tiomanipi. "Drying Chokecherries." South Dakota State University, Extension Extra Archives, 2007. https://openprairie .sdstate.edu/extension_extra/486/.

Saitoh, Fumiyo, Masana Noma, and Nobumaro Kawashima. "The Alkaloid Contents of Sixty *Nicotiana* Species." *Phytochemistry* 24, no. 3 (1985): 477–80.

Savinelli, Alfred. *Plants of Power: Native American Ceremony and the Use of Sacred Plants*. Summertown TN: Native Voices, 2002.

Sayers, June, Robert Thompson, and Rob Lusteck. "Phytoliths from Food Residues Provide the Oldest Date for Use of Wild Rice in Minnesota." Paper presented at annual meeting of the Geological Society of America, Minneapolis, October 2011.

Sayre, Matthew P. "Chronicling Indigenous Accounts of the 'Rise of Agriculture' in the Americas." In *Rethinking Agriculture: Archaeological and Ethnoarchaeological Perspectives*, edited by Timothy P. Denham, José Iriarte, and Luc Vrydaghs, 231–40. New York: Routledge, 2016.

Schaefer, Kimberly A. "Prehistoric Subsistence on the Coast of North Carolina: An Archaeobotanical Study." PhD diss., University of North Carolina at Chapel Hill, 2011.

Schaetzl, Randall, and Sharon Anderson. *Soils: Genesis and Geomorphology*. Cambridge: Cambridge University Press, 2005.

Schambach, Frank F. 1999. "Spiro and the Tunica: A New Interpretation of the Role of the Tunica in the Culture History of the Southeast and the Southern Plains, AD 1100–1750." In *Arkansas Archaeology: Essays in Honor of Dan and Phyllis Morse*, edited by Robert C. Mainfort Jr. and Marvin D. Jeter, 169–224. Fayetteville: University of Arkansas Press, 1999.

Schauss, Alexander G. "Emerging Knowledge of the Bioactivity of Foods in the Diets of Indigenous North Americans." In *Bioactive Foods in Promoting Health–Fruits and Vegetables,* 71–84. Cambridge MA: Academic Press, 2010.

Schmid, Magdalena Maria E. "Archaeological Applications of Radiocarbon Chronologies and Statistical Models: Dating the Viking Age Settlement of Iceland (Landnám)." PhD diss., University of Iceland, 2018.

Schneider, Fred. "Corn in the Crib Is Like Money in the Bank: George F. Will and the Oscar H. Will & Company, 1917–1955." *North Dakota History* 76, no. 1–2 (2009): 2–25.

———. "Prehistoric Horticulture in the Northeastern Plains." *Plains Anthropologist* 47, no. 180 (2002): 33–50.

Schneider, Fred E., and Mary Jane Schneider. "Sunflowers and Native Americans of North Dakota." *South Dakota Archaeology* 19–20 (1996): 142–53.

Schneider, Mary Jane. "An Investigation into the Origin of Arikara, Hidatsa, and Mandan Twilled Basketry." *Plains Anthropologist* 29, no. 106 (1984): 265–76.

———. "Native American Traditional Art." In *Encyclopedia of the Great Plains,* edited by David J. Wishart. Lincoln: University of Nebraska Press, 2011. http:// plainshumanities.unl.edu/encyclopedia/.

———. "Plains Indian Basketry." In *The Art of Native Basketry: A Living Legacy,* edited by Frank W. Porter III, 109–34. Westport CT: Greenwood Press, 1990.

———. "Regional Differences in Plains Indian Painting." *Great Plains Quarterly* 2, no. 3 (1982): 131–45.

Scott, Douglas D., Thomas D. Thiessen, Jeffrey J. Richner, and Scott Stadler. *An Archeological Inventory and Overview of Pipestone National Monument, Minnesota.* Lincoln NE: U.S. Department of the Interior, National Park Service, Midwest Archeological Center, 2006.

Scully, B. T., and D. H. Wallace. "Variation in and Relationship of Biomass, Growth Rate, Harvest Index, and Phenology to Yield of Common Bean." *Journal of the American Society for Horticultural Science* 115, no. 2 (1990): 218–25.

Seager, Richard, and Martin Hoerling. "Atmosphere and Ocean Origins of North American Droughts." *Journal of Climate* 27, no. 12 (2014): 4581–606.

Seeram, Navindra P. "Berry Fruits: Compositional Elements, Biochemical Activities, and the Impact of Their Intake on Human Health, Performance, and Disease." *Journal of Agricultural and Food Chemistry* 56, no. 3 (2008): 627–29.

Shay, C. T. *Itasca Bison Kill Site: An Ecological Analysis.* St. Paul: Minnesota Historical Society, 1971.

———. "Medicinal Plant Remains from Archaeological Sites in Southern Manitoba and Adjacent Areas." In *Painting the Past with a Broad Brush*, edited by David L. Keenlyside and Jean-Luc Pilon, 425–71. Ottawa: Canadian Museum of Civilization, 2009.

———. "Perspectives on the Late Prehistory of the Northern Plains." In *The Woodland Tradition on the Western Great Lakes: Papers Presented in Honor of Elden Johnson*, edited by Guy E. Gibbon, 113–33. Minneapolis: University of Minnesota Publications in Anthropology, 1990.

———. "Pioneers on the Forest Fringe: The Wood Economy of the Red River Settlement, 1812–1883." *Manitoba History* 78 (Summer 2015): 2–12.

———. "Plants and People: Past Ethnobotany of the Northeastern Prairie." In *The Prairie: Past, Present and Future; Proceedings of the Ninth North American Prairie Conference*, edited by G. Clambey and R. H. Pemble, 1–7. Moorhead MN and Fargo ND: Tri-College University Centre for Environmental Studies, 1986.

———. "Postglacial Vegetation Development in Northwestern Minnesota and Its Implications for Prehistoric Human Ecology." Master's thesis, University of Minnesota, 1965.

Shay, C. T., S. Coyston, and M. Waddell. "Paleobotanical Studies at The Forks: Analysis of Seeds, Charcoal and Other Organic Remains." *Journal of Manitoba Archaeology* 1, no. 1 (1991): 62–92.

Shay, C. T., and M. Kapinga. "*Cenococcum geophilum* Sclerotia from an Archaeological Site in Western Canada." *North American Archaeologist* 18, no. 4 (1998): 363–70.

Shay, C. T., L. P. Stene, J. M. Shay, and L. C. Wilson. "Palaeoecological Studies, Proposed Rafferty Dam Area." Saskatchewan Research Council, 1989.

———. "Preliminary Report of Paleoecological Investigations, Proposed Rafferty Dam Area, Southeastern Saskatchewan." *North Dakota Archaeological Association Journal* 4 (1990): 43–75.

———. "Report of Palaeoecological Investigations, Proposed Rafferty Dam Area." Western Heritage Services, Saskatoon, 1992.

Shay, C. T., L. P. Stene, J. M. Shay, L. C. Wilson, M. Kapinga, and S. Coyston. "Final Report of Palaeoecological Investigations in the Proposed Rafferty Dam Area, Southeastern Saskatchewan." Saskatchewan Heritage Foundation, 1995.

Shay, C. T., L. P. Stene, and L. C. Wilson. "Palaeoecological Investigations in the Proposed Rafferty Dam Area, Southeastern Saskatchewan: An Interim Report, April to December, 1989." Saskatchewan Research Council, 1990.

Shay, J. M. *Annotated Vascular Plant Species List for the Delta Marsh, Manitoba and Surrounding Area.* Occasional Publication No. 2, University of Manitoba Field Station (Delta Marsh), 1999.

Shay, Jennifer M., Marjorie Herring, and Barbara S. Dyck. "Dune Colonization in the Bald Head Hills of Southwestern Manitoba." *Canadian Field Naturalist* 114, no. 4 (2000): 612–27.

Shay, Jennifer M., and C. Thomas Shay. "Prairie Marshes in Western Canada, with Specific Reference to the Ecology of Five Emergent Macrophytes." *Canadian Journal of Botany* 64, no. 2 (Jan. 2011): 443–54.

Shepard, Glenn H., Jr. "Psychoactive Botanicals in Ritual, Religion and Shamanism." In *Encyclopedia of Life Support Systems*, vol. 2, *Ethnopharmacology*, edited by E. Elisabetsky and N. Etkin, 128–82. Oxford: UNESCO/EOLSS, 2005.

Sherman, Sean, and Beth Dooley. *The Sioux Chef's Indigenous Kitchen.* Minneapolis: University of Minnesota Press, 2017.

Sherwood, Sarah C., and Jefferson Chapman. "The Identification and Potential Significance of Early Holocene Prepared Clay Surfaces: Examples from Dust Cave and Icehouse Bottom." *Southeastern Archaeology* 24, no. 1 (2005): 70–82.

Sherwood, Sarah C., Boyce N. Driskell, Asa R. Randall, and Scott C. Meeks. "Chronology and Stratigraphy at Dust Cave, Alabama." *American Antiquity* 69, no. 3 (2004): 533–54.

Shuman, Bryan N., and Jeremiah Marsicek. "The Structure of Holocene Climate Change in Mid-Latitude North America." *Quaternary Science Reviews* 141 (June 2016): 38–51.

Silver, Nate, and Reuben Fischer-Baum. "Which City Has the Most Unpredictable Weather?" FiveThirtyEight, December 4, 2014. https://fivethirtyeight.com/features/which-city-has-the-most-unpredictable-weather/.

Simms, Steven R. "Acquisition Cost and Nutritional Data on Great Basin Resources." *Journal of California and Great Basin Anthropology* 7, no. 1 (1985): 117–26.

Simon, Mary L., Thomas Emerson, Dale McElrath, and Andrew Fortier. "A Regional and Chronological Synthesis of Archaic Period Plant Use in the Midcontinent." In *Archaic Societies: Diversity and Complexity across the Midcontinent*, edited by Thomas E. Emerson, Dale L. McElrath, and Andrew C. Fortier, 81–114. Albany: State University of New York Press, 2009.

Singer, Andrew C., David E. Crowley, and Ian P. Thompson. "Secondary Plant Metabolites in Phytoremediation and Biotransformation." *Trends in Biotechnology* 21, no. 3 (2003): 123–30.

Sitting Bull. "The Spring." In *In a Sacred Manner I Live: Native American Wisdom*, edited by Neil Philip. New York: Clarion Books, 1997.

Slaughter, Linda. *Leaves from Northwestern History: Early Life of the Sioux Warrior Sitting Bull*. Bismarck: State Historical Society of North Dakota, 1906.

Small, Ernest. *Culinary Herbs*. Ottawa: Canadian Science Publishing, National Research Council Press, 2006.

Smith, Bruce D. "Eastern North America as an Independent Center of Plant Domestication." *Proceedings of the National Academy of Sciences* 103, no. 33 (Aug. 15, 2006): 12223–28.

———. "The Initial Domestication of *Cucurbita pepo* in the Americas 10,000 Years Ago." *Science* 276, no. 5314 (May 9, 1997): 932–34.

———. "Neo-Darwinism, Niche Construction Theory, and the Initial Domestication of Plants and Animals." *Evolutionary Ecology* 30, no. 2 (2016): 307–24.

Smith, Bruce D., C. Wesley Cowan, and Michael P. Hoffman. *Rivers of Change: Essays on Early Agriculture in Eastern North America*. Tuscaloosa: University of Alabama Press, 2007.

Smith, Daryl. "Iowa Prairie: Original Extent and Loss, Preservation and Recovery Attempts." *Journal of the Iowa Academy of Science* 105, no. 3 (1998): 94–108.

———. *The Tallgrass Prairie Center Guide to Prairie Restoration in the Upper Midwest*. Iowa City: University of Iowa Press, 2010.

Smith, G. Hubert. *The Explorations of the La Vérendryes in the Northern Plains, 1738–43*. Lincoln: University of Nebraska Press, 1980.

Smith, Huron H. *Ethnobotany of the Menomini Indians*. Bulletin of the Public Museum of the City of Milwaukee, vol. 4, no. 1. Milwaukee WI: Greenwood Press, 1923.

Smith, Jeffrey L., and Janice V. Perino. "Osage Orange (*Maclura pomifera*): History and Economic Uses." *Economic Botany* 35, no. 1 (1981): 24–41.

Snell, Alma Hogan. *A Taste of Heritage: Crow Indian Recipes and Herbal Medicines*. Lincoln: University of Nebraska Press, 2006.

Souris Basin Development Authority. *Rafferty/Alameda Environmental Impact Statement*. Saskatoon SK: Souris Basin Development Authority, 1987–88.

Spencer, Jessica D. "An 8,000-Year Fire and Vegetation History of an Oak Savanna in East Central Minnesota." Master's thesis, University of Utah, 2012.

Speth, John D. "When Did Humans Learn to Boil?" *PaleoAnthropology* (2015): 54–67.

Sproule, T. A. "A Paleoecological Investigation in the Post-Glacial History of the Delta Marsh, Manitoba." Master's thesis, University of Manitoba, 1972.

Spurr, Stephen H. "Forest Fire History of Itasca State Park." *Minnesota Forestry Notes*, no. 18 (June 15, 1953).

Steinbring, Jack H. "Dating Rock Art in the Northern Midcontinent." *American Indian Rock Art* 12 (1993): 15–29.

St. George, Scott, and Erik Nielsen. "Palaeoflood Records for the Red River, Manitoba, Canada, Derived from Anatomical Tree-Ring Signatures." *The Holocene* 13, no. 4 (2003): 547–55.

St. Pierre, Mark, and Tilda Long Soldier. *Walking in the Sacred Manner: Healers, Dreamers, and Pipe Carriers—Medicine Women of the Plains.* New York: Touchstone Press, 1995.

Strong, W. L., and L. V. Hills. "Late-Glacial and Holocene Palaeovegetation Zonal Reconstruction for Central and North-Central North America." *Journal of Biogeography* 32, no. 6 (2005): 1043–62.

Struever, Stuart, ed. *Prehistoric Agriculture.* Garden City NY: Natural History Press, 1971.

Summerhayes, Colin, and Dan Charman. "Introduction to Holocene Climate Change: New Perspectives." *Journal of the Geological Society* 172, no. 2 (2015): 251–53.

Sun, C. S., and James T. Teller. "Reconstruction of Glacial Lake Hind in Southwestern Manitoba, Canada." *Journal of Paleolimnology* 17, no. 1 (1997): 9–21.

Sundstrom, Linea. *Boulder Effigy Sites in South Dakota: History, Description, and Evaluation.* Pierre: South Dakota State Historical Society Cultural Heritage Center, 2006.

Sutton, Bruce D., David A. Carlson, Jeffrey A. Lockwood, and Richard A. Nunamaker. "Cuticular Hydrocarbons of Glacially-Preserved Melanoplus (Orthoptera: Acrididae): Identification and Comparison with Hydrocarbons of M. sanguinipes and M. spretu." *Journal of Orthoptera Research* 5 (August 1996): 1–12.

Swarts, Kelly, Rafal M. Gutaker, Bruce Benz, Michael Blake, Robert Bukowski, James Holland, Melissa Kruse-Peeples, et al. "Genomic Estimation of Complex Traits Reveals Ancient Maize Adaptation to Temperate North America." *Science* 357, no. 6350 (2017): 512–15.

Swift, M. J., O. W. Heal, and J. M. Anderson. *Decomposition in Terrestrial Ecosystems.* Oxford: Blackwell Scientific, 1979.

Syms, E. Leigh. "The Devils Lake–Sourisford Burial Complex on the Northeastern Plains." *Plains Anthropologist* 24, no. 86 (1979): 283–308.

Talalay, Laurie, Donald R. Keller, and Patrick J. Munson. "Hickory Nuts, Walnuts, Butternuts, and Hazelnuts: Observations and Experiments Relevant to Their Aboriginal Exploitation in Eastern North America." In *Experiments and Observations on Aboriginal Wild Plant Food Utilization in Eastern North America,* edited by Patrick J. Munson, 338–59. Indianapolis: Indiana Historical Society, 1984.

Tankersley, Kenneth B. "Variation in the Early Paleoindian Economies of Late Pleistocene Eastern North America." *American Antiquity* 63, no. 1 (1998): 7–20.

Teague, Lynn S. *Textiles in Southwestern Prehistory*. Albuquerque: University of New Mexico Press, 1998.

Teller, James T. "Proglacial Lakes and the Southern Margin of the Laurentide Ice Sheet." In *North America and Adjacent Oceans during the Last Deglaciation*, edited by William F. Ruddiman and Herbert E. Wright Jr., 39–70. Boulder CO: Geological Society of America, 1987.

Teller, James T., and Lee Clayton, eds. *Glacial Lake Agassiz*. Geological Association of Canada Special Paper 26. Ottawa: Geological Association of Canada, 1983.

Teller, James T., and William M. Last. "Late Quaternary History of Lake Manitoba, Canada." *Quaternary Research* 16, no. 1 (1981): 97–116.

Teller, James T., and David W. Leverington. "Glacial Lake Agassiz: A 5000-Year History of Change and Its Relationship to the δ^{18}o Record of Greenland." *Geological Society of America Bulletin* 116, no. 5–6 (2004): 729–42.

Terrell, Edward E., Paul M. Peterson, James L. Reveal, and Melvin R. Duvall. "Taxonomy of North American Species of *Zizania* (Poaceae)." *SIDA, Contributions to Botany* 17, no. 3 (1997): 533–49.

Thadani, Meera B., ed. *Medicinal and Pharmaceutical Uses of Natural Products*. Winnipeg MB: Cantext Publications, 1996.

Theler, James L., and Robert F. Boszhardt. *Twelve Millennia: Archaeology of the Upper Mississippi River Valley*. Iowa City: University of Iowa Press, 2005.

Therrell, Matthew D., and Makayla J. Trotter. "Waniyetu Wówapi: Native American Records of Weather and Climate." *Bulletin of the American Meteorological Society* 92, no. 5 (2011): 583–92.

Thomas–Van Gundy, Melissa A., and Gregory J. Nowacki. "Landscape-Fire Relationships Inferred from Bearing Trees in Minnesota." In *General Technical Report NRS-GTR-160*, U.S. Department of Agriculture, Forest Service, Northern Research Station, 2016.

Thompson, Amanda Jo, and Kathryn A. Jakes. "Replication of Textile Dyeing with Sumac and Bedstraw." *Southeastern Archaeology* 21, no. 2 (2002): 252–56.

Thompson, David. *The Writings of David Thompson: The Travels, 1850*. Seattle: University of Washington Press, 2009.

Thoms, Alston V. "Rocks of Ages: Propagation of Hot-Rock Cookery in Western North America." *Journal of Archaeological Science* 36, no. 3 (2009): 573–91.

Thorn, Vanessa. "Phytoliths in Paleoecology." *Geology Today* 23, no. 4 (2007): 153–57.

Thresh, Robert, and Christine Thresh. *An Introduction to Natural Dyeing*. Santa Rosa CA: Thresh Publications, 1972.

Tibbits, Clark, ed. *Aging in the Modern World: Selections from the Literature of Aging for Pleasure and Instruction*. Ann Arbor: University of Michigan, 1957.

Todt, Donn L., and N. Hannon. "Plant Food Resource Ranking on the Upper Klamath River of Oregon and California: A Methodology with Archaeological Applications." *Journal of Ethnobiology* 18, no. 2 (1998): 273–308.

Townsley, Jesse R. "BP: Time for a Change." *Radiocarbon* 59, no. 1 (2017): 177–78.

Trimble, Donald E. *The Geologic Story of the Great Plains*. U.S. Geological Survey Bulletin 1493. Washington DC: Government Printing Office, 1980.

Turner, Nancy J. "The Food/Medicine/Poison Triangle: Implications for Traditional Ecological Knowledge Systems of Indigenous Peoples of British Columbia, Canada." In *Social-Ecological Diversity and Traditional Food Systems: Opportunities from the Biocultural World*, edited by Ranjay K. Singh, Nancy J. Turner, Victoria Reyes-García, and Jules Pretty, 1–31. New Delhi: New Delhi Publishing Agency, 2014.

———. "Roots of Reflection: Spiritual Aspects of Plant Harvesting, Ethnoecological Practice and Sustainability for Indigenous Peoples of Northwestern North America." In the proceedings of the conference Des êtres vivants et des artefacts, April 9–10, 2014, *Les actes de colloques du musée du quai Branly*, no. 6. Paris, 2016.

Turner, Nancy J., Yilmaz Ari, Fikret Berkes, Iain Davidson-Hunt, Z. Fusun Ertug, and Andrew M. Miller. "Cultural Management of Living Trees: An International Perspective." *Journal of Ethnobiology* 29, no. 2 (2009): 237–70.

Tushingham, Shannon, and Jelmer W. Eerkens. "Hunter-Gatherer Tobacco Smoking in Ancient North America: Current Chemical Evidence and a Framework for Future Studies." In *Perspectives on the Archaeology of Pipes, Tobacco and Other Smoke Plants in the Ancient Americas*, edited by Elizabeth A. Bollwerk and Shannon Tushingham, 211–30. New York: Springer International, 2016.

Tyler, Varro E., Lynn R. Brady, and James E. Robbers. *Pharmacognosy*. 9th ed. Philadelphia: Lee & Febiger, 1988.

Upham, Warren. *The Glacial Lake Agassiz*. U.S. Geological Survey Monograph 25. Washington DC: Government Printing Office, 1896.

Uprety, Yadav, Hugo Asselin, Archana Dhakal, and Nancy Julien. "Traditional Use of Medicinal Plants in the Boreal Forest of Canada: Review and Perspectives." *Journal of Ethnobiology and Ethnomedicine* 8, no. 1 (2012): 1–14.

U.S. Geological Survey. *Missouri Coteau Wetland Ecosystem Observatory: Understanding Effects of Land-Use and Climate Change on Wetland Ecosystems of the Prairie Pothole Region.* N.d. https://www.sciencebase.gov/catalog/item /52f0ffd9e4b0f941aa181fc6.

Valko, Marian, Dieter Leibfritz, Jan Moncol, Mark T. D. Cronin, Milan Mazur, and Joshua Telser. "Free Radicals and Antioxidants in Normal Physiological Functions and Human Disease." *International Journal of Biochemistry and Cell Biology* 39, no. 1 (2007): 44–84.

Vallès, Joan, Sònia Garcia, Oriane Hidalgo, Joan Martín, Jaume Pellicer, María Sanz, and Teresa Garnatje. "Biology, Genome Evolution, Biotechnological Issues and Research Including Applied Perspectives in *Artemisia* (Asteraceae)." *Advances in Botanical Research* 60 (December 2011): 349–419.

van der Valk, A. G., ed. *Northern Prairie Wetlands.* Ames: Iowa State University Press, 1989.

VanStone, James W. *Ethnographic Collections from the Assiniboine and Yanktonia Sioux in the Field Museum of Natural History.* Chicago: Field Museum of Natural History, 1996.

———. *Material Culture of the Blackfoot (Blood) Indians of Southern Alberta.* Chicago: Field Museum of Natural History, 1992.

———. *The Simms Collection of Southwestern Chippewa Material Culture.* Chicago: Field Museum of Natural History, 1988.

Varney, R. A., Kathryn Puseman, and Linda Scott Cummings. *Pollen, Macrofloral, and Protein Residue Analyses at Sites 42DA1269 and EG10 (42DA1294, CJ), Northeastern Utah.* Golden CO: PaleoResearch Institute, 2003.

Veni, George. "Revising the Karst Map of the United States." *Journal of Cave and Karst Studies* 64, no. 1 (2002): 45–50.

Vennum, Thomas. *Wild Rice and the Ojibway People.* St. Paul: Minnesota Historical Society Press, 1988.

Vogt, David. "Medicine Wheels of the Great Plains." In *Handbook of Archaeoastronomy and Ethnoastronomy,* edited by Clive Ruggles, 541–50. New York: Springer, 2015.

Wales, Nathan, Melis Akman, Ray H. B. Watson, Fátima Sánchez Barreiro, Bruce D. Smith, Kristen J. Gremillion, M. Thomas P. Gilbert, and Benjamin K. Blackman. "Ancient DNA Reveals the Timing and Persistence of Organellar Genetic Bottlenecks over 3,000 Years of Sunflower Domestication and Improvement." *Evolutionary Applications* 12, no. 1 (2019): 38–53.

Walker, J. R., Raymond J. DeMallie, and Elaine Jahner. *Lakota Belief and Ritual.* Lincoln: University of Nebraska Press, 1991.

Walker, Renee B., Kandace R. Detwiler, Scott C. Meeks, and Boyce N. Driskell. "Berries, Bones, and Blades: Reconstructing Late Paleoindian Subsistence Economy at Dust Cave, Alabama." *Midcontinental Journal of Archaeology* 26, no. 2 (2001): 169–97.

Walker, Renee B., and Boyce N. Driskell, eds. *Foragers of the Terminal Pleistocene in North America.* Lincoln: University of Nebraska Press, 2007.

Walker, Renee Beauchamp. "Late Paleoindian through Middle Archaic Faunal Evidence from Dust Cave, Alabama." PhD diss., University of Tennessee, 1998.

Walters, Anna Lee. *The Spirit of Native America: Beauty and Mysticism in American Indian Art.* San Francisco: Chronicle Books, 1989.

Walton, Izaak. *The Compleat Angler, or, the Contemplative Man's Recreation.* London: Cassell, 1886. Originally published by Richard Marriot (London), 1653.

Wandsnider, LuAnn. "The Roasted and the Boiled: Food Composition and Heat Treatment with Special Emphasis on Pit-Hearth Cooking." *Journal of Anthropological Archaeology* 16, no. 1 (1997): 1–48.

Wang, Wei-Ming. "On the Origin and Development of *Artemisia* (Asteraceae) in the Geological Past." *Botanical Journal of the Linnean Society* 145, no. 3 (2004): 331–36.

Warkentin, Germaine. *Canadian Exploration Literature: An Anthology.* Vol. 3. Toronto: Dundurn, 2007.

Warren, Robert E. "Thunderbird Effigies from Plains Village Sites in the Northern Great Plains." In *Plains Village Archaeology: Bison-Hunting Farmers in the Central and Northern Plains,* edited by Stanley A. Ahler and Marvin Kay, 107–25. Salt Lake City: University of Utah Press, 2007.

Watson, Patty Jo. "Archaeology and Anthropology: A Personal Overview of the Past Half-Century." *Annual Review of Anthropology* 38 (October 2009): 1–15.

———. "In Pursuit of Prehistoric Subsistence: A Comparative Account of Some Contemporary Flotation Techniques." *Midcontinental Journal of Archaeology* 1, no. 1 (1976): 77–100.

Watson, Patty Jo, and Mary C. Kennedy. "The Development of Horticulture in the Eastern Woodlands of North America." In *Reader in Archaeological Theory: Post-Processual and Cognitive Approaches,* edited by David S. Whitley, 223–40. London: Psychology Press, 1998.

Wedel, Waldo R. "George Francis Will—1884–1955." *American Antiquity* 22, no. 1 (1956): 73–76.

Weiland, Andrew W. "Marshelder (*Iva annua* L.) Seed Morphology and Patterns of Domestication in Eastern North America." Master's thesis, Ohio State University, 2013.

Weitzel, Elic M. "Declining Foraging Efficiency in the Middle Tennessee River Valley Prior to Initial Domestication." *American Antiquity* 84, no. 2 (2019): 191–214. https://www.doi.org/10.1017/aaq.2018.86.

Weitzner, Bella, and Gilbert Livingstone Wilson. *Notes on the Hidatsa Indians Based on Data Recorded by the Late Gilbert L. Wilson.* Anthropological Papers of the American Museum of Natural History, vol. 56, part 2. New York: American Museum of Natural History, 1979.

Weller, Milton W. *Freshwater Marshes: Ecology and Wildlife Management.* Minneapolis: University of Minnesota Press, 1994.

Wells, P. V. "Scarp Woodlands, Transported Grassland Soils, and Concept of Grassland Climate in the Great Plains Region." *Science* 148, no. 3667 (April 9, 1965): 246–49.

Wendt, Keith M., and Barbara A. Coffin. *Natural Vegetation of Minnesota at the Time of the Public Land Survey, 1847–1907.* Biological Report No. 1, Minnesota Department of Natural Resources, 1988.

Whelan, Mary K. "The Archaeological and Ethnohistoric Evidence for Prehistoric Occupation." In *The Patterned Peatlands of Minnesota,* edited by Herbert E. Wright, Barbara Coffin, and Norman E. Aaseng, 239–49. Minneapolis: University of Minnesota Press, 1992.

———. "The 1837 Ioway Indian Map Project: Using Geographic Information Systems to Integrate History, Archaeology and Landscape." Master's thesis, University of Redlands, 2003.

White, N. 2002. "The Malaria Medicine Chest." *Wellcome News Supplement* 6 (2002): 10–11.

Whiteford, Andrew Hunter. "Mystic and Decorative Art of the Anishinabe (Chippewa/Ojibwa)." *Arctic Anthropology* 28, no. 1 (1991): 74–83.

Whitlock, Cathy, and Chris Larsen. "Charcoal as a Fire Proxy." In *Tracking Environmental Change Using Lake Sediments: Volume 3, Terrestrial, Algal, and Siliceous Indicators,* edited by John P. Smol, H. John, B. Birks and William M. Last, 75–97. New York: Springer, 2001.

Whittaker, R. H. *Communities and Ecosystems.* 2nd ed. New York: Macmillan, 1975.

Whittaker, R. H., and G. E. Likens. "The Biosphere and Man." In *Primary Productivity of the Biosphere,* edited by H. Leith and R. H. Whittaker, 305–28. New York: Springer-Verlag, 1975.

Whittaker, William E. "The Palace Site and the Appearance of House Basins in the Middle Archaic." *Plains Anthropologist* 61, no. 239 (2016): 250–72.

Widga, Chris. "Middle Holocene Taphonomy and Paleozoology at the Prairie-Forest Border, the Itasca Bison Site, MN." *Midcontinental Journal of Archaeology* 39, no. 3 (2014): 251–79.

Will, George F. *Archaeology of the Missouri Valley*. New York: American Museum of Natural History, 1924.

Will, George F., and George E. Hyde. *Corn among the Indians of the Upper Missouri*. St. Louis MO: William Harvey Miner, 1917.

Will, George F., and Herbert J. Spinden. *Mandans: A Study of Their Culture, Archaeology and Language*. Cambridge MA: Peabody Museum of American Archeology and Ethnology, Harvard University, 1906.

Williams, Gerald W. "References on the American Indian Use of Fire in Ecosystems." U.S. Department of Agriculture, 2005. https://www.nrcs.usda.gov/Internet/FSE_DOCUMENTS/nrcs144p2_051334.pdf.

Wilson, Gilbert L. *Buffalo Bird Woman's Garden: Agriculture of the Hidatsa Indians*. St. Paul: Minnesota Historical Society Press, 1987. Originally published by the University of Minnesota, 1917.

———. *The Hidatsa Earthlodge*. Edited by Bella Weitzner. Anthropological Papers of the American Museum of Natural History, vol. 33, part 5. New York: American Museum of Natural History, 1934.

———. *Uses of Plants by the Hidatsas of the Northern Plains*. Edited by Michael Scullin. Lincoln: University of Nebraska Press, 2014.

———. *Waheenee: An Indian Girl's Story*. Lincoln: University of Nebraska Press, 1981. Originally published by Webb (St. Paul MN), 1921.

Wilson, Michael C. "The Household as a Portable Mnemonic Landscape: Archaeological Implications for Plains Stone Circle Sites." In *Beyond Subsistence: Plains Archaeology and the Postprocessual Critique*, edited by Philip Duke and Michael C. Wilson, 169–92. Tuscaloosa: University of Alabama Press, 1995.

Winter, Joseph C., ed. *Tobacco Use by Native North Americans: Sacred Smoke and Silent Killer*. Norman: University of Oklahoma Press, 2000.

Winter, Thomas C. "Hydrologic Studies of Wetlands in the Northern Prairie." In *Northern Prairie Wetlands*, edited by Arnold van der Valk, 16–54. Ames: Iowa State University Press, 1989.

Wishart, David. J. "The Great Plains Region." In *Encyclopedia of the Great Plains*, edited by David J. Wishart. Lincoln: University of Nebraska, 2011. http://plainshumanities.unl.edu/encyclopedia/.

Wissler, Clark. *Material Culture of the Blackfoot Indian*. New York: American Museum of Natural History, 1910.

Withycombe, Donald A., Robert C. Lindsay, and David A. Stuiber. "Isolation and Identification of Volatile Components from Wild Rice Grain (*Zizania aquatica*)." *Journal of Agricultural and Food Chemistry* 26, no. 4 (1978): 816–22.

Wolfe, Stephen A., David Huntley, and Jeff Ollerhead. "Optical Dating of Modern and Late Holocene Dune Sands in the Brandon Sand Hills, Southwestern Manitoba." *Géographie Physique et Quaternaire* 56, no. 2–3 (2002): 203–14.

Wolfe, Stephen A., Olav B. Lian, Christopher H. Hugenholtz, and Justine R. Riches. "Holocene Eolian Sand Deposition Linked to Climatic Variability, Northern Great Plains, Canada." *The Holocene* 27, no. 4 (2017): 579–93.

Wood, W. Raymond. "Plains Trade in Prehistoric and Protohistoric Intertribal Relations." In *Anthropology on the Great Plains*, edited by W. Raymond Wood and Margot Liberty, 99–109. Lincoln: University of Nebraska Press, 1980.

Wood, W. Raymond, and Alan R. Woolworth. *The Paul Brave Site (32SI4), Oahe Reservoir Area, North Dakota*. River Basin Surveys Papers No. 33, Bureau of American Ethnology Bulletin 189. Washington DC: Government Printing Office, 1964.

Wright, James V. *A History of the Native People of Canada*. Gatineau QC: Canadian Museum of Civilization, 2006.

Wright, Katherine I. "Ground-Stone Tools and Hunter-Gatherer Subsistence in Southwest Asia: Implications for the Transition to Farming." *American Antiquity* 59, no. 2 (1994): 238–63.

Wymer, DeeAnne. "Trends and Disparities: The Woodland Paleoethnobotanical Record of the Mid-Ohio Valley." In *Cultural Variability in Context: Woodland Settlements of the Mid-Ohio Valley*, edited by Mark F. Seeman, 65–76. Kent OH: Kent State University Press, 1992.

Xu, Xinwei, Christina Walters, Michael F. Antolin, Mara L. Alexander, Sue Lutz, Song Ge, and Jun Wen. "Phylogeny and Biogeography of the Eastern Asian-North American Disjunct Wild-Rice Genus (*Zizania* L., Poaceae)." *Molecular Phylogenetics and Evolution* 55, no. 3 (2010): 1008–17.

Yansa, Catherine H. "The Timing and Nature of Late Quaternary Vegetation Changes in the Northern Great Plains, USA and Canada: A Re-assessment of the Spruce Phase." *Quaternary Science Reviews* 25, no. 3 (2006): 263–81.

Yansa, Catherine H., and James F. Basinger. "A Postglacial Plant Macrofossil Record of Vegetation and Climate Change in Southern Saskatchewan." In *Holocene Climate and Environmental Change in the Palliser Triangle: A Geoscientific Context for Evaluating the Impacts of Climate Change on the Southern Canadian Prairies*, edited by Donald S. Lemmen and Robert E. Vance, 139–72. Ottawa: Geological Survey of Canada, 1999.

Yao, Liu H., Y. M. Jiang, Je Shi, F. A. Tomás-Barberán, Nivedita Datta, Riantong Singanusong, and S. S. Chen. 2004. "Flavonoids in Food and Their Health Benefits." *Plant Foods for Human Nutrition* 59, no. 3 (2004): 113–22.

Yarnell, Richard A., and M. Jean Black. "Temporal Trends Indicated by a Survey of Archaic and Woodland Plant Food Remains from Southeastern North America." *Southeastern Archaeology* 4, no. 2 (1985): 93–106.

Yellowhorn, Eldon Carlyle. "Awakening Internalist Archaeology in the Aboriginal World." PhD diss., McGill University, 2002.

Yost, C. L., M. S. Blinnikov, and M. L. Julius. "Detecting Ancient Wild Rice (*Zizania* spp. L.) Using Phytoliths: A Taphonomic Study of Modern Wild Rice in Minnesota (USA) Lake Sediments." *Journal of Paleolimnology* 49, no. 2 (2012): 221–36.

Zarrillo, Sonia, and Brian Kooyman. "Evidence for Berry and Maize Processing on the Canadian Plains from Starch Grain Analysis." *American Antiquity* 71, no. 3 (2006): 473–99.

Zedeño, M. Nieves, Richard W. Stoffle, Fabio Pittaluga, Genevieve Dewey-Hefley, R. Christopher Basaldú, and María Porter. *Traditional Ojibway Resources in the Western Great Lakes: An Ethnographic Inventory in the States of Michigan, Minnesota, and Wisconsin.* Tucson: Bureau of Applied Research in Anthropology, University of Arizona, 2001.

Zedeño, María Nieves. "Art as the Road to Perfection: The Blackfoot Painted Tipi." *Cambridge Archaeological Journal* 27, no. 4 (2017): 631–42.

Zeder, Melinda A. "Domestication as a Model System for Niche Construction Theory." *Evolutionary Ecology* 30, no. 2 (2016): 325–48.

———. "Domestication as a Model System for the Extended Evolutionary Synthesis." *Interface Focus* 7, no. 5 (2017): 1–15.

Zeder, Melinda A., Eve Emshwiller, Bruce D. Smith, and Daniel G. Bradley. "Documenting Domestication: The Intersection of Genetics and Archaeology." TRENDS *in Genetics* 22, no. 3 (2006): 139–55.

Zohary, Daniel. "Unconscious Selection and the Evolution of Domesticated Plants." *Economic Botany* 58, no. 1 (2004): 5–10.

INDEX

Italicized page numbers refer to illustrations. The letter t *following a page number denotes a table.*

marsh, 8, 10, 45, 54, 59, 60, 76, 119. *See also* Delta Marsh

marsh elder, 76, 78, 88–89t, 95, 106, *107*, 109

marsh marigold, 123, *124*

maygrass, 109, 111–12, *111*

medicine, 3, 91, 133, 138, 141, 145–49

Menominee, 122, 170

Mexico, 99, 106, 114, 115

microscope, 17, 18, 32, 79; scanning electron (SEM), 79, *80*

milkweed, 70, 168, 173, 174

Minnesota, 5, 6, 12, 13, 53, 61, 91, 92

Mississippi River, 21, 58, 60–61

Missouri River, 5–6, 38, 58, 104, 106, 134, 159, 162

Moose Jaw SK, 11, 36–37, 45, *46*

moraine, 8. *See also* glacial landforms

moss, 89, 90, 174

Nabhan, Gary, 2, 43, 101

nettle, 76, 143, 168, *169, 170*

Newt Kash Hollow Shelter, 97–98

North Dakota, 8–9, 10, 19, 58, 71, 135

northern plains, *4, 5, 12, 19*, 27, 88, 193n1; archaeology in, 73; human history of, 23, 43, 87, 88–89t, 92, 140, 163; vegetation of, *44*, 119, 141, 158; weather and climate in, 21, 33, 36–37

nuts, 92, 93, 97, 126, 133

oak, 32, 33, 67, 91, 159, *160, 161*; acorns, 97, 120, *121*; bark, 172, 174; for crafts, 145, 162, 172, 174, 224n17

oak, bur, 53, 61, 133

oak savanna, 45, 66, 68

Ohkwamingininiwug, 90

Ojibwe. *See* Anishinaabe

Omaha, 25, 71, 172, 176

Osage orange, 97, 159

paper birch, 61

parkland, 45, 53, 88, 141

Pawnee, 25, 104, 152, 153, 164, 176

Pembina River, 19, 51

pemmican, 51, 129

phytoliths, 81, 94, 132

pigweed, 76, 134

pine, 18, 45, 61, 62, 94

pipes, 151, 158

pipestone, 112, 152

plains porcupine grass, 49, *49*

plant roots: for crafts, 90, 154, 163, 171, 172; for food, 88t, 120, 125, 129, *130*, 133–34; for medicine, 91, 138, 147; in soil, 15, 33, 54, 115

plants: domestication of, 81, 88t, 89, 95–117, 208n37; partnering with, 95–96; remains of, 6, 76, 77, 93, 143, 212n96

pollen, 15–19, 55, 89, 94, 123; diagram, *18*

poplar, 76, 89, 145

poplar, balsam, 47, 53, 61

pottery, 24, 51, 75, 78, 81

prairie, 66, 70, 76, 119–20, 141, 158, *173*; history of, 88t, 91–92; mixed-grass, 35, 48, *120*; shortgrass, 48; tallgrass, 24, 48, 63, 65–66, 68–70, *118*; transition to forest, 19, 53, 66–67, *67*

prairie pothole, 10, 59, *60*

prairie sagewort, 141–42, *142*. *See also* sage, wild

prairie turnip, 129, *130*. *See also* Indian breadroot; tipsin

prickly pear cactus, 48, 93

pumpkin, 58, 99, 117

Qually Pond, 15–16

radiocarbon dating, 47, 79–80, 92
raspberries, 78, 120, 127, 133, 134
Red River, 5, 6, 27, 31, 53, 56, 63, 123
Red River Settlement, 27, 196n16
rose, prairie, 40, 76, 78, 139, 143

sage, wild, 89, 141, 142, *142*, *145*; uses for,
    136, 143, 147, 149, 152, 174
Saskatchewan, 5, 10, 11, 47, 73, 91, 132, 143
saskatoon. *See* juneberry (saskatoon)
sedges, 54, 61, 76
seeds: charred, 76, 81, 96, 99, 143,
    204n7; as food, 76, 93, 126, 134,
    137; fossils of, 55, 89; and germi-
    nation, 136, 147. *See also* plants:
    remains of
Seibold Lake, 8–9
Shay, Jennifer, 28–31, 35, 74, 122
shelter. *See* homes
silverberry, 50, 136
skeleton plant, 52, *52*
smoke, for healing, 149
smoke hole, 58, 165, 166
smoking, 146, 151
Snell, Alma, 129, 165
snowberry, western, 50, 76, 143
snowshoes, 40, 128
soil, 13–15, *14*
Souris River, 51, 73–76
South Dakota, 5, *26*, 45, 91, 132, *158*, *162*,
    200n7
Spirit Sands, 51–53

spiritual connections, 3, 43, 133, 157
spirituality, 43, 119, 143, 148, 149, 151,
    175, 180
spruce, 8, 9, 19, 88–89t, 91, 141; uses of,
    90, 131, 163; woodlands, 8, 9, 45
spruce, black, 61
spruce, white, 51, 61, *91*
Spruce Woods Provincial Park, 52
squash, 88–89t, 96, 99, *100*, 101, 136–38, 147
stimulant, 91, 146
stinging nettle. *See* nettle
stone artifacts. *See* tools
strawberry, wild, 76, 134, 139
sumpweed. *See* marsh elder
sunflower, 88–89t, 104–6, *105*, 136–37,
    139, 140
sweetgrass, 49–50, 145, 149, *150*

textiles, 106, 168–71, 172
Three Sisters, 117
Thunderbird, 24–25, *25*
till, 8. *See also* glacial debris and deposits
tipi, 25, 159, 164–65
tipsin, 129, 153, *154. See also* Indian
    breadroot; prairie turnip
tobacco, 58, 104, 146, 148, 151
tokens (charms), 90, 152
tools, 75, 90, 92, 93, 112, 129, *130*, 136, *136*,
    157–61
toys, 90, 157, 175–76
trade, 58, 88–89t, 92, 112, 140, 151, 159
Trans-Canada Highway, 47, 53
travois, 164–65, 175
tree rings: and analysis of drought, 33–
    34; and analysis of floods, 32–33, *32*
trickster, 94, 122